Visual Research Methods
in the Social Sciences

Visual Research Methods is a guide for students, researchers and teachers in the social sciences who wish to explore and actively use a visual dimension in their research. This book offers an integrated approach to doing visual research, showing the potential for building convincing case studies using a mix of visual forms including: archive images, media, maps, objects, video and still images. The book offers a critical review of some of the key theoretical ideas which underpin visual research and in particular the critical analysis of urban landscapes and visual identities.

Examples of the visual construction of 'place', social identity and trends of analysis are given in the first section of the book, whilst the essays in the second section highlight the astonishing creativity and innovation of four visual researchers. Each detailed example serves as a touchstone of quality and analysis in research, with themes ranging from the ethnography of a Venezuelan cult goddess to the forensic photography of the skeleton of a fourteenth-century nobleman. They give a keen sense of the motives, philosophies and benefits of using visual research methods.

This volume will be of practical interest to those embarking on visual research as well as more experienced researchers. Key concerns include the power of images and their changing significance in a world of cross-mediation, techniques of analysis and ethical issues, and how to unlock the potential of visual data for research.

Stephen Spencer is a Senior Lecturer in Sociology at Sheffield Hallam University. He has worked in both Further and Higher Education in Australia, with a background in anthropology and cultural and media studies. His previous works include *Social Identities: Multidisciplinary Approaches* with Gary Taylor (Routledge, 2004); *Race and Ethnicity: Culture, Identity and Representation* (Routledge, 2006); and *A Dream Deferred: Guyanese Identity Under the Colonial Shadow* (Hansib Press, 2006).

Visual Research Methods in the Social Sciences

Awakening visions

Stephen Spencer

 Routledge
Taylor & Francis Group

LONDON AND NEW YORK

First published 2011
by Routledge
2 Park Square, Milton Park, Abingdon, Oxon, OX14 4RN

Simultaneously published in the USA and Canada
by Routledge
711 Third Avenue, New York, NY 10017

Routledge is an imprint of the Taylor & Francis Group, an informa business

Typeset in Times New Roman by
Keystroke, Station Road, Codsall, Wolverhampton
Printed and bound in Great Britain by
TJI Digital, Padstow, Cornwall

British Library Cataloguing in Publication Data
A catalogue record for this book is available from the British Library

Library of Congress Cataloging-in-Publication Data
Spencer, Stephen.
    Visual research methods : in the social sciences / by Stephen Spencer. –1st ed.
        p. cm.
    Includes bibliographical references and index.
    1. Visual sociology.   2. Social sciences–Research.   I. Title.
    HM500.S64 2010
    302.2'22–dc22   2010018743

ISBN: 978–0–415–48382–7 (hbk)
ISBN: 978–0–415–48385–8 (pbk)
ISBN: 978–0–203–88386–0 (ebk)

Contents

SECTION II
Research practices in focus **167**

List of figures

All photographs, and models, by Stephen Spencer unless otherwise attributed.

Cover image: Public art – back wall of Rare and Racy, Sheffield, by Phlegm (Spencer, 2010).

3 Mapping society: a 'sense of place'

4 Visualising identity

5 Visual analysis

Model 2 Micro and macro relationships   *135*

Model 3 Levels of visual ethnogaphic research   *141*

SECTION II – PRACTITIONER ESSAYS

Panizza Allmark

Sarah Atkinson

Roger Brown

Roger Canals

Glossary

About the author

Stephen Spencer has a background in Communications and Cultural Studies and is a Senior Lecturer in Sociology at Sheffield Hallam University, having worked as a lecturer in both Higher and Further Education in Australia and the UK. His research into ethnic conflict in the Caribbean led to the publication of *A Dream Deferred: Guyanese Identity Under the Colonial Shadow* (Hansib, 2006). In the same year *Race and Ethnicity: Culture, Identity and Representation* (Routledge, 2006) was especially concerned with the way in which people are classified, and in particular the role of images in popular culture as a means of circulating mythical concepts of 'race' and multicultural identity. As well as these sole authored texts, a co-edited monograph for CSAP, *Reflecting on Practice: Teaching 'Race' & Ethnicity in Further and Higher Education* (2006) sought to capture the experiences of teaching issues of race and ethnicity in diverse settings. More recent research has focused on visual methodologies for research and teaching and the production of videos on consumerism, media representation of the Iraq conflict, homeless Aborigines in Darwin and the complex meanings of multiculturalism. Research in Nova Scotia in 2007 led to the publication of *Identities in Transition: Five African Canadian Women Discuss Identity*, a video published in *EliSS* Journal, CSAP, Online Publication, Vol. 1, Issue 2, Autumn 2008.

The practitioner essays

Dr Panizza Allmark

Dr Panizza Allmark is a senior lecturer and course coordinator for Mass Communications and Media and Cultural Studies at Edith Cowan University, Western Australia. Panizza is a documentary photographer and has exhibited widely and published in the field of cultural studies. She is also the co-editor of *Continuum: Journal of Media & Cultural Studies*. Her output has included articles on gender and sexuality, art and photographic discourse, and her work has been exhibited in New York, Urbino in Italy, Buenos Aires and in several galleries in Australia. Panizza's current work includes a photographic study of border towns on the Thai–Burma border and interviewing and photographing Burmese Buddhist peace freedom activist Ashin Sapaka.

Dr Sarah Atkinson

Dr Sarah Atkinson is Principal Lecturer in Broadcast Media at the University of Brighton. Sarah is also a new media practitioner working within the field of interactive visual and sonic arts. She has a PhD from Brunel University. 'Telling Interactive Stories' is a practice-based thesis, which theoretically and practically investigates the field of digital fictional interactive storytelling. Sarah has also published articles around the area of interactive film, video and cinema. Dr Atkinson's *Crossed Lines* is an original fictional interactive film amalgamating multi-linear plots, a multi-screen viewing environment, an interactive interface and an interactive story navigation form. It has been exhibited at the Electronic Literature Organisation conference at the Washington State University, US; the Digital Interactive Media in Arts and Entertainment conference arts show in Athens; The Interrupt arts show in Providence, US; the Euro ITV arts show in Belgium and the International Digital Interactive Storytelling conference in Portugal.

Roger Brown

Roger Brown is a Senior Lecturer in Photography at Staffordshire University, Faculty of Arts. He is a practising and exhibiting documentary and studio still life photographer and research-active in the fields of visual anthropology, visual sociology, visual archaeology and hermeneutic philosophy. Roger Brown is also a PhD doctoral research candidate in the practice, aesthetics and theorising philosophical hermeneutics of documentary photography, visual ethnography and visualising archaeology. His doctoral thesis is entitled 'Documentary Photography and the Hermeneutic Philosophy of Paul Ricoeur, 1913–2005'. He has a growing number of publications including Cassella, Brown, Lewis and Lucking (2008) 'HASDiP: The Hulton Abbey Skeleton Digitisation Project, A Teaching & Learning Resource'; DVD, JISC/HEA E-Learning research programme; 'Digitally visualising archaeological remains from the Hulton Abbey Archaeological Excavations' (Boothroyd and Klemperer, 2004). Roger's recent exhibitions include, in 2008 at Waterside South: *Identity & Regeneration* and an Arts Council & RENEW North Staffordshire regeneration partnership *Place, Space & Identity* 1 Community Arts project, Wellington Community Centre and St Marks Church, Wellington, Hanley, Stoke-on-Trent, Staffordshire.

Dr Roger Canals

Roger Canals is a Postdoctoral Professor and researcher at the University of Barcelona where he currently teaches the Anthroplogy of Art (and specialises in Visual Anthroplogy).

Dr Canals's varied research interests include: visual anthropology, anthropology of religion (studies in African-American cults in South America and abroad), ethnographic cinema, and anthropology of art. His published work includes: 'Double debt. Prints in the Cult of María Lionza (Venezuela)' in *Performance and Representation in South American Shamanic Societies* in C. Alès & M. Harris (eds), (Oxford, Berhghan Books), in press, 'Les avatars du regard dans le culte à María Lionza (Venezuela)' in *L'Homme. Revue française d'anthropologie*, Éditions de l'École des Hautes Etudes en Sciences Sociales (Paris, in press). In addition, he has produced, directed and filmed two ethnographic videos, *The Blood and the Hen* and *María Lionza: The Many Faces of a Venezuelan Goddess*. Roger Canals's current projects include further research on the diaspora of María Lionza's cult in other Caribbean countries and in Barcelona. This research will lead to a new ethnographic film and a number of articles on the place of African-American religions in a globalised world. He is also preparing the publication of his first book on the representations of María Lionza in Venezuela.

Acknowledgements

This book is the result of several projects; the main ones are listed at the end of the introduction. It also draws on an unpublished PhD report for some of its critical themes about research. The biggest debt is clearly to the four authors for providing their practitioner essays which make up Section II of the text. These are essays that demonstrate the diversity and innovation to be found in visual research today and the wealth of critical insights which underpin such work. In addition to these four contributors I would like to thank several other collaborators, notably Keith Radley, Lloyd Samuels, Dave Surridge and Richard McCarter, for their video, still images and drawings which are featured in this book.

Every effort has been made to contact the copyright holders for their permission to reprint material in this book. The publisher would be grateful to hear from any copyright holder who is not acknowledged and will undertake to rectify any errors or omissions in future editions of the book.

Introduction

This book is intended primarily for students, particularly those in the later years of social science degrees or those pursuing postgraduate research. Increasingly, forms of visual research are being examined and the potential benefits are attractive. Of course, I also hope it will be of interest to lecturers and researchers like myself, who teach in the social sciences; in anthropology, sociology, cultural and media studies or in qualitative research methods where these disciplinary areas often collide.

Why should researchers in the social sciences focus their attentions on visual methods? There are two compelling reasons for becoming a 'visualista'.[1] Firstly, that the visual is recognised as central to the human condition and to expressions of humanity which pre-date language, affecting our emotions, identities, memories and aspirations in a most profound way. We are visual beings in a world which is a visual array of meaning. Secondly, despite this, social sciences have undervalued the visual, or relegated its use to mere subsidiary illustrations to written text. However, in the last two decades, the interest in the visual dimension of social life has rapidly increased; the potential of visual methods to provide a deeper and more subtle exploration of social contexts and relationships is recognised, allowing us to see the everyday with new eyes.

This book aims to provide a guide to the thinking and planning processes involved for employing different forms of visual research in the project of understanding and representing crucial issues in social life. Arguably we are not only an 'interview society' (Atkinson and Silverman, 1997) but also an obsessively visual one verging, at times, on the voyeuristic. Academic knowledge and scholarship, once so logocentric (emphasising the written and spoken word), is changing and developing, driven by rapid innovations in media and educational technologies, marking a cultural shift towards a society which is concerned with the visual recording of everyday social behaviours. The camera's intrusion into every aspects of life is witnessed in the ascendency of reality TV and trends in surveillance. Most academics now rely on more immediately visual displays using PowerPoint and bespoke websites, blogs and galleries on Flickr or video clips from YouTube, where before they would have presented in a more formal verbal style.

While the earliest cave paintings demonstrate that visual representations are as old as human culture itself, it is language which has developed as an 'essentially perfect' (Sapir, 1966: 1) means of communication in every society. We believe in language; it is a bond which unites cultures, delineates relations of belonging, identity and difference. Language is one of the facets of culture we are most motivated to learn, enabling relative precision in the description of complex concepts, emotions and other internal states. Pictures, on the other hand, are less reliable as vehicles for conveying simple messages; a painting can of course incorporate conventional codes and symbols, but a clear 'reading' of the combination of elements and how they are intended by the artist may be difficult to assess and open to multiple interpretations. Similarly, while the photographic image is 'indexical', that is, a sign which is directly connected to that which it portrays rather than one where the interpretation is based on arbitrary convention (like the '?' question mark or the other linguistic signs which have no natural relationship to the things they denote) the meaning we deduce from such an image is equally open to speculation.

So perhaps it is not surprising that most social research has seen visual attributes of social life as less reliable or harder to categorise or generalise, and if used they have been an addendum to the verbal discussion and traditional language-based methods of research. Marcus Banks suggests: 'the study and use of visual images is only of use within broader sociological research enterprises, rather than as ends in themselves' (Banks, 2001: 178). Research is often enhanced by the inclusion of visual material which gives a broader context, allowing a more detailed understanding of everyday social life. Key issues and questions in sociology and anthropology can be examined in a manner which adds intimate, particular and substantial detail to the exploration of social actions which may be habitual and commonplace, and hence easily overlooked. Indeed the visual saturation of western culture makes the visual a valid object of research in its own right. This focus on visual aspects is considered by some theorists (Jenks, 1995; Mitchell, 1994) to be indicative of a markedly 'visual turn' which has come to characterise the era.

This text has been developed for those who wish to engage with the visual elements of social phenomena as a valuable resource for supplementing the traditional tools of qualitative methods for understanding about society, culture and the increasingly visual nature of our everyday lives.

Structure of the book

The aim of this text is not to give a definitive grasp of the whole field – there are already several books which might serve as more comprehensive guides to the terrain; among the best are works by Gillian Rose (2007), Marcus Banks (2007), Jon Prosser (1998), Sarah Pink (2007) and Doug Harper (2005). While owing a debt to these pioneers and making reference to their insights, by contrast, this book focuses on selected examples which allow discussion of the processes and problems inherent in using and developing visual research as a practice. The chapters deal with reflections on the process of research and the nature of imagery drawing from several pieces of action research (outlined below). There is an emphasis on tentative development based on exploratory samples from the author's recent fieldwork experiences and, in addition, visual case studies and essays about practice from four innovative researchers.

Chapter 1 considers some different aspects of visual phenomena, airing some preliminary theoretical concepts. Chapter 2 explores the potential uses of visual methods within a qualitative methodological framework, as well as issues of ethical and analytical validity. Chapters 3 and 4 highlight two crucial areas of social life: respectively, constructions of 'place' and social identities. In each case, facets of these areas of enquiry are illustrated through actual research samples, in the hope of offering a suite of ideas and approaches which will inspire researchers in the field. Chapter 5 discusses the analytical task and gives examples of semiotic and discourse analyses in action with follow-ups from some of the projects already outlined. Analysis does not realistically begin only after the data has been collected, it is implicit in the rationale and aims of the research and often already visible in the construction of researcher-produced images and video pieces. Finally, in Section II of the book, four very different and original visual researchers give a brief account of their own research journeys.

Section I

To illustrate my tentative steps in visual research I have used examples from several pieces of visual-based case study research I have been involved with in the last few years. These are cited not necessarily because they are exemplars (in fact they have many weaknesses not least in some cases less than professional audio-visual results) but because they might demonstrate the gradual development of a more critical visual approach and developing a sociologically adapted eye (although this might sound like disciplinary blinkers!). The initial reason for turning to video was to be able to bring vivid case material into my teaching as inspiration for both subject knowledge and research techniques and theoretical understanding of complex issues.

1. Spencer, S., Sawyer, S. and Surridge, D. (2003) *War and Propaganda: Closing the Public Mind*

A short unpublished video examining the management of media during the Iraq war of 2003, protest, and public reactions to media coverage, theories of media influence and the propaganda model. This is an unpublished resource used in teaching which is based on a series of interviews with three professors of media: Bob Franklin (Cardiff University), David Miller (Glasgow University Media Group) and Richard Keeble (University of Lincoln). In addition, the video draws on a number of street interviews with the public in Sheffield.

2. (i) *Framing the Fringe Dwellers* **(2004), Academic video. Available on C-SAP Website (http://www.teachingrace.bham.ac.uk/video_resources/)**

(ii) *Framing the Fringe Dwellers: Visual Methods for Research & Teaching Race & Ethnicity: A Sample Case Study* **(2006), in Max Farrar and Malcolm Todd (2006)** *Teaching Race in Social Sciences – New Contexts, New Approaches***, C-SAP Monograph, Birmingham.**
[Available Online] http:// www.c-sap.bham.ac.uk/resources/publications/ monographs/ teaching_race/

Australia has a complex indigenous heritage encompassing several hundred 'Aboriginal' groups with unique languages and traditions. However, the consequences of invasion rates of incarceration and the legacy of the 'stolen generation' (forcible removal of Aboriginal children), and continuous pressure from developers on already small parcels of land, has had a catastrophic impact on many communities, dislocating them from their traditional areas and leading to many indigenous people being trapped in an impoverished and pressured state. There is often a struggle to obtain even the most basic amenities in the midst of mono-cultural Australian affluence. This film (also a journal article and chapter in a book) focused on one specific site of this heritage, Darwin, in the Northern Territory, an area with a larger proportion of diverse indigenous peoples than other states of Australia. Yet these disparate groups enjoy an uneasy existence on the edges of the city in a few poorly resourced and crowded housing estates or in informal camps. It is an existence which at times brings them into conflict with the local government, the white community and concerns for the image of the city and the burgeoning tourist trade.

This video focused on the case of indigenous people in Darwin and was used as a vehicle for theoretical and practical reflections on exploratory attempts to use the medium (digital video and stills) both for research and to address issues in the teaching of race and ethnicity. There are two key concerns which the use of video is well suited to address. Firstly, the need to present voices of people who are affected by regimes of racism, social exclusion and powerlessness; to hear their story and to present their viewpoint while giving some cultural context to the case. This study raises a number of important questions about visual ethnography and the importance of developing an ethical and engaged practice which embraces collaborative and intersubjective approaches to research.

3. Spencer, S. and Radley, K. (2006) *Under the Skin of Multiculturalism***, Academic video. Available on C -SAP website: http://www.teachingrace. bham.ac.uk/video_resources/**

The intention behind this project was to create a video resource for learning and teaching which addressed some of the issues arising from the often bewildering and contradictory interpretations of 'multiculturalism'; exposing doubts, fears and the lived realities of an increasingly diverse society. The team set out to develop a visual approach charting the twists and turns in cultural and political discourses of diversity; from a sense of celebration and enjoyment of difference and the often palliative perceptions of multiculturalism through to current concerns about segregation, militancy and terrorism. Drawing on archive films, stills, live interviews and original music, the video provides a visually interesting and provocative account. Street interviews, voices from individuals in different communities (South Asian, African and African-Caribbean) as well as academics from the UK, US and Europe have been sampled to present a range of definitions and interpretations of multiculturalism. Especially of interest are the debates about the perceived tension between equality and difference, core and peripheral views of identity and citizenship, and anxieties over secularism and religion. This project was designed as a flexible series of materials for students and lecturers to open up debate into serious issues of race and ethnicity; the video exposes assumptions and embedded values, asking about the social and political realities which drive the changes.

4. *Drifting Visions & Dialectical Images: Everyday Paradoxes in a Northern City* (2009) (Illumina Issue 3, Dec 2009 e-journal, Edith Cowan University)

This project is a visual study of Sheffield exploring the contradictions and visual paradoxes of a city which is deeply scarred by transitions, the chaos of deindustrialisation and the constant attempts at re-invention. This article is largely reproduced in a section of Chapter 3. This is also an ongoing project which includes video, and a website which was constructed by colleague Dave Surridge – http://vissoc.org.uk

5. Spencer, S. and Samuels, L. (2010) *Looking for Africville*

An academic video and article examining the story of Africville; an early, autonomous community of largely African-Canadian settlers in Nova Scotia. The experiences of Africville residents survive through their powerful accounts of an area which was stigmatised and neglected by mainstream white society and eventually destroyed. At the centre of this case study is a piece of visual ethnography, employing video, stills archive materials and interviews. The specific focus of the paper is an examination of particular facets of qualitative visual research; the uses of walking and movement in ethnographic records, and the focus on oral narratives and how these may contrast with the 'official' histories.

Section II

Having experienced the range of new visual research which is happening at several conferences since 2006, I wanted to include space in this book to give a sense of the dynamism and creativity of visual research. Therefore, I approached four innovative researchers from across the social science disciplines to give a short account of the philosophies and purposes behind their practices with reflections on specific projects they have undertaken. The work ranges through sociological and cultural studies to anthropology, as well as specific discussion of hermeneutics of the visual, film genres, narrative structures and of course photographic aesthetics and practice.

Panizza Allmark – Edith Cowan University, Western Australia: *Towards a* photographie féminine: *photography of the city*

Allmark explores the city photographically, developing an embodied approach which breaks from the rational and comfortable masculine tradition of the landscape as beautiful, picturesque or transcendent. She challenges this with a feminist counter-aesthetic of the uncanny which portrays the city as an indeterminate and potentially ominous space. A wide-ranging discussion of the city includes examples from London, Las Vegas and Buenos Aires, while examining the relationship of photography to identity, through a subtle use of the stylistic documentary tradition developed by Atget, a seminal photographer of the early twentieth century, and innovative political practice.

Sarah Atkinson – University of Brighton: *Multiple cameras, multiple screens, multiple possibilities: an insight into the interactive film production process*

Crossed Lines (Dir: Sarah Atkinson) is an original fictional interactive film amalgamating multi-linear plots, a multi-screen viewing environment, an interactive interface and an interactive story navigation form. It has been exhibited at the Electronic Literature Organisation conference at the Washington State University, US; the Digital Interactive Media in Arts and Entertainment conference arts show in Athens; The Interrupt arts show in Providence, US; the Euro ITV arts show in Belgium and the International Digital Interactive Storytelling conference in Portugal. This essay reflects upon the creative processes of devising, scripting, directing and authoring the interactive film installation in which the viewer is given control over the flow, pace and ordering of the video-based narratives. The entire production process from script-writing to the final installation took place over a four-year period and involved nine principal cast members, numerous crew personnel, technicians, programmers, various cameras, audio-recording equipment, cutting-edge computer processors, reams of cable and a precariously soldered telephone. The complexities of undertaking and delivering such a project are reflected upon and discussed within this essay from the first-person perspective of the artist herself.

Roger Brown: *Photography as process, documentary photographing as discourse*

Recent discussions about photography concentrate on two perspectives: as a method in a complex of sociological methodology, and as a text to be variously evaluated, analysed and de-coded (Banks, 2007; Rose, 2007). Both views rest on the assumption that photographs offer a representation of knowledge and a correspondence to an empirical truth. Rarely is the making of photography discussed, yet there is much to be learnt from doing so (Becker, 1994; Banks, ibid.). This article focuses on the process of making documentary photographs of sociological value. On what Maynard refers to as the process of photographing and thinking through photography and Rorty as edification (Maynard, 2000; Rorty, 2009). Referring back to Szarkowski and his five-fold aesthetic of photography I shall argue that photographing is a process of thoughtful and ethical social interaction and hermeneutic whose value combines observation and aesthetics, or as Ruskin put it many years ago, 'a mutual dependency on Form and Mental Expression' (Ricoeur, 1991; Ruskin, 1853).

Roger Canals, an anthropologist and film maker, University of Barcelona: *Studying images through images: a visual ethnography of the cult of María Lionza in Venezuela*

Visual anthropology has been defined as a discipline which integrates three different fields: the study of images as an object, the use of images as an ethnographic method and the construction a visual discourse (through film or photography) to present the conclusions of the research. The aim of this article is to give an ethnographic example of how these three dimensions of visual anthropology can be combined in an innovative and creative way. From 2005 to 2007, I was doing fieldwork in Venezuela on the representations of María Lionza, one of the most important goddesses of the country. My objective was to study both the iconography and the social role of this image, but rapidly I realised that I could only achieve this goal critically using images during my fieldwork and constructing an anthropological discourse in which images had an autonomous position.

The ingredients are varied but collectively address some of the crucial issues of visual research touching on methodology and ethics, and the boundary between individual subjectivity and developing a visual practice which adds valid expression and in-depth analysis to the social sciences.

Section I

Visual research and social realities

1 Visualising social life

No object is mysterious. The mystery is your eye.

Elizabeth Bowen

An evolving visual culture

In this chapter the problems and potentiality of visual forms are examined to pave the way for an understanding of how visual methods might reveal many aspects of social life. It has been suggested that we are living in a visually saturated culture (Gombrich, 1996; Mirzeoff, 1999) and that late modernity has undergone a 'visual turn' towards an increasingly 'ocularcentric' culture (Jay, 1994; Jenks, 1995; Mitchell, 1994). There have been changes in the form and fluidity of new media technologies permitting a succession of new forms of visual experience. This plasticity of digital communications allows the simultaneous experience of visual, audio, verbal data as fluid and easily manipulated, whether via a webcam, embedded video or audio on PowerPoint slides or video networking at a conference.

> Mass societies have now come to rely on the electronic broadcast media as the centrifugal force of democracy. This new public sphere can be regarded as the mediasphere – a critical 'culturescape' in which meanings flow through various channels of human and technologically enhanced modes of communication (Lewis, 2005; Lewis and Lewis, 2006). The mediasphere is the compound of the media and the public sphere, the conflux of macro and micro processes of communication and social engagement.
>
> (Lewis, 2007: 5)

The 'mediasphere'[1] (see Hartley, 2002) includes the total output of the media and encompasses the smaller public sphere. In turn there is constant movement of communication between the mediasphere and the much broader web of cultural meanings (Lotman's 'semiosphere' conceived as the total universe of culture, language and text). These imaginary zones are useful to account for the way in which communications from within the public spheres are mediated as meanings vacillate between them leading to the active reconfiguration of written, textual and visual systems. One effect of globalisation has been the two-way ripple effect of movement from the centre to periphery, as possibilities for new cultural identities are introduced to cultures on the periphery (via electronic images and affluent tourism), while at the same time the periphery moves to the centre – for example the flow of economic migrants, and aspects of (for example) black, working-class culture taken up by white suburban youth. The focus on 'visual culture' as a viable area of study acknowledges the reality of living in a world of cross-mediation; our experience of culturally meaningful visual content, fluid multiple forms, and codes which migrate from one form to another, are bringing about profound and dynamic changes to social human systems.

> Today, rapidly growing technologies such as Internet, mobile computing and sensor web have enabled new patterns of human interactions, from social networks to physiological functions. A cogent example is the rapid 'evolution' of our thumbs from holding to controlling mobile systems, just in a few recent years.
>
> (Cai and Terrill, 2006: 235)

These changes have accelerated the study and critical analyses of visual social phenomena. The focus here is particularly on the qualitative uses of visual material in research, and the interdisciplinary nature of visual research which straddles anthropology, sociology and cultural studies, history, and social geography (amongst others). This chapter discusses the power of the image, emphasising its value as both complementary to more traditional modes of research, and as a field of study in its own right.

Is seeing believing?

There are examples where overt visual signs are ignored in favour of other contextual factors which determine our interpretation of a situation. A classic example of *not* believing one's eyes is the experiment of Solomon Asch (1951, 1955) (see Figure 1) in which an experimenter enlists the help of a group as confederate to agree that a line on a card (below left) was the same length as line 'B' on the comparison card (below right). Then a 'naïve' subject joined the group to take part in what was said to be a 'vision test'. Each member of the class was asked whether the line on the left corresponded most closely to either line A, B or C, and to state their answer aloud. Each of the group, in turn, as instructed, gave the answer as 'B'. One would assume that given the very obvious evidence of their own eyes most individuals would resist the pressure of conformity; however, when faced with the unanimously incorrect answer from each of the group members, 75 per cent of the naïve participants conformed, giving the 'wrong' answer to at least one question – they appeared not to believe their eyes. On the other hand perhaps it should not be surprising that shared values, beliefs and perceptions should be so powerfully persuasive, overriding individual perception and rationality. Seeing is not a biological process but a

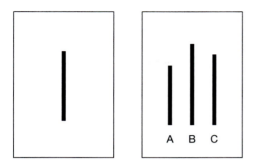

Figure 1 Picture based on the cards used in the Asch conformity experiments (Spencer, 2010).

socially and culturally learnt one, group conformity has survival value and verbal assurances are powerful, we believe in language, language can unite or exclude and in many situations people see what is socially expedient and turn a 'blind eye' to things which are less socially acceptable.

Images operate at the most basic level of human perception, and yet there is still a great deal we do not understand about the complex process of recognition and attribution of meaning. The idea that the picture both in our heads and the representations of photography or painting, for example, can somehow transfix and influence us like false idols which need to be smashed is reflected in Wittgenstein's ambivalent if not iconophobic comment: 'A *picture* held us captive. And we could not get outside of it, for it lay in our language and language seemed to repeat itself to us inexorably' (Wittgenstein, 1976: 48; Mitchell, 1994: 12). Philosophical concerns have centred on the relationship between the linguistic and pictorial, and in particular attacking the image as idolatry, false consciousness or a form of fantasy. Indeed, a strong thread in the understanding of visual culture is one of cultural pessimism that conceives of mass culture as passively in thrall to mass media spectacles; celebrity, sport and even warfare help to maintain a collective social order.

It seems clear that the visual evidence of photographs or video is only a partial representation of the reality which we perceive, a reality which is intimately linked to social values and culture, a reality which is collectively constructed. The meaning of the image, however beguiling the quality, and however it may seem to resist reduction to one or another model of interpretation, is a construction of culture both in its production and interpretation. This seductive authenticity of photography and video may be persuasive and authoritative, but the image can be used to privilege different meanings. The famous 'Point of View' advert for the *Guardian* newspaper nicely illustrates this. An event is recorded from several camera angles and at first sight appears to record a skinhead mugging an older smartly dressed middle-class man carrying a briefcase, until the camera pans out and we see the 'real' story, which is the imminent collapse of scaffolding and building materials above the man's head. From this wider perspective the street thug becomes a hero. Visual messages are potentially open to multiple interpretations. In this example the advert manipulates the cultural class-based stereotypes of respectability and delinquency to foreground the initial negative interpretation. Yet, as photographer Roger Brown reminds us, while photographs can be used to deceive or disguise, at the same time they present 'truthfulness to the appearance of things' and 'explicitness':

> I think one of the great gifts of photography is not Realism or Objectivity but a Truthfulness to the appearance of things. Photography is not Realism – it has what the essayist Raymond Tallis calls Explicitness, a defining human characteristic he reminds us. It is something we all want to believe in. Recording all that is before the lens. This IS what Great Aunt Nelly looks like. Hey, that is the Apollo 14 lander, Antares, on the Moon in 1971. This is the full orb of the earth, seen and photographed for the first time ever from Apollo 17 in 1972. It is an explicitness that upsets a lot of people even today. But we muck about with it at our peril. It is reported that the Apollo astronauts don't really remember space – what they remember are the photographs!
>
> (Brown, 2009)

Another famous example of the power of an image and the potential for fabrication is the photo of US Marines raising the flag on the summit of Mount Suribachi during the battle for Iwo Jima. It is popularly portrayed as a paradigm example of media manipulation, although in fact the image was genuine but taken on the second raising of the flag after the original flag was lowered and hidden to prevent a naval official from taking possession of it as a souvenir. Clint Eastwood's recent film *Flags of Our Fathers* focuses on the pivotal importance of this image for influencing the course of US public opinion, selling war bonds and creating an icon of mythical heroism for a battle in which thousands of US and Japanese troops were slaughtered.

Historically photographs have been an indispensable tool of rationalisation providing the reductive realism behind the bureaucratic ordering of society and the institutions of social control: family, school, criminal justice and the medical system. Through constellations of institutions everyday life is regulated and bodies are trained and rendered docile through a 'micro physics of power' (Foucault, 1977: 26). Marxist critic John Tagg argues that photography became a central technique in this regulatory system:

> The bodies – workers, vagrants, criminals, patients, the insane, the poor, the colonised races – are taken one by one: isolated in a shallow, contained space; turned full face and subjected to an unreturnable gaze; illuminated, focused, measured, numbered and named; forced to yield to the minutest scrutiny of gestures and features. Each device is the trace of the wordless power, replicated in countless images, whenever the photographer prepares an exposure, in police cell, prison, mission house, hospital, asylum or school.
>
> (2003: 260)

Similarly scientific disciplines used photography as part of their regimes of truth to catalogue and verify. Anthropology used visual records of indigenous peoples to represent their everyday lives sometimes with a focus on a presumed hierarchical ordering of 'race'. The tendency in some of these early examples is to present photographic imagery as a direct representation of reality. The two examples below illustrate this tendency. In the photograph of Australian aborigines the group is posed and framed as a family group, completely naked and isolated in a harsh desert landscape. The accompanying text stated: 'Reserves are set aside for them, and they receive Government protection, but whether they will survive is doubtful' (Wheeler, 1935). The drawing (below) by Landseer shows four portraits of 'Negroes' and a skull demonstrating the essentialist vision which suggests that such varied physical types might all be reducible to a common physiognomy. Ironically the drawing seems to undermine this essentialised piece of pseudo-science – the features shown are so obviously not reducible to one 'physical type'.

However, a more critical and conscious perspective began to develop in the later twentieth century recognising the highly constructed nature of images, and fed by a postmodern awareness of 'the indignity of speaking for others' (Gilles Deleuze in Foucault, 1977: 209). There is a danger in treating imagery (especially photographs and video) as authoritative evidence; as Prosser warns:

A family of aborigines in Central Australia. (Wheeler, H. ed. (1935?) *Peoples of the World in Pictures* in Spencer 2006 page 18)

'Negro race'

plate from Baron Cuvier's *Natural History* (1890) in Spencer 2006 page 40

Figure 2 Visions of 'race': (a) Hammerton, J. (c. 1932); (b) Cuvier's *Natural History*, illustration by Edward Landseer (c. 1890).

'A photograph does not show how things look. It is an image produced by a mechanical device, at a very specific moment, in a particular context by a person working within a set of personal parameters' (2006: 2).

Visual representation is always 'political', whether intentionally manipulated and censored, or through the embedded discourses and conventional codes which constitute and articulate meaning in our social institutions. More directly 'propagandist' manipulation of imagery, from gilded portraits to 'spin' and media management, has been occurring throughout history from Louis XIV to Tony Blair. The art of statecraft includes what John Thompson (1994) has called the 'management of visibility'. Different forms of 'mediated publicness' have become increasingly part of the art of politics, ensuring that politicians are kept out of harm's way, allowing professional 'flak catchers' to take the brunt of negative publicity and 'spin doctors' to massage the media.

Aesthetics of the visual

Interwoven with the political use of images, to catalogue, to confer verification, to affirm ideology, there is the aesthetic and artistic dimension of images. The unique character of the visual communicates at a different level to the verbal. The contrast between visual imagery and written explanation is similar to the classical distinction between mimesis (showing) and diegesis (telling) which is so important in the arts and literature. There is evidence that visual is part of a poetic process of expression and interpretation which 'encourages the use of metaphor and the empathetic communication of knowledge and experience that cannot be expressed using words alone' (Pink 2004: 10). This poetic use of imagery creates feelings and texture; the imagery speaks directly to the individual's inner self evoking memories, reflections and feelings. For example, Rosy Martin and Jo Spence developed a therapeutic use of photographic practice – 'phototherapy'. Her work, based on enactment and framed within a feminist practice of the performative body, explores identities, sexualities, ageing, desire, shame and sense of place (see e.g. 'Phototherapy and re-enactment: the performative body', 2001). In her series *Too Close to Home?* (2000/2003) images of everyday domestic objects take on eerie significance: a kitchen cupboard from which a bunch of keys hang, a white picket gate in an overgrown hedge seem filled with the hidden biographies of their users in their worn, mundane, still presence. Such meanings are hard to articulate in language and the images may provide a conduit for emotions; the scar tissue of the habitual resignation to ordinary life.

Similarly, Susan Hogan's research has examined the uses of imagery in social art therapy, describing pregnant women's use of expressive drawings to examine existential issues of identity and elusive feelings which are difficult to articulate in language (see Hogan, 1997: 2001). In this less tangible realm of the poetic with its resonances for the individual the image may not easily be reduced to a rational object; as Gaston Bachelard suggests:

the "objective" critical attitude stifles the "reverberation" and rejects on principle the depth at which the original poetic phenomenon starts. As for the psychologist, being deafened by the resonances, he keeps trying to *describe* his feelings. And the psychoanalyst, victim of his method, inevitably intellectualises the image, losing the reverberations in his efforts to untangle the skein of his interpretation.

(1964: xxiv)

That there is a tension between the use of images as aesthetic and political objects becomes clear from the commentaries of visual sociologists and anthropologists. Several visual sociologists have experienced an ambivalence with the discourse of art. Panizza Allmark, whose work straddles the boundaries between politics and aesthetics, comments on the uneasy consequences for her work being viewed as art: 'Within the art forum at times it tends to lose its textual political base, as images are open to be read in many ways, and the images may be rendered within a passive aesthetic status' (see Section II).

Culture, image and meaning

The poster below, which was part of a CRE campaign in the late 1990s, demonstrates some of the inherent problems in discussion of the image. Consider

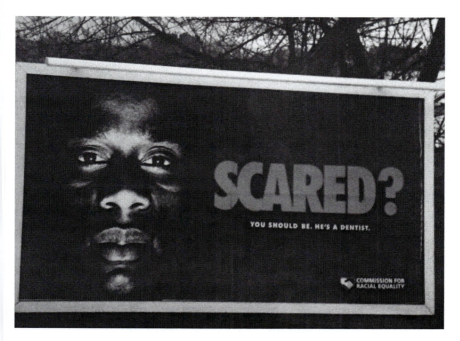

Figure 3 Commission for Racial Equality poster, *Scared?* 1999, Sheffield (Spencer, 2006: 23).

the image – it operates quite differently to words in a language. It has content – even a rather abstract image, like the face, has an immediate reality and is more concrete than the words beside it. The fact of the concreteness of the image, its immediate sensual reality, means that its expression will not make a full transition from object-language to meta-language. By contrast the word 'SCARED?' is part of a system which has an entirely arbitrary relationship to that which it denotes. All language operates at this level (with the exception of onomatopoeic words like cuckoo, woof, etc.). A further example of this elementary truth about the difference between language and image can be seen in the use of colour. The redness of the word 'SCARED?' affects us immediately (although its meaning in this context is ambiguous) but the redness of this word is very different from the redness of an image (a flag, stoplight, sunset or blood); the impact it might have derives from a complex series of cultural associations and conventional codes that might be related to the colour, compounded and co-related to the semantics of the word and the holistic interpretation of all of the elements in the billboard poster.

The photographic image is considered by some to be 'indexical', that is, a sign which is directly connected to that which it portrays rather than one where the interpretation is based on arbitrary convention (like the '?' question mark or other linguistic signs which have no natural relationship to the things they denote). However, it is highly contentious to describe a photograph in this way and has been a constant source of debate. Although the image thus created is to *some degree* an accurate and explicit record of the world, the seductive realism of photography has long been associated with the potential for manipulation and propagandist purposes. This has arguably reached a new peak with the so-called 'digital revolution' permitting ever more potential for subtle manipulation of the image, and the enormous proliferation of images which seem to erode the value and craft of the traditional photographer. Secondly, whatever the production process the image is always potentially polysemic, and hence the suggestion that the image is a direct emanation of 'the real' ignores the question of multiple interpretations and different reading positions. These issues will be addressed in several places in this book, but the problem of navigating these confounding currents should not be an obstacle to the enormous research value of visual representation. As Luc Pauwels warns: 'many researchers (of both ends of the spectrum) are overlooking the vast expressive potential of visual representations that opens up the way to scholarly argumentation and new avenues of expressing the unspeakable and unquantifiable' (2010: 572–73).

Given these lingering anxieties about the status of representation perhaps it is not surprising that most social research has seen visual attributes of social life as less reliable, harder to categorise or generalise, and if used they have been an addendum to the verbal discussion and traditional language-based methods of research. Marcus Banks suggests: 'the study and use of visual images is only of use within broader sociological research enterprises, rather than as ends in themselves' (Banks, 2001: 178).

While images are not elements in an entirely arbitrary code, neither are they tied to a simple one-to-one relationship with some referent in the real world. The interpretation of images like the face in Figure 3 is based upon the associations and cultural knowledge the viewer may have access to. Therefore they too can be seen as elements in a code, and this code can be manipulated to achieve certain effects, but, as in the case of this poster, there is always a possibility that the choice of image will not have the intended resonances or nuances of meaning with its target audience. This example demonstrates that there are often mismatches in the codes used and unrealistic expectations that the message will be interpreted and responded to in the manner the source of the message anticipated.

Intertextuality

How an individual interprets an image will depend on their accumulated cultural knowledge: 'every text and every reading depends on prior codes.' Kristeva argued that: 'Whatever the semantic content of a text its condition as a signifying practice presupposes the existence of other discourses. [. . .] This is to say that every text is from the outset under the jurisdiction of other discourses which impose a universe on it' (Kristeva, quoted in Culler, 1981: 116).

We 'read' the images in front of our eyes through the pictures we have in our heads. No two people have the same repertoire of cultural experience; individual subjectivity is complex and unique – hence responses will vary depending on this association to a universe of discourse which shapes interpretation. In the example of the poster image an observer will decode the features of the image through associations to existing cultural knowledge. Experience imposes a set of available frames of reference. So an observer's perception of an image (or indeed any social sign) is constrained by rhetorical forms which exist and circulate in a culture. These frames for seeing are sometimes referred to as tropes.

'Tropes' are similar to figures of speech, like metaphors or analogies; once we see one image in relation to the visual framework or trope it suggests, a strand of interpretation is brought into play. Roland Barthes declared that 'no sooner is a form seen than it *must* resemble something: humanity seems doomed to analogy' (cited in Silverman and Torode, 1980: 247). For example, the face in the poster might invoke images from film genres which then snap an interpretive framework into place, shaping the way the elements in the text are read. This is not dissimilar to the foreground/background effect by which ambiguous figures will perceptually vacillate. But the interpretation of the poster image is more than merely formal readings of a line drawing; depictions like this poster have been intentionally crafted to resonate with certain popular discourses of 'blackness'. In this case there is an intentional manipulation of these tropes attempting to expose a supposedly automatic conditioned response linking blackness with criminality and fear. However, the eerie lighting and stark choice of features looming from a black background does not offer many alternative viewpoints: it verges on parody or stereotype, which undermines the apparent (high-minded) intention of exposing our knee-jerk reaction to a black male. Further, although our perception of images is inevitably tied to the shaping influence of accumulated cultural knowledge, this also points to the fact that each individual's repertoire will vary. Stuart Hall suggested that 'texts' (any cultural form) can be read from a variety of inherently political 'reading positions' adopted by the individual. In 'Encoding/decoding' (1980), Hall argued that the dominant ideology is typically inscribed as the *preferred reading*[2] in a media text, but that this is not automatically adopted by readers. Hall (1980) identifies three broad frames of interpretation: the dominant (or 'hegemonic') reading, negotiated reading and oppositional ('counter-hegemonic') reading. Media sociologist David Morley further emphasised the context-specific nature of these reading practices, suggesting that a particular individual or group might employ different 'decoding strategies' when faced with a specific topic or a social context in which media material is presented. So in one context the same person may use an oppositional reading, but in another context 'read' the same content through a dominant (hegemonic) lens (Morley, 1981a: 9; 1981b: 66–67; 1992: 135).

So again in relation to the poster campaign, we might envisage a spectrum of reading positions, but the context of reading itself – a billboard on a busy road – will inevitably mean that the majority of those who pass in a car will barely register the image, or else it will merge into the more general transitory reception given to advertising hoardings. If walking down the road towards the poster, we might have a longer look at it and be faced by a sense of puzzlement. We might imagine that, like some poster ads, this is some sort of 'teaser' ad for a film or a TV drama, as the product line or branding are not readily identifiable. Closer consideration might bring a 'political' reading when the image resonates with the cultural baggage of the individual – affirming or challenging predictions of what the poster is trying to do. It seems quite possible that the reader might end up unclear as to the ultimate purpose of the campaign. In fact the ostensible purpose was to encourage a public protest: a sense of outrage at the popular and degraded portrayal of black identity and our readiness to jump to conclusions. Unfortunately in this case the majority of complaints received were from dentists. Perhaps, also, a campaign like this is heavily dependent on the wider political debate about diversity; perceptions and rhetoric around national identity and multiculturalism are a constantly shifting terrain.

Model 1 is an attempt to examine some of the features of the image as a communicative message attempting to identify some of the processes by which images generate, affirm or reproduce meanings and identities within a culture. Images, language and other signs are encoded by a sender and decoded by a receiver (clearly reflexive and reversible roles). The manner in which the message is understood has to do with the perception of codes, context and intention in the readings of the signs passed between the sender and receiver and back again. In the model the poster on a billboard was produced in a specific time by a specific agency with particular intentions. The outer frame of the model employs Shannon and Weaver's 'Communication Decision' model to demonstrate that there are

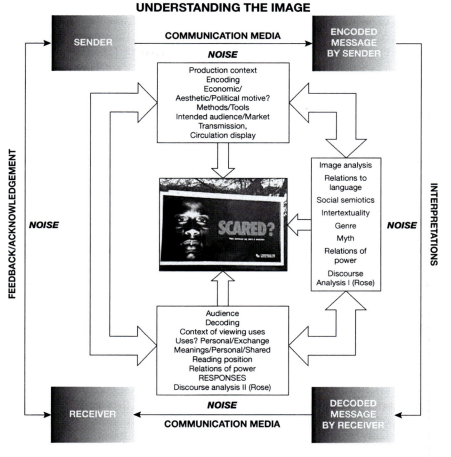

Model 1 Understanding the image

complex cultural codes being employed in the process of interpreting meaning. Both senders and receivers need to possess similar forms of cultural knowledge to avoid 'noise' (which signifies any interference which distorts the message) in the transmission of communication between either party, to achieve some symmetry in the intended message and the manner in which it is interpreted. The problem with images is that they are 'open texts' which are potentially polysemic. However, as discussed, their meanings are frequently fixed by the available intertextual associations made by the reader of the image. Although, in turn, such associations depend on the specific reader's positionality,[3] cultural knowledge and life experience, which will determine the reading position taken.

The possibility of 'noise' in the interpretation of the image could be a result of 'aberrant decoding',[4] a term coined by Umberto Eco (1965). Eco suggests that if we do not have access to the repertoire of codes the artist or author had we might be interpreting the message from entirely the wrong standpoint. Fiske gives the example of prehistoric cave paintings in which the animals thus depicted had been considered to look as if they were lighter than air and floating in an ethereal manner. Fiske (1989b: 78–79) cites Margaret Abercrombie (1960) who suggests to the contrary that the animals are being drawn when they are dead and lying on their sides on the ground. Our cultural codes which tend to avoid connotations of death and prefer images of living animals have led us to misinterpret these images. In the case of the poster in Model 1, it could be argued that the authors of the image deliberately tried to evoke a sense of menace by choosing a starkly lit black face juxtaposed next to a bold red 'SCARED?' – hence giving the prompts to encourage an alienated reading of this as a black face without a biography, suggesting the image is an icon standing for 'blackness'. The error of our decoding is made apparent in the much smaller white lettering: 'YOU SHOULD BE. HE'S A DENTIST' – which makes 'him' at once a specific person again. Looking at each of these in turn sheds light on how images and ways of seeing circulate to make sense of social life and our own identities. A matrix of social processes operates to convey dominant values reproducing and regulating meaning.

However, it is necessary to emphasise that visual methods are as problematic as other approaches and do not provide some magical conduit into an unmediated social reality. Rather, imagery is always potentially preyed upon for expedient political uses.

In a capitalist society which is structured along lines of unequal power and organised in terms of domination and exploitation, the status quo is maintained through systems of representation which reflect this as normal and unremark-able. Kress and Hodge argue that these divided material conditions manifest themselves in the ambiguous forms of ideology which they term 'ideological complexes': 'An ideological complex exists to sustain relationships of both power and solidarity, and it represents the social order as simultaneously serving the interests of both dominant and subordinate' (1988: 3).

The poster example demonstrates the complex alternative meanings which can be produced from images, and the analysis of its constitutive elements and intertextual relationships may suggest a 'preferred reading'. Images 'speak' to us, they link to constellations of other signs – hence they are 'rhetorical'.

This example highlights several key facets of the image: images have a materiality and immediateness (they can represent objects). This gives the image a different 'ontology to words and language' (see Canals, Section II). The images' explicitness presents an apparently unarguable reality, yet paradoxically this indexical relationship of images to actual reality has the potential for systematic distortion like any other medium in the hands of those who wish to persuade or shape attitudes. The next section examines images as agents of social control or at least as players in this dual ideological role.

Surveillance, spectacles and simulations

One of the most commented-on aspects of western culture and to an extent a growing feature of global society is the prominence of surveillance. Jeremy Bentham's 1785 vision of the panopticon was a design for prisons, said to be derived from the plan of a military school in Paris. The building comprised a central tower in the middle of a circular building lined with cells open to the scrutiny of the warder. The concept of the design is to allow an observer to oversee all prisoners without the prisoners being able to tell whether they are being watched, thus conveying what has been called the 'sentiment of an invisible omniscience'(Lang, 2004: 53). Bentham conceived of this as a structure which would make the need for state violence obsolete as control would be possible by the simple ordering of public space. The principles of this design were taken up by several prison regimes; at Port Arthur prison in Tasmania, for example, with its radical and cruel approach to the moral education of criminals. In the chapel cubicles were set up dividing prisoners from one another and directing their view onto the priest, while the partitions dividing each cubicle prevented them from seeing the men next to them. A warder seated on a raised platform would have an unobstructed view of the congregation.

The design of prisons, as a 'moral architecture' rendering the individual transparent to the gaze of the warder, is thought to have been influential on the architecture of other buildings, factories, schools and hospitals, and some suggest that shopping malls, too, have a similar architecture with a central domed tower and radiating arms of the malls (see e.g. Davis, 1990, 'The Panopticon Mall').

The notion of a social subject totally exposed before the omniscient gaze of an authoritarian society which has the vested power to order, shape and control has been influential in western culture. In Orwell's dystopian novel, *Nineteen Eighty-Four*, even the thought processes of citizens are scrutinised. Foucault's *Discipline and Punish* (1977) examines 'panopticism' as a movement in an evolving discourse of disciplinary society. Elements of this vision seem particularly prescient in Britain today. There are estimated to be around 4.2 million CCTV cameras in Britain – about one for every 14 people (BBC News, 2006). These are located in every main street and in public buildings like Job Centres where some have sensors which activate them if they detect aggressive voice tones over a certain decibel level (*Independent*, 2007). In addition, they are being used privately in people's homes to monitor domestic abuse or to gather evidence about neighbours.

While originally a term used by Christian Metz (1982) to discuss the very different visual spectacle of cinema as distinct from theatre, 'scopic regime' has come to mean the generic ways of looking, mediated by the particular technology employed as well as the shaping influence of dominant discourses within a particular culture. More ambitious theoreticians have posited general systems of visuality constructed by a cultural/technological/political apparatus mediating the apparently given world of objects in a neutral perceptual field. In this more totalising usage, 'scopic regime' indicates a non-natural visual order operating on a pre-reflective level to determine the dominant protocols of seeing and being on view in a specific culture.

Theoretically the relationship of the look to power relations has been of interest in social sciences and media studies and in particular the way in which different groups are positioned in cinema and photography. Laura Mulvey's work used Freudian and Lacanian theory of scopophilia[5] (the desire to look – voyeurism) in the analysis of cinema. Typically films tended to present women as the object to be looked at and men are the 'bearer of the look' ([1992] 2001: 346). The look is indicative of the dominant subject positions of men and women in society. Literature, film and other media position women as subordinate and passive, men as the active protagonists who present the locus of control through their objectifying 'male gaze'. Sarah Atkinson gives reference to this aspect of visual media in her Section II discussion citing Hitchcock's *Rear Window* as a famous example of the voyeuristic theme in cinema (see also Chandler, 2010).

French situationist philosopher Guy Debord (1967: 44) described everyday life as 'a permanent opium war'. Modern capitalism was an 'immense accumulation of spectacles' and what was once 'truly lived has become mere representation' (Ali, 2006). Spectacular defining events are likely to capture our attention. Edward Bernays (considered one of the founders of public relations) recognised the power of a fabricated spectacle to shape public opinion. In a 1929 campaign to promote smoking to women (at the time there was a very negative, stigmatised view of women who smoked), Bernays drew on psychoanalytical thought (his uncle was Sigmund Freud) and he staged an event employing debutantes and models to pose as suffragettes as part of the annual New York Easter Parade. At a prearranged signal from him they would light up cigarettes. Bernays had alerted all the main news agencies that a group of Suffragettes were planning to protest by lighting up 'torches of freedom'. The mass spectacle was reported across America and reputedly, thousands of women took up smoking as a result.[6]

The media tends to focus on those events which are 'newsworthy' rather than commonplace. The more subtle processes which are harder to portray in visual media don't lend themselves to the iconic photo-image or the 'sound bite' news feature. How can a gradual process of everyday lived reality be portrayed? By the values of news corporations they are redundant. Les Back (in an interview in 2006, below) suggested that sociology too needed a more careful focus which did not miss the profound aspects of everyday life in favour of a focus on the spectacular, the 'big issues' in social sciences.

> Les Back: I think both politics and sociology is drawn to a kind of unhealthy fascination with the spectacular; the violent outburst, the biggest news, the loudest voice, the most exotic example. I think we need to find another way of engaging with the ways in which people live through and across, within, beyond sometimes, the differences which they inherit and that they make everyday. I'm not sure we've got a language to describe that, because they are the remarkable things that are not remarked upon because they are not spectacular.
>
> (In Spencer and Radley (2006) *Under the Skin of Multiculturalism*, interview at CRONEM Conference, 15 June)

The power of the spectacle to focus attention and create mythical narratives to invade all aspects of social reality is never more alarming than in the case of 'war'. We have limited resources when it comes to news from distant parts of the world. Despite the proliferation of media channels there is a high degree of media consolidation with ownership in the hands of relatively few global corporations. So if we depend on news sources to understand what is happening around the world it is fair to assume that what we are presented with is a culturally-specific frame of reference for interpreting often complex political situations with equally complex historical origins. We are confronted with media imagery which tends to be built around narratives that have been filtered, censored and shaped in terms of what is seen as appropriate to the sensitivities of the home nation. In the case of the 2003 invasion of Iraq it could be argued that there was a mythical narrative of 'war' (when it was, in fact, a swift invasion of a fairly defenceless country in which many thousands of Iraqis died).

Several writers have claimed that the 2003 Iraq war was not really a war but a series of spectacles staged to provide images of heroic battle (akin to the epic conflicts of the Second World War. The media is central in the illusion: Professor Richard Keeble at Lincoln University explained how carefully the conflict was choreographed to build the heroic impression of warfare:

> There was no war in the Gulf in 2003. Rather, a myth of heroic, spectacular warfare was manufactured, in large part, as a desperate measure to help provide a raison d'être for the (increasingly out-of-control) military industrial complexes in the US and UK – and to hide the reality of a rout of a hopelessly overwhelmed 'enemy' army. The links between mainstream journalists and the intelligence services are crucial factors in the manufacture of the myth. But it is not essentially a massive elite conspiracy. Rather, the myth's origins lie deep within complex military, historical, economic and political forces which it is crucial to identify. Moreover, the manufacture of the 'war' myth has profound implications for any study of the political and military origins of the conflict and press representations.
>
> (Keeble in Allan and Zelizer, 2004: 43)

What Keeble is suggesting here is of primary importance to the discussion of visual culture, and current media portrayals specifically, and it does vindicate some of the postmodern concerns about spectacles and simulations.

Jean Baudrillard (1983: 2) defines simulation[7] as follows: 'Simulation is no longer that of a territory, a referential being, or a substance. It is the generation by models of a real without origin or reality: a hyperreal. . . . It is no longer a question of imitation, nor duplication, nor even parody. It is a question of substituting the signs of the real for the real.' In Baudrillard's view this interpenetration of reality by fantasy was apparent everywhere, and starkly noted during the Gulf War in 1991 that the war had never happened and that it was just a video game. Similarly the 2003 invasion was more like 'reality TV' – as Armando Iannucci explains:

It has been said that if the first Gulf War (the allied intervention when Iraqi forces invaded Kuwait) was a video game the 2003 invasion of Iraq was more like a reality TV show. At first sight these seem just the glib throw away comments the stock in trade of arrogant postmodern analysis. Baudrillard was talking about the anaesthetising effects of broadcast news; real conflict in 1991 was turned to animated computer game, encouraged by Pentagon briefings that focused on graphically generated images of bombs hitting their targets. Because we were denied the close-up reality of war, we felt detached. It was like watching a battle on Playstation, and the language of 'collateral damage' and 'softening up' convinced us we were participating in a virtual game.

To an audience in UK there is some truth in them. The fact that such events are presented as a spectacle viewed thousands of miles away in living rooms in cities and countries removed geographically, culturally and ideologically from their epicentre raises the suspicion that these are events taking place in another space, another reality. These are images so stage-managed, choreographed, packaged and mediated that they could indeed be said to have the character of media simulations, virtual reality games or the postmodern sense of myth.

(Armando Iannucci, the *Guardian*, Monday, 28 April 2003)

Some claims from postmodernism are nihilistic and seem to lead to a cul-de-sac in the discussion of social change; however, it is clear that to some degree there has been an interpenetration of fiction with fact, real and the imagined, the material and the symbolic. For example, some video gaming companies have based their computer animations on footage of actual warfare which has then been modelled and simulated. The results are increasingly realistic and aim to re-create as closely as possible the experience of combat in different theatres of warfare. 'Shock and Awe' (the concept of the initial extreme bombing campaigns on Baghdad) is now a brand name used in dozens of products. The United States Patent and Trademark Office received at least 29 trademark applications in 2003 for exclusive use of the term. 'The first came from a fireworks company on the day the United States started bombing Baghdad. Sony registered the trademark the day after the beginning of the operation for use in a video game title, but later withdrew the application and described it as "an exercise of regrettable bad judgment"' (*Seattle Post Intelligencer*, 2003). The term has also been used as a level in the video game *Call of Duty 4*, and is reputedly being used in a variety of other products, including insecticide sprays, bowling balls, shampoo and condoms. Perhaps this trivialisation and commodification of horrific events is not surprising given the intense stage management of such spectacles. In the last 20 years, media management of warfare has become crucial in maintaining public support. These wars are not about territory:

They are about winning access to resources; oil in Iraq, without damaging the resource that you're trying to get. Therefore you can't leave it to clumsy conscript soldiers who are mere cannon fodder; you have to send in trained specialists. You use sophisticated weaponry. You're looking to start and finish the thing in a couple of weeks . . . journalists can't just walk round. How do they get the story? Well, governments say we have two answers to that. One is we will embed you in a fighting unit. What this means is that a journalist works, lives and fights, and reports from behind – at the line, at the fighting line, with a group of soldiers. And he literally brings not only the political but the physical perspective. And so we see images of someone being bombarded by 'the enemy'. We see people, our side, being killed. Everything is reported from "our side". As viewers we are pulled in, not only to the physical but the ideological position of 'our side'.

The second way to do it is that journalists who won't be embedded can go along and be briefed by rather good-looking guys in military uniforms; slick press briefers, who stand in front of plasma screens where digital images flash in front of them, on sets and stages and briefing platforms designed by Hollywood set designers. And all of this is conducted – 'our' side of the war is given. Information is withheld for so-called 'military reasons', and they're used as a platform to abuse, stereotype and ridicule our enemies.

(Professor Bob Franklin in Spencer, 2003)

The US Special Forces' 'rescue' of Private Jessica Lynch is another example of how a story can be filtered and embellished for dramatic effect (produced as a heroic rescue with allusions to the Hollywood blockbuster film *Saving Private Ryan*). In fact although Private Lynch had been taken prisoner she was given specialist medical treatment for traffic accident injuries, and she had never sustained bullet or stab wounds as the US claimed:

'We heard the noise of helicopters', says Dr Anmar Uday. He says that they must have known there would be no resistance. 'We were surprised. Why do this? There was no military, there were no soldiers in the hospital. . . . It was like a Hollywood film. They cried, "Go, go, go", with guns and blanks and the sound of explosions. They made a show – an action movie like Sylvester Stallone or Jackie Chan, with jumping and shouting, breaking down doors.' All the time with the camera rolling. The Americans took no chances, restraining doctors and a patient who was handcuffed to a bed frame.

(Kampfner, 2003)

These examples further highlight and critically reveal the way in which imagery can be harnessed to propagandist causes, disguising the real motives of wars and their devastating consequences on civilians. All of this indicates that, despite the many benefits of using images, there is the possibility that the viewer may be prone to a misapprehension that video, film or photographs open a window into the lives of people without any of the barriers and obstacles inherent in other accounts especially those which are written. We are, after all, experiencing the nuances of non-verbal codes which are lost in written forms. However, while there are many benefits for the researcher in the use of video or still pictures, it must be remembered, as Marcus Banks suggests, that:

> Images are no more transparent than written accounts and while film, video and photography do stand in an indexical relationship to that which they represent they are still representations of reality, not a direct encoding of it. As representations they are therefore subject to the influences of their social, cultural and historical contexts of production and consumption.
>
> (Banks, 1995)

Our culture is one which gives great authority to TV images. There is the understandable belief that film and video simply record events, delivering an unmediated view of reality. Live coverage of events as they occur, for example, in a war zone, is often presented uncritically as incontrovertible evidence.

This popular conception that the visual media are an authoritative source is, as Fiske suggests, a covert form of propaganda. The impossibility of objectivity and the consequent irrelevance of notions of bias (based as they are upon an assumption that non-bias is possible) 'should not blind us to the ideological role that the concept of "objectivity" plays' (Fiske, 1989: 288). This power to shape perception of events has long been recognised and exploited – it is certainly true that media images have an extraordinary power which endures in the memory. In a 2003 interview, Bob Franklin, Professor of Journalism Studies at Cardiff University, made the point that the visual power of TV can be greatly influential and hence prone to active censorship when oppositional political views might be broadcast:

SS. Would you argue that T.V. perhaps is accorded greater value and authority than other forms of media?

B.F. Absolutely . . . It's very, very hard for a radio journalist or a print journalist to produce an image that's as evocative as a young child running down a road, on fire with napalm. And I think governments understand that. And I think it's precisely why, when the government – Douglas Hurd, then Conservative Home Secretary – banned eleven paramilitary organisations and parties in Northern Ireland, the ban applied only to television.

(Spencer, 2003, Interview with Professor Bob Franklin)

How can such images be understood? Sontag makes the point that the moral impact of such pictures depends on the political consciousness of the viewer: 'Without a politics, photographs of the slaughter-bench of history will most likely be experienced as, simply, unreal or as a demoralising emotional blow' (1978: 19). More than this, perhaps, images may be trivialised or ignored – indeed there may be no communicative bridge to allow their real significance to emerge. Forty years ago John Berger's groundbreaking 1970s book and TV series *Ways of Seeing* made this point, showing the total disconnect in his powerful contrast between the publicity dream in glossy advertising and images of East Pakistani refugees in a Sunday supplement. As he flicked through the pages he pointed out how intrinsically hollow were the appeals for aid when encountered in this context; skeletal fly-covered victims sandwiched between the glamorous publicity images for Martini or Pimms.

> What happens in East Pakistan, or for that matter Birmingham, any historic event, anywhere is always on the far side of the frontier of the publicity dream. What happens 'out there', happens to strangers whose fate is meant to be different to ours, what happens in the dream is meant to happen to us.
>
> (Berger, 1972)

We can understand the images discussed above as products of particular scopic regimes. In the case of 'SCARED?' the dominant modes of seeing are being manipulated to highlight the scopic principles through which 'we' (a possibly privileged white audience) look at 'them' (the marginalised, black, 'other'). Although in this case there are indications that the design misrecognised the audience's response and the ambiguity of the image (which may have been intentional) made the final product look either crudely discriminatory or puzzling. This brief detour into the disturbing, postmodern realms of the spectacle demonstrates again why a critical sociology of the image is important, because developments in media technologies and sophistication of production make the line between reality and fiction increasingly hard to detect.

The comfort of things: images and objects

The images discussed in many of the research contexts cited so far are frequently images of objects; artefacts which are significant in the context in which they were revealed: statues, postcards, posters, signposts, family albums and so on. Hartley's pictures of how TV sets were 'dressed' in the family house are good examples of how TV, the focus of visual attention, performs a different function in the home, as a public object. They were adorned: 'Often their polished wooden tops were shrines of family remembrance, with photos of absent children, wedding pictures or formal portraits, enhanced by an assortment of flowers, ornaments, trophies and doilies neatly arranged into a votive altar' (1992: 108). This material context suggests that objects have 'biographies' (Appadurai, 1986; Banks, 2007). They have histories and a range of complex connections with people and their lives: 'they have previous entanglements with the lives of other people which may prove important to their current roles in society when encountered by the researcher' (Banks, 2007: 60).

In a recent study Daniel Miller chose a London street at random and visited 30 households to examine these micro worlds in their own right, the forms of connectivity and the role that objects play in the lives of the inhabitants. His encounters with people and their relationship to the things in their lives present a vision not of people as greedy materialists but as highly sensitive to the significance favourite objects have, sustaining and affirming their lives not as mere status symbols. One woman's aesthetic repudiation of her parents' coldness and snobbery takes the form of a love for McDonald's 'happy meal' toys and

IKEA furniture. Another part-Aboriginal street resident uses his laptop as a means of resolving a deep-seated cultural contradiction about materiality: wanting to give away things which most would keep and at the same time wanting to create an archive about his Aboriginal mother and his own Aboriginal heritage.

'The laptop seems almost perfect as the solution to his ambitions in life; as the contemporary completion of a cosmological tussle with materiality which was once central to the lives of his aboriginal ancestors' (Miller, 2009: 72). Other studies have also examined this 'domestication' of technology (e.g. Lally, 2002; Moores, 2005) not only through the publicity which eases the hardware's induction into the rhythms of domestic life, but also by exploring the process by which they are integrated into the household. The constant leapfrogging of technologies – their exponential increase in capacity and decrease in size – can render goods swiftly obsolete or socially embarrassing. Within the family, product use of computers, stereos, ipods, TVs, DVD players, game consoles and so on may be divided along gendered or generational lines. Computers are often perceived as essential for a child's educational attainment but parents may become increasingly worried about their distracting use for the purposes of entertainment or social networking potential.

Parent-to-child relationships of competition and collaboration are significant factors in the uses and meanings of consumer products. Hence 'consumer durables' can become key actors in the fabric of everyday life.

In another street-based study of 'things', Robert Williams and his 10-year-old son Jack Aylward bring an artistic and scientific passion to the forensic analysis and cataloguing of everyday material objects. The cabinet of collected objects (*Historico-Naturalis et Archaeologica* ex-Dale Street) is an attempt to archive many different facets of everyday life of Dale Street in Lancaster. Transcending the boundaries of the traditional museum, the Williams have created a repository of folk memories, not mere suburban detritus but a celebration of the things which are meaningful in our lives. These are objects which have their own biographies, indeed many objects come into being through use: 'Any object is always actualised in a specific moment of use, which produces both the object and the sort of person looking at it' (Rose, 2007: 220). With an obvious passion for natural histories like Gilbert White's *Natural History of Selborne* (cited as one of the key influences), the collection elevates the everyday by treating it with the same forensic fervour usually reserved for items in exotic collections in museums. Cataloguing the material objects from the everyday life of a suburban city street; from cigarette packets and tennis balls to genus of beetles and snail shells and conkers, test tubes containing 'squashed bees', mobile phone SIM cards, and the skeleton of a mouse. Each item is labelled and dated, with details of location and catalogue numbers. This form of bricolage[8] demonstrates the extraordinary diversity of one street.

Anthropologically objects can be considered to have a social life because they are linked to the system of production, and through consumption and exchange they can be imbued with value, both monetary and social status; they can thereby enter the constellation of goods which represent worth and identity. Arun Appadurai (1986) discussed the 'commodity' role of objects as only one possible phase in a complex social journey of the object. Everyday objects are another window into people's lives, narratives, sense of identity and belonging. Objects can be aspirational; like collectors' items, imbued with the promise contained in the sleek, well-manufactured lines of consumer luxury, a car or a camera. They can play roles in the ongoing narratives of relationships, forms of exchange,

Figure 4 Cabinet display *Historico-Naturalis et Archaeologica*, Dale Street, Karen Slinger photographer; copyright Robert Williams (Principal Lecturer, Fine Art, and Programme Leader, Fine Art, at the School of Art and Design, Faculty of the Arts, University of Cumbria) and Jack Aylward-Williams, 2009.

symbols of forgiveness, or eternal love, they can be customised, modified and disposed of or destroyed in a moment of anger or as an act of spite.

These studies are centred on the world of things, setting out to examine the everyday in detail. Miller's study demonstrates that people's uses of material things are complex and transcendent and not easily reduced to some form of false consciousness or commodity fetishism. The Williams' project is a sort of collective celebration of things unremarkable in themselves but, when gathered together and set out with such custodial care, exert a remarkable presence, a pride in the shared lives that they represent.

Roger Canals' work takes a critical anthropological approach, showing how spiritual values associated with the folk goddess María Lionza are transformed into concrete representations: figurines, paintings, or enacted in spirit possessions or by dance troupes and actors. This process is a form of 'ritual condensation', a term coined by Edmund Leach to explain the process whereby thought objects are converted into material objects often through ritual processes.

The ritual object gives a tangible and visible presence to referents which exist on a different, transcendental plane, whether these referents are 'real', imagined, concrete or abstract. In some rites the unseen spirits are personified or enacted through symbolic objects; in Catholic Eucharist, for example, the body and blood of Jesus passes into the host and the wine. Canals' film *The Blood and The Hen* shows an example of a healing ritual where blood, smoke and water are used to channel unseen supernatural forces. Fiske and Hartley (1978) point out that ritual condensation could be said to occur in TV programmes in which abstract concepts about interpersonal relationships are rendered into concrete form. Using the example of successive rolling out of US cop dramas *Ironside*, *Kojak* and *Starsky and Hutch*, they argue that the articulation of moral or deviant behaviour is enacted, each cop show subsuming the role of 'bard' and, through ritual condensation of societal values the characters of the key protagonist seem to embody societal values of morality and justice.

The role of material culture in our lives is complex and provides an important emphasis in visual studies, showing that when the taken-for-granted furniture of our existence comes under scrutiny the findings can be very revealing. Following this initial foray into the dimensions of the image we can now begin to identify some tentative benefits of visual research.

Benefits of visual approaches

First, the visual has an explicitness and immediacy which delivers a multisensory impact. This immediacy of the visual affects us in a profound and elusive way – before the sense-making apparatus, the cognitive processing, there is a pre-reflective reaction, as several writers and researchers have noted. There seems to be some accord that there is something indefinable about the visual, grounding it in material reality. It is an immediate and authentic form which verbal accounts are unable to fully encompass. Pink (2007: 135) argues for the primacy of sensory experience in ethnographic research:

Scholars across the social sciences and humanities are currently acknowledging the benefits of accounting for the senses . . . in a research agenda that emphasises the inevitable interconnectedness of the senses and the multisensoriality of human experience. . . . This body of research has demonstrated the impossibility of separating the visual from the other senses in human perception, knowledge, understanding and practice.

Second, and as a result of this, visual records can create vivid and authentic personal narratives. In one example (Spencer and Radley, 2006) we interviewed several prominent sociologists and recorded their responses about the meaning of multiculturalism and identity politics. The resulting video material added drama and life to an account of concepts which when read in a textbook or an editorial may be far less engaging, and often couched in language constrained by academic conventions. Similarly, watching 'real' people from different communities talk about their lived experiences is refreshing to students because it captures an *embodied* expression, not abstract truisms about 'community'. When personal stories from experience and theoretical discussions are united, the result is powerful. This approach is not a substitute for other forms of academic engagement, but the variety of concerns and expressions stimulate greater interest and focus attention. Video narrative records are a powerful visual form bringing an authenticity of lived experience to the issue. They are, arguably, empowering as stories are told in people's own words. Critical Race Theorists have long recognised the power of individual voices to provide a 'counter-story' to expose and challenge consensus (Ladson-Billings and Tate, 1985; Delgado, 1998; McDonald, 2003). In the next chapter, several examples of the power of visual narratives will be examined.

Third, building on these points, visual material provides a form of 'thick description'[9] which helps in the exploration and understanding of theoretical ideas. Clifford Geertz adapted the concept 'thick description' in his approach to ethnographic study to suggest a more penetrating approach which recognised the multiple layers of our social reality. Drawing on Ryle's analysis of the complex motives behind the simple gesture of two boys winking, he demonstrates how more in-depth examination of social actions can be very revealing. It is not a case of enumerating 'social facts' about behaviour – such an approach remains superficial, he suggests – but about understanding the significance of such phenomena to the social actors and meanings revealed about the broader society.

Doing ethnography is like trying to read (in the sense of 'construct a reading of') a manuscript – foreign, faded, full of ellipses, incoherencies, suspicious emendations, and tendentious commentaries, but written not in conventionalised graphs of sound but in transient examples of shaped behavior.

(Geertz, 1973: 10)

Imagery is explicit and specific, capturing the instance in action. As suggested above, photography is not untainted realism, but sometimes it might present us with ways of seeing the world which rupture the familiarity of the everyday, insisting on a closer look at those things beneath the mundane surfaces. As Allmark (Section II) suggests, the value of her photographic practice is that it 'conveys dialectical images that pose questions, rather than presenting answers. It is about contemplation of the world we live in rather than confirmation of how it is.' This is to suggest that images and video might be used to capture and foreground the processes of complex dialectical change which is going on continuously. This quality of some images to depict the processes of social change could assist in the development of a more critical discursive approach for looking at the norms and values tacitly portrayed in society and in social products and representations. By looking beneath the surfaces of social relations the complex motives and meanings behind behaviour are revealed, creating what bell hooks (1997) has called 'enlightened witnesses' of cultural forms. We cannot avoid the bombardment of images but we can develop a critical distance from them. Perhaps visual methods are an important part of the development in a critical sociological practice of seeing and producing images; to question rather than to confirm, to pick apart the motives and examine the techniques used in advertising, news production and political rhetoric as well as questioning those institutions which are seen as impartial, objective and beyond bias.

Summary

To understand the image and ways of seeing and constructing meaning requires a discussion of the social and cultural context in which imagery is used and in which conventions of representation are developed in culturally bounded ways. Seeing is never innocent in that it occurs within already ascribed cultural boundaries; nonetheless, the materiality and *explicitness* of the image is power-fully persuasive. For this reason images have been indispensable in the sciences and are a vital tool of political and commercial rhetoric.

In the case of anthropology and ethnology, early use of images, despite the veneer of objectivity, operated in many cases from within a culture which was built upon the active colonial domination of large areas of the world, and could be seen to actively legitimate ideas of superiority through pseudo-sciences of racial hierarchy. The image *is* political: it presents a picture of the world, presenting events from a point of view – 'spectacles' can be staged or selectively chosen to support or affirm an ideological platform. Imagery can position the subject and regulate social relations as a form of social control – in an obvious way through the burgeoning practices of surveillance. CCTV cameras and reality TV shows explore intimate areas of public life, and at the time of writing, the news that remotely controlled drone 'spy' planes which are too high to be seen are being introduced to further regulate traffic and prevent fly tipping in the UK. However, at a more embedded psycho-social level, gendered or 'raced' practices of looking exert implicit influence on social relationships. Scopic regimes – modes of looking – are associated with pleasure as well as power, the gaze of the shopper and tourist, the flaneur or voyeur, are structured by global processes of consumption and the seemingly inexhaustible supply of images. Such modes of looking are interwoven with aesthetic and popular cultural tropes and genres in art, cinema and advertising. Finally we have seen that the image is also beguilingly real and that this apparently irreducible materiality 'innocents' interpretation: objects themselves take on an autonomous existence in a capitalist society. The 'visual turn' does seem to herald different and startling trends. What does the dawning of this new visual era mean? Mitchell says it is not clear but more critical work is urgently needed:

> Most important is the realization that while the problem of pictorial representation has always been with us, it presses inescapably now and with unprecedented force, on every level of culture, from the most refined philosophical speculation to the most vulgar productions of the mass media. Traditional strategies of containment no longer seem adequate, and the need for a global critique of visual culture seems inescapable.
>
> (Mitchell, 1994: 16)

This chapter has demonstrated several different aspects of images and their uses as research evidence. It is clear from this brief account that images and video open up complex, reflexive and multi-faceted ways of exploring social realities. These are just a few of the uses that make visual methods a powerful complement to other traditional approaches. Having ascertained that visual methods offer some unique insights less accessible to traditional methods, how should research progress, and in what processes, designs and methodologies could visual research be used? Chapter 2 will begin to address these questions.

2 The research process and visual methods

The real voyage of discovery consists of not in seeking new landscapes but in having new eyes.

Marcel Proust

The visual researcher

In the first chapter the individual's perception of images was shown to be a complex, cultural and social process. Analyses of the visual dimensions of social life to attain a 'thick description' are characteristic of a qualitative approach which is recognised to be the best approach when a complex and in-depth detailed understanding of an issue is required. Furthermore, Cresswell suggests that the qualitative mode of research is one through which:

> we want to empower individuals to share their stories, hear their voices, and minimise the power relationships that often exist between a researcher and the participants in a study. To further de-emphasise a power relationship, we may collaborate directly with participants by having them review our questions, or by having them collaborate with us during the data analysis and interpretation phases of research.
>
> (2007: 40)

In terms of visual research a collaborative use of imagery or video footage is recognised as essential. As with any research method, visual approaches ought not to be chosen without discussion of their validity to the research question and ethical sensitivity. Social science researchers are confronted by a bigger and more confounding problem: the question of 'how far one can ever really understand the social world?' Guba and Lincoln (1994: 108) suggest three key questions which should be considered in order to ensure depth of engagement with the underlying philosophy of research:

*   **The ontological question**
    What is the form and nature of reality and, therefore, what is there that can be known about it?

- **The epistemological question**
  What is the nature of the relationship between the knower or would-be knower and what can be known?
- **The methodological question**
  How can the inquirer go about finding out whatever he or she believes can be known?

Ontologically the use of visual data raises questions about the perception and interpretation of what we believe to be social reality. For example, as discussed earlier, the mediasphere, political ideologies and rapid technological changes all raise questions about how social reality can be understood. How influential are visual media in the construction of individual and community identities and what are the processes by which individuals interpret social and cultural phenomena as meaningful to their lives? As discussed in Chapter 1, imagery has the potential to distort and serve political and ideological ends. Sociologically it could be argued that the task is to work with 'visions' people have constructed of the world which depend on the frames of meaning, tropes and discursive structures they have available to them. Giddens introduced the concept of the 'double hermeneutic' which recognises that sociologists are interpreting how people have already made interpretations of social life:

> sociology's unique perspective: '. . . deals with a universe which is already constituted within frames of meaning by social actors themselves, and reinterprets these within its own theoretical schemes, mediating ordinary and technical language.'
>
> (1976: 162)

Furthermore, this is not only a one-way process; people take the ideas and concepts of sociology and draw them back into the public sphere where they may become popular currency in the description of social phenomena; rather undermining the sociological project of creating a critical distance from the commonsense of social life.

This description of the reflexive nature of sociological research, recognising fields of overlapping and socially constructed knowledge, partly addresses the question of 'epistemology'[1] and what can be known about the social phenomenon or beings in question. Cresswell explains the epistemological issue as:

> another philosophical assumption for the qualitative researcher. It addresses the relationship between the researcher and that being studied as interrelated, not independent. Rather than 'distance', as I call it, a 'closeness' follows between the researcher and that being researched. This closeness, for example, is manifest through time being in the field, collaboration, and the impact that that being researched has on the researcher.
>
> (2007: 247)

This closeness is often mediated in visual research by the shared codes used in visual culture and in an immediate sense by the use of the camera in the specific research context, as the discussion below demonstrates.

The visual gives evidence of existence; while, like any other form of evidence, it can be manipulated and distorted, it nevertheless provides an array of evidence which might suggest the reality of objects and their relative importance. Yet the verisimilitude of photography, we know, is also problematic because while photographic images are a 'true' representation in terms of the mechanical or chemical or electronic processes involved, the human eye and brain which framed and composed the image (not to mention the complex mediated processes of interpreting such an image) make such images no more objective or truthful a representation than any other medium of communication. As with the transitions in our understandings of the physical world the understanding tends to be that it very much depends on our individual subject position and the choice of paradigm that an observer chooses.

Prosser and Schwartz (1998) give guidance to the use of photographs within the research process. The discussion is clear and wide ranging and for the student provides useful scenarios of how the visual researcher might operate:

> I am walking along a city street. In one pocket I have a camera and a notebook and in the other two lenses and extra rolls of film. A young couple are peering into a jeweller's shop. I take out the camera and begin shooting, using the wide angle lens and a slow shutter speed to freeze the couple and turn other shoppers into a blur, suggesting and emphasising the couple's stillness and intimacy. I change to a short telephoto, shift position and shoot against the light to accentuate their intimacy and body language. The couple's reflection in the window catches my eye and I switch to a standard lens and shoot some more, aware that the couple is analogous to a theoretical concept derived from interviews with other couples conducted earlier in the study. I put the camera away, take out my notebook and . . .
>
> (Prosser and Schwartz, 1998: 116)

This is a compelling sketch of the active visual researcher armed with technical expertise and tools for the job constantly making connections between the emerging theoretical strands of the study and the visions unfolding before their eyes, and making decisions about framing, camera angle and lighting to accentuate the reading of the scene and its coherence to the premises already laid down in the project. This example demonstrates the active construction of the image and the complex interplay between photographic techniques and theoretical concerns. More than ten years on the example is still compelling, but the awareness of technical and ethical aspects of visual research has changed significantly. Prosser and Schwartz's example encourages us to reflect on the complex relationships between the research subjects and the process of recording their behaviours photographically, but also on the evolving conscious processes of the researcher. Harper has suggested that visual sociology offers us an arena to consider 'postmodern critiques of ethnography and documentary photography and, in so doing, to fashion a new method based on the understanding of the social construction of the image and the need for collaboration between the subject and the photographer' (2005: 747).

Critical discussions about visual research have multiplied as have the number of researchers employing visual methods. Digital cameras, with technical versatility and capacity unheard of in 1998, are now readily and cheaply available. This has led to an avalanche of visual material produced by, often, self-taught photographers and video makers. This is a situation which some professional photographers and film makers may decry, being concerned about a loss of technical standards or aesthetic quality of the imagery produced (once the province of a few skilled and doggedly patient individuals). When interviewed in 2001, Jean Rouch, one of the pioneers of French visual ethnography and 'cinéma vérité', was asked about the proliferation and accessibility of video cameras which permit anyone to shoot video. His response was angry and bewildered, a King Canute figure insisting that the tide recedes:

Interviewer: What about responsibility . . . with these video cameras anyone can film?

Rouch: It's not true. We don't shoot with these cameras. This does not work. This is not a camera . . . It's not true. We fight against this. You have to shoot with a real camera. And I demand that we ban all these instruments and the people shoot with the real thing . . . with a viewfinder through which you see the film you are shooting. Not with these things . . . they don't work.

(Jean Rouch on the Future of Visual Anthropology, 2001: YouTube clip)

This could be interpreted as a professional with a passion for realism who feels that video is not a serious form, because it can be captured almost casually without the discipline of film making. Digital imagery *is* cheaper and easier to produce, manipulate and control, but is said to lack the smoothness and depth of colour and texture that film has. Just pointing a video camera which does not allow the framing of a shot can seem haphazard, implying a different relationship to the social scene one attempts to record.

The relationship of the individual researcher/photographer to their cameras and the act of photographing is a theme which will receive thought in Section II. Particularly valuable are the viewpoints of professional photographers who are also social scientists and how they have developed their practice. Roger Canals' experience of fieldwork with a camera also noted the way the presence of a camera brought opportunities and became a tool of networking to 'provoke' situations. Panizza Allmark (Section II) described her camera as: 'a defensive utensil against loss of subjectivity', suggesting that within her practice the creative subject and her camera are fused in an intuitive relationship. Both of these reflections recall Jean Rouch who also used the camera to create 'cine-provocations'. The camera became a catalyst that made things happen that would otherwise be hard to reveal. To Rouch, the process of film making was a 'cine-trance' where he no longer distinguished between the camera, himself and his environment (Sjöberg, 2006).

Jean Rouch in the 1950s developed what he called cine-fictions – later termed 'ethnofictions' (Stoller, 1992: 143) – explorations of the borderlands between fact and fiction comprising dramatic reconstructions of the everyday lives of the people he had come to know through his work in West Africa. The intention to capture lived experience in the most honest way appears to blur the boundaries between cinéma vérité, non-fiction documentary and fictional narratives. In a panel conversation (Coover, 2009: 237) Kelly commented that good fiction attained 'a sort of phenomenological intensity of plenitude, or intimacy which is so hard to achieve with non-fiction'. This is an important point and suggests that capturing the experience of the human condition at its most profound is not only the province of objectivist science (even if this was strictly possible) and where visual records are concerned there is truth in fiction as well as fiction in truth.

The example deliberately chosen by Prosser and Schwartz pictures the researcher/ photographer engaged in fieldwork, surreptitiously recording a couple absorbed by the display in a jeweller's window, would be difficult to conceive of today. In the last few years there has been a heightened concern about the integrity of research and the ethical implications of using imagery without the explicit knowledge and agreement of the people involved. In the same article Prosser and Schwartz highlight the ethical and epistemological problems of a visual researcher as detached observer, acknowledging the problems of the covert photographer, describing the use of telephoto lenses to avoid detection as 'outsider arrogance' (ibid.: 120).

For visual anthropologists working in the earlier part of the twentieth century the understanding of the aesthetic and ethics of photography and ethnographic film were at an early stage of development. Pioneers like Flaherty (*Nanook of the North*), Evans-Pritchard (studies of the Nuer) and Bateson and Mead (studies in Bali) have been criticised as objectivist, voyeuristic and fabricating social life for the camera. Anthropology at certain historical moments can be seen as re-affirming social Darwinist or colonialist views of racial hierarchy, potentially exploitative approaches to otherness. However, as Pink (2003: 185) points out, it is important to recognise that these are studies which need to be understood 'in the historical contexts of their production and viewing'. Certainly at different historical moments their work existed within a very different universe of meaning.

Another observation about visual studies of different cultures is that they have a tendency to expose the cultural categories of the film maker and anthropologist more than the culture in question. Dennis O' Rourke's film *Cannibal Tours* examines this. Following a group of affluent tourists who visit communities along the Sepik River in New Guinea seeking authentic 'primitive' culture, the sardonic eye of the camera exposes the impact of tourism and its profound effect; producing and reproducing distorted images of the indigenous people who constantly re-invent their culture to please the tourist cameras. Indeed as the epigram at the beginning of the film – a quote from Camus – so eloquently states: 'There is nothing so strange, in a strange land, as the stranger who comes to visit it.' The relationship between the viewer and the viewed is a critical issue that the visual researcher must consider before, during and after the research.

Getting started

Clearly the nature of the research question and the phenomenon under research largely dictate what is appropriate and valid. Sometimes images or visual forms of communication may be central to the research; several examples in this volume address issues which are implicitly visual. There is a great deal of research examining the visual representations of specific groups. In these cases the focus on visual themes is often *intrinsic* to the purpose of the research; it is not merely based on a personal preference for using a camera rather than the pursuit of other forms of research; the significance of visual culture itself has taken centre stage.

Research generally begins with a question, sense of puzzlement or curiosity. Frequently the issues arise from the individual researcher's unique circumstances and observations of everyday life. Of course the research may be part of a formal contract or bid, but usually the choice of method follows from the formation of an intellectual problem. It is rare to choose a method and then cast around for a suitable problem to solve; the practice of visual research opens up new vistas for researchers and may implicitly guide the form and direction of research. What I mean by this is that the experience of visual research can itself have a marked effect on the researcher's perceptions of social reality and hence preface the gradual development of a new way of looking at the social world. The visual researcher develops an 'eye' through active experimentation. Taking pictures – producing images – and criticising them helps to learn the limitations and possibilities of the medium. As a purposeful visual aptitude develops other images from TV, advertising, public information campaigns, and the whole gamut of commercial and public imagery we are exposed to every day, are viewed through the eyes of an 'enlightened witness' (hooks, 1997). This means that the 'taken-for-granted' nature of these images is recognised instead for *implicit* as well as explicit social and political meanings. In addition, the work of other image makers and how they achieved their effects, their underlying perspective or milieu, becomes more apparent to the critical and refined eye. Allmark in Section II briefly outlines a reflexive approach through which she first takes pictures at an 'instinctual level', and later: 'The challenge lies in delving deeper to what makes the subject and photograph interesting. How does it conform to what has been done before? How does it build upon, comment on, and develop wider critical inquiry?' As Grady (2001: 103) exclaims in a nutshell: 'the more you shoot, the more you see.' Visual sociologists bring a critical eye to the interpretation of images; developing the sociological imagination (C. Wright Mills, 1957) requires a form of free association 'guided but not hampered by a frame of reference internalised not quite into the unconscious' (Hughes, 1971: vi). All of these observations suggest that an active visual practice which recognises the constructed nature of images, and of the meanings and values they come to represent, might allow the researcher to adopt a more alert and critical stance to the maelstrom of images circulating in our culture which are generated by complex interwoven discourses.

It is useful to differentiate between the forms of image-based research. Fieldwork can include: imagery created or found by the researcher in the course of their endeavours, or imagery created by the respondent. Jon Prosser (1998) has introduced these terms as the four Rs of visual research:

- Researcher-found visual data
- Researcher-created visual data
- Respondent-generated visual data
- Representation and visual research

Found imagery could include: graffiti, cartoons, newspaper photographs, internet imagery, etc. Respondent-generated might include drawings, photographs and videos which have been produced by respondents or may indicate the use of photographs, videos or objects introduced to elicit a response during an interview. For example, in a tape-recorded interview with my grandmother (then in her nineties) in West Yorkshire, I recorded her impressions as she leafed through a family album which contained images going back to her childhood in the early 1900s. The album served as a mediating context for the interview, aiding a more detailed recall of events and people. Each image evoked vivid narratives which traditional interviewing techniques would not so readily elicit.

In addition, the fourth 'R' allows a broader field of analysis. Harper (2005) suggests the use of imagery in cultural studies analyses is a form of 'indirect ethnography' because it taps into the wider culture; the style and texture and values of everyday social reality. For example, teenage magazines from the 1970s, women's magazines from the 1950s or a copy of a men's magazine in the late 1990s: imagery from each of these evokes a sense of the mediated values of the era, the politics of gender and popular culture scripted as appropriate or popular at the time. Indeed, there is an obvious overlap between 'researcher-found' and representational imagery, except that the former is usually found in the narrower case under examination and the latter is part of the broader manifestation of the culture. The use of found images and their subtexts and contradictions can reveal volumes about historical, political, social and moral values of the time. Images from popular culture, cinema, TV, advertising and postcards can show social construction at work and the accretion of meanings around visual forms. A sense of intertextuality is vital in understanding the metaphorical and metonymic use of visual forms to explain an issue, showing how images and cultural objects are nomadic and are changed and reinterpreted for different social users. The visual researcher becomes attuned to the realm of representation and to the construction of sign systems which affirm, regulate and reproduce social values and identities (see discussion on symbols of identity in Chapter 4).

Using images can be much more than a 'largely redundant visual representation of something already described in the text' (Banks, 2001: 44); using visuals to describe elements within the text may add depth and emphasis to a written description. Also, as Rose (2007: 239) suggests, the inclusion of imagery as an *excessive* and *supplemental* element to the research, where it is not a feature directly anchored to the text, may allow the images to reveal their unique qualities. Certainly these are 'methods which give more space to the photographs themselves to have their own, perhaps rather unpredictable effects in the research process' (ibid.: 247).

Rose's observation is significant; it does indeed appear that images are not immediately exhausted; there is a sort of slow release of meaning, and this may lead to revision or reconsideration of research findings. Arguably, when research data diverge from expectations this could be claimed to demonstrate greater validity (see Ratcliff, 1995), and a more vigorously inductive approach rather than one which merely discovers what was expected. Longer research trajectories might also provide opportunities for the resonances of imagery to gradually unfold within the research. Banks recently spoke of 'letting images breathe' (Banks, 2009). An image can have long-term effects on how other research data are interpreted as it reveals perhaps unexpected significance.

So far it seems that visual methods offer some unique insights not readily accessible to traditional methods, and further that through active 'image work' a critical 'sociological eye' (Hughes, 1971) can be developed to perceive visual displays as intrinsically significant signs of the way society is ordered. How then can visual research become an integral part of qualitative methodologies? In the discussion below, four methodologies are examined and discussed in relation to visual methods. The four broad methods – phenomenology, ethnography, case studies and narrative – are not mutually exclusive; indeed they can be combined as strategies and are approaches which can be complementary or nested. For example, a case study approach may focus on a phenomenon and explore this through narratives elicited by an ethnographic approach. However, the discussion below will focus on the characteristic features of each approach and demonstrate some visual approaches which might enhance the validity and allow valuable insight into the social world.

Phenomenology

Phenomenology is an umbrella term which includes a variety of methods and stems from the transcendental philosophy of Husserl (although possible roots go back to Aristotle[2]) and the quest to reach into the inner reality of social life and know the underlying authentic truths of a person's experience. As Husserl famously put it: 'to return to the things themselves' (Husserl, 1931) – the view that it is possible to capture the 'essence' of a person's interior experiences, life worlds, their unique perspective and interpretation. The questions of whether essences are a viable object for research or whether untainted versions of a social actor's experience can really be obtained may highlight the idealism in the original conception of Husserl. However, the intention of informing the researcher's ignorance of phenomena, behaviours and social contexts, without the assumptions of theory, is a useful starting point for research. Such a view is arguably valuable 'for understanding subjective experience, gaining insights into people's motivations and actions, and cutting through the clutter of taken-for-granted assumptions and conventional wisdom' (Lester, 1999: 1).

Alfred Schutz developed Husserl's concept of Lebenswelt (lifeworlds) showing that, for the phenomenologist, the social actor's understanding of their world is one of intersubjectively constructed meanings, while such constructs are, nonetheless, different from rational scientific thought:

> common-sense thinking as well as in science, involves mental constructs, syntheses, generalizations, formalizations, idealizations specific to the respective level of thought organization.
>
> (Schutz, 1962: 58)

The purpose of the phenomenological approach, then, is to illuminate the specific, and to understand phenomena as they are perceived by social actors in context. In the human sphere this normally translates into gathering 'deep' information and perceptions through inductive, qualitative methods such as interviews, discussions and participant observation, and representing it from the perspective of the research participant(s) (Lester, 1999). To this extent, the approach produces a description of the research participant's experience which is as accurate as possible – it does not presume to analyse this by imposing a theoretical framework on the data; it is a naturalistic, deep description attained through a relatively unstructured approach.

Social knowledge, then, is an intersubjective construction; a constantly changing dialogue, through which individuals negotiate their sense of self-identity and social/cultural meanings. Therefore, as Cresswell (2007: 60) suggests, the sort of problem most suited to phenomenological research is one which would seek to understand the collective experiences of individuals to a phenomenon. Finlay outlines the values associated with phenomenological accounts in Polkinghorne's work:

> Polkinghorne (1983) offers four qualities to help the reader evaluate the power and trustworthiness of phenomenological accounts: vividness, accuracy, richness and elegance. Is the research vivid in the sense that it generates a sense of reality and draws the reader in? Are readers able to recognise the phenomenon from their own experience or from imagining the situation vicariously? In terms of richness, can readers enter the account

emotionally? Finally, has the phenomenon been described in a graceful, clear, poignant way?

(Finlay, 2008: 7)

These are qualities which research strives to attain. Visual methods, at times, demonstrate this richness; an image can make the account explicit and vividly manifest the material context in which people's lifeworlds are constructed.

The following example is a moment in research where a certain image is revealed as especially significant. Such an image might epitomise the understanding of the research context; it might be considered as a 'specified generalisation' (Becker, 2002; Rose, 2007). Spencer (2006a: 55) used several images to evoke a more nuanced understanding of a phenomenon. The battered statue of Queen Victoria (see Figure 5) is an icon which captures the divisive nature of British colonial rule, and in the wake of independence, a sort of self-contempt and nostalgia which is the result of the struggle between the once subject groups. Such 'specified generalisations' provide a tangible referent to the case, something specific and iconic which extends and adds depth to the issue. However, without the accompanying interview (see below) the special significance of the statue would not have been apparent. It is one visible element in a popular narrative about the exposed ethnic rifts in a postcolonial society. The Indian Guyanese in this time period had been denied access to the political system as a corrupt African-Guyanese regime hung onto power by election fraud. Since independence the country had become increasingly polarised along ethnic lines. Hence the resurrection of the battered statue held all sorts of complex meanings for the speaker.

The interpretative process, as Prosser and Schwartz (1998: 126) remind us, 'begins well before viewing a photograph, and takes place, for example, when decisions are made as to *what* and *how* the photographs are to be taken'. Sometimes, as in the case of the image of a statue above, the image represented an immediate, self-evident significance as an iconic sign, in this case for the process of colonialism and ethnic rivalry. However, to an outsider the visual presence of the statue means little without other sources of information.

There is a degree of serendipity in the discovery and selection of images and their emergence as 'specified generalisations'; where they might instantaneously communicate a complex process, or anchor an interview to material and historical realities. Furthermore the process is rarely linear; the significance of images may emerge when we have sensitivity enough to recognise their portent, and in turn, the recognition of embedded layers of meaning in an image may suggest appropriate research strategies and resonances with theoretical concepts. The caveat for recording images of people is that without the moral obligations of informed consent and transparency any insights may seem empty and miss the point of ethnographic research which is essentially a collaborative craft.

Video ethnography, photo-documentation, researcher-found images and respondent generated images are all forms of visual research which enhance the vividness, accuracy, richness and elegance of phenomenological accounts.

'Look what they do to the mother!' Indian-Guyanese bus driver commenting on the defaced statue of Queen Victoria in Georgetown.

Bus Driver (East Indian): 'See see, thas how this country run like . . . Queen Victoria they pushed he to the back of the Promenade Gardens.'

SS: 'They chucked her out?'

Driver:. 'Queen Victoria – the mother'.

SS: 'Yeah I heard'.

Driver: 'Queen Victoria who gave us this country – its independence – put her at the back . . .'

SS: 'Desmond Hoyte[3] pulled her out again?'

Driver: 'Not Desmond Hoyte! No. Not Desmond Hoyte – the people – is the people. When they elect a new mayor for this town, the people call on the mayor, "Why have you got the queen, the statue at the back of . . ." Burnham[4] used to go shit on her . . .

This government just trying to squeeze this nation, they trying to see this nation wasting – they just going over the world and just asking for aid and help and all them ting. What are they doing with our own resource?'

Conversation on a minibus, Georgetown, 15 April 1991

Figure 5
Defaced statue of
Queen Victoria in
Georgetown, Guyana
(Spencer, 2006: 55).

Several examples will be given but first it is important to understand the relationship with some methodological strategies which could be seen as tributaries flowing from the broad course of phenomenological intent: ethnography, case study and narrative studies.

Ethnography

'Ethnography' traditionally denotes the detailed analytical and descriptive studies carried out by anthropologists, often with a focus upon 'exotic' cultures. Classic examples include studies in New Guinea, South Pacific and African countries. However, ethnography has undergone many changes since the time of the seminal studies of, for example, Malinowski or Evans Pritchard. Ethnography has turned its focus onto the everyday culture at 'home', while still retaining and using the guidelines for participant observation drawn up in the classic 'exotic' studies. Toren (1996) stresses that in ethnography the intensity of involvement and participation in the lives of others is as important as the role played by observation, and *everything* can be significant because the most potentially mundane and everyday activities can be as revealing as the spectacular ceremonies and rituals (which often seem like the mainstay of anthropology to lay perceptions). As Toren explains: 'The idea is that everyone, everywhere, including ourselves, is the locus of relations in which we engage with others and in which others engage with us. So, however small and circumscribed the situation upon which the ethnographer initially focuses, it will inevitably prove to have ramifying implications in respect of collective processes that go well beyond that initial focus' (1996: 104). Willis and Trondman (2002: 394) emphasise the essential 'this-ness' and 'lived-out-ness' of ethnographic accounts. Further, they underline the importance of capturing embodied knowledge of '"the nitty-gritty" of everyday life, of how "the meat is cut close to the bone" in ordinary cultural practices' (ibid.: 398).

Turning this scrutiny on our own 'home' environments is more difficult because the everyday, taken-for-granted aspects of our culture are particularly difficult to recognise and observe. The ability of visual depictions to capture these seemingly unremarkable signs of everyday life is one of the particular strengths of visual ethnography. As Toren suggests, it is the unremarkable details that may later provide more profound ramifications, demonstrating the coherence and intersubjective meanings of the groups under examination. These details may be documents which circulate within an organisation, graffiti or a piece of street art on the walls of a particular neighbourhood, images or signs pinned up in a workplace, a resurrected statue in a postcolonial nation, or the décor and favourite objects chosen by a particular family in a suburban street.

Ethnography can be understood as essentially a reflexive project. The challenge is 'to grasp the native point of view, his reaction to his life, to realise his vision of his world' (Malinowski, 1961: 25), but this vision must be: 'from the vantage point of everyday life' (Jenkins, 2008: 5). The importance of the impact of political and cultural changes and how these are expressed through daily lives, interactions and representational forms of a group or groups is the stuff of ethnography. The problem is how ethnographers can possibly access and understand these in the terms of their own culture. There is an implied reflexivity in much ethnography which makes it a far cry from traditions of positivism which attempted to objectify the research encounter and bring back a description intact; untainted by the researcher's distorting subjectivity.

To present an interpretation of the social context, not as a dusty artefact for a museum but as part of a living reality, makes the traditional positivist divide between the observer and the observed impossible. As Pink suggests, ethnography is intimately linked to subjectivity, and reflexivity is a central feature of the process. . .

> not simply a mechanism that neutralises ethnographer's subjectivity as collectors of data through an engagement with how their presence may have affected the reality observed and the data collected. Indeed, the assumption that a reflexive approach will aid ethnographers to produce objective data represents only a token and cosmetic engagement with reflexivity that wrongly supposes subjectivity could (or should) be avoided or eradicated. Instead, subjectivity should be engaged with as a central aspect of ethnographic knowledge, interpretation and representation.
>
> (Pink, 2007: 23)

Embracing the subject position of the researcher has become more acceptable following the postmodern critique of ethnography as always a construction, a 'fiction', merely the ethnographer's version of reality (see e.g. Tyler in Clifford and Marcus, 1986), but the effect of postmodern theorising as Dickens and Fontana (2004: 220) argue is to strengthen ethnography rather than to dismiss it:

> postmodernism broadens the field of ethnography by accentuating awareness of research practices, problematising the role of the ethnographer as author, and drawing attention to ethnographic reporting procedures.

It may be that the critical effect of postmodern thinking has had some positive outcomes. One is to call for a greater scrutiny of the ethnographer's motives and practice, particularly in terms of the asymmetry of power relations. This is noticeable in visual ethnography where there has been a great deal of criticism of the objectivist vision of the other which was commonplace up to the 1970s. There are many examples of static, stereotyped images of indigenous people (as discussed earlier) rendered voiceless and devoid of active subject status in the process of representation, passively posed for the eye of the camera. Examples of this imperialist cataloguing are abundant and reflect thinking in the social sciences which still laboured under the sign of the colonial project. Reflexivity as a feature of qualitative research methods in the social sciences is a relatively new phenomenon, and one that still comes under fire from positivist criticism (see Denzin, 2009).

Employing multiple sources to examine the phenomena in question from many rather than one privileged or expert viewpoint may be another valid response to this critique of ethnography as merely reproducing the dominant power relations and privileged viewpoints. The use of a variety of methods to document the dynamics of culture can be very successful. For example, the interpretation of the situation for indigenous Australians in Darwin (Spencer, 2006a) drew broadly from a combination of 'researcher-created' (Prosser, 2006) still imagery, participant observations, interviews with people in an informal community, and also with academics and activists, video clips, newspaper headlines, archive materials (nineteenth-century caricatures) as well as government statistics and literary and anthropological representations. The resulting accounts create a composite examination of the political and sociological debates around this complex yet specific case. The interpretation of other cultures is an *intersubjective* process, in which the subject positions of the researcher and the informants both contribute to the account. Sarah Pink makes this point clearly when she suggests that:

> It is not solely the subjectivity of the researcher that may shade his or her understanding of reality, but the relationship between the subjectivities of researcher and informants that produces a negotiated version of reality.
>
> (Pink, 2007: 24)

The importance of an approach which allows for more careful interaction and does not assume meaning from visual spectacles of the other but from an intersubjective examination of visual phenomena is illustrated nicely by the work of Bernard Siegel (Collier and Collier, 1986: 127–130). Siegel's study of contemporary indigenous American culture (the Picuris Pueblo in New Mexico) revealed that the aspect of culture which had most engaged previous anthropological researchers, the elaborately costumed ritual of the 'deer dance' was of less interest to the group than a running race which was held annually at the same time. Siegel discovered this by actively using the images of these events in interviews and eliciting responses to them from the Picuris.

Collier states that not only does this correct the anthropological misdiagnosis about a ceremonial event which had appeared to take centre stage because of its *ubiquitous visual nature*. The aspect of timeworn tradition in the trappings of costume and masks, the complex theatre of dance and the use of symbols are powerful themes in the understanding of traditional oral cultures which are the stuff of traditional anthropology. Only by using the photographs of these two events in interviews was their true importance revealed. The deer dance, with its opportunities for rich cultural signification would 'trap the eye' of the anthropologist, giving a distorted view. This example demonstrates the importance of combining several approaches to counteract a tendency to look through one narrow disciplinary discourse:

Photographs by themselves do not necessarily provide information or insight. Without Siegel's disciplined use of the photographs, nothing would have come of them.

(Collier and Collier, 1986: 129)

Case studies

There is considerable controversy around the case study; is it a broad strategy or a specific method? Can it be viable to focus on a bounded microcosm of society? Can any valid inferences be drawn from a case or cases to inform broader questions about a specific phenomenon? By its very nature the case is a unique instance, an integrated and usually well-defined and bounded system. The value of cases is not to try and generalise to a population but their capability in uncovering causal paths and mechanisms, and through richness of detail, identify causal influences and interaction (Garson, 2008). It is debatable how far case study results can be indicative of more general trends in social phenomena as by their nature they examine specific instances in detail. Yin (2003) explains that it is a mistake to try and select a 'representative' case or set of cases, because: 'The problem lies in the very notion of generalising to other case studies. Instead the analyst should try to generalise to "theory" analogous to the way a scientist generalises from experimental results to theory' (Yin, 2003: 38). Therefore the criticism of case study research, namely that the results are not widely applicable in real life, can be refuted because analytical generalisations are appropriate and make good use of the in-depth specificity of the case study.

It is clear from this short description of the case study that there are fundamental differences between ethnography and the case study. The case study is an instance in the flow of social life: scrutinised from different angles and providing critical insights into theoretical explanations for social phenomena. Case studies may be considered to have different intentions to ethnography:

Ethnography is inward looking, aiming to uncover the tacit knowledge of culture participants. Case study is outward looking, aiming to delineate the nature of phenomena through detailed investigation of individual cases and their contexts.

(Cohen, 2003)

Yet case studies frequently use ethnographic approaches to test or generate theoretical explanations; setting boundaries to the project perhaps based on an event or a local situation. In the discussion about ethnography above it is suggested that clustering information from different sources gives the specific case under scrutiny greater validity. However, this begs the question as to whether an outsider can merely act as conduit for other social realities, and, as the above suggests, present raw experience of other cultures. It would be naïve in the extreme to suggest that recording voices, stories and aspects of daily life is done without researcher bias. Perhaps the purpose of research is rather to mediate between different constructions of social reality. The researcher's own construction of reality is inevitably part of the description. Ideally, the resulting account: 'allows interpretations and influences to pass in both directions' (Davies, 1999: 6). Case studies can be described as an 'umbrella term for a family of research methods having in common the decision to focus on enquiry around *an instance in action*' (Adelman *et al.*, 1980: 49, italics added). The action basis of the cases chosen is important, as it lifts the discussion of processes – historical, cultural, social and political – out of the often abstract context of scholarly literature and canons of thought, into the lived reality. The theoretical literature is important, but as discussed above, many students struggle to comprehend theoretical concepts. Cases give voice to the experience of oppression, discrimination – or equally liberation and realised identity – of real people. These 'instances in action' are compelling and create a vivid context for theoretical discourses; especially when the account is supported by visual and audio recording in context.

Drawing on people's lived experiences, relationships and forms of social organisation the language and other expressive sign systems used, the case approach provides rich phenomenological data. As case study research proceeds, connections and interrelations among meanings and social identities and theoretical explanations may begin to emerge. Strengths of this approach are firstly the ability to develop in-depth specificity and insight into complex issues, while at the same time their great convenience is the use of fewer resources and the contained nature of the case which can be an excellent illustration and test of theoretical ideas. The nature of the case lends itself especially to the use of multiple methods. One piece of case study research concerned the conditions and views of indigenous Australians in an informal camp near Darwin. The small community was involved in a campaign to resist threats of eviction from 'One Mile Dam' (the small informal plot allocated for their use in the 1970s). The study focused on these issues and the way in which they were represented in the local press (Spencer, 2005; 2006). The use of visual dimensions was valuable, showing clearly how entrenched attitudes have a historical basis in popular stereotypes prevalent and constantly reaffirmed by white Australian tabloid media. In other words, while the ethnographic detail of the people at 'One Mile Dam' are part of a specific bounded case, the social values which produce and reproduce these conditions can be found in the imagery and texts which link the local and specific case to the broader socio-historical reality of Australia. This specificity of the case study makes visual records of their dynamics, where these are possible, particularly suitable. As Banks (2007) suggests, 'Visual methodologies relentlessly particularise, highlight the unique, go beyond the standardization of statistics and language' (2007: 119). Yet case studies can be strongly contextualised and in this instance multiple data sources were used, including a range of visual and textual ones: newspapers, posters, video interviews with the residents, personal observations, historical records and caricatures from satirical nineteenth-century magazines. These sources highlighted aspects of the case which appeared to show similarities over time; stereotypes of Aboriginal people as unsuited to 'modern' urban lifestyles, as 'at one with nature', and as adversely affected by alcohol which, as noted in the late 1800s, was similar to the rhetoric and popular press in the early twenty-first century. This example will be discussed in more detail in Chapter 5, but the value of a case approach for illuminating and challenging theoretical ideas became clear as well as the power of visual methods in the form of video recordings which captured the stories of a marginalised group in the social context in which their struggle against eviction and neglect took place.

Narrative research

> Stories surround us, not only in novels, films, memoirs and other cultural forms which *explicitly* present themselves in terms of stories, but also in therapeutic encounters, newspaper articles, social theories and just the everyday ways in which people make sense of all of the discrete and diverse elements of a life.
>
> (Lawler, 2007: 32)

Narratives are a basic means of making sense of reality and working to structure, and give order to events. All societies have them: 'they are "simply there, like life itself"' (Fiske, 1989a: 128). Structuralist thinkers like anthropologist Claude Levi-Strauss and Russian Formalist Vladimir Propp theorised a deep level of core structural principles which produced all narrative forms. Propp (1927), for example, analysed 100 folk tales and showed that they all conformed to the identical narrative structure; he identified 31 *narratemes* (narrative units) that comprised the structure of many of the stories. Fiske demonstrated that these universal themes are present in British and American TV shows; dramas and soap operas interestingly show conformance to their underlying structural morphology. Fiske claims that 'the cultural specificity or ideology of a narrative lies in the way this deep structure is transformed into apparently different stories, that is, in which actions and individuals are chosen to perform the functions and character roles' (Fiske, 1989a: 138). This is similar to the division which structuralist Ferdinand de Saussure theorised between the *langue* and the *parole*. The *langue* denotes a system of generative rules like a grammar and the *parole* is the particular variety, utterance or story which is composed from these underlying rules. Some narrative structures are widely influential within western culture, as Fiske (1987) in *Television Culture* sets out to show there are unspoken conventions which make up news 'stories' and other televisual genres.

Narrative themes structure and sequence visual as well as language-based texts. Whether the text is *Romeo and Juliet*, a sixteenth-century romantic play, or *Star Wars*, a science fiction film from the 1980s, underlying narrative themes are what give them meaning and relevance (and they are composed from the same deep structural elements). TV news, for example, imposes its own narratives on world events often from an ideological or ethnocentric perspective. Visual research can examine the influence of the media we are exposed to. Researchers have examined how the multiple narratives of news programmes, documentaries and advertising might influence the viewing public. For example, Kitzinger and the Glasgow Media Group demonstrated the manner in which visual narratives appear to condition perceptions of how we think about social events. Greg Philo's method used a series of 12 still photographs depicting scenes from the 1984–85 miners' strike, with the objective of examining audience perception of the events and their likely order and portrayal in the news. Kitzinger developed this technique in 'the news game', in which news images are used as prompts for focus group work – the images which are on cards are arranged in order by the respondents to tell stories, and again appear to demonstrate the individual's recognition of habitual narratives which may have been internalised. They found that the way in which individuals arranged the images to represent the story as they imagined it had been reported tended to reproduce the heavily one-sided reporting in their placement of the images, portraying the miners as violent aggressors rather than victims. This technique revealed the power of the news, suggesting to people:

> The order in which to think about events and issues. In other words it 'sets the agenda,' decides what is important and what will be featured. More crucially it very largely decides what people will think with: TV controls the crucial information with which we make up our mind about the world.
>
> (Philo *et al.*, 1982: 1)

Such approaches contribute a significantly original perspective to the understanding of media messages, drawing on ideas of narrative and using images to highlight the many possible meanings available and the restricted readings imposed by, for example, mainstream news channels. Creative use of visual materials can be used to explore the process of making sense of a scene, and examine the complex process of attributing meaning to visual cues. Allmark's photograph (Figure 6) positions a newspaper in an everyday setting. Such images could be used to reveal the manner in which we make sense of images and fit them into our existing framework of knowledge; they are complex semiotic commentaries on the pervasiveness of the media in our understanding of serious social and political issues. When presented with these images, students tend to speculate on the intended meanings of the images and extend the contexts into narratives, demonstrating the shared (and divergent) codes by which we read such images (see Spencer, 2007). In the image below the oblique visual cues are anchored by the newspaper, which seems to take a central role, and the headline shapes our perception. The timing of this particular narrative is significant. Perhaps, when the image was first seen in 2006, the headline, title and context would have overwhelmingly lead us to interpret this as referring to the London underground '7/7' bombs of 7 July 2005. However, five years on, the image may begin to drift from its contextual moorings: could it be talking about the recent violence of the G20 demonstrations in London, or even the mayoral race, congestion charges, another gun or knife crime, or some other story?

Figure 6 'After the Incidents, No. 1' (Allmark, 2006).

Cresswell suggests several types of narrative research – pointing out the division between 'analysis of narratives' in which generic themes are recognised across stories or groups of certain kinds of stories, and 'narrative analysis', in which descriptions of events or occurrences are gathered and then constructed into a story with an abiding theme or plot. In Section II of this book Sarah Atkinson's work *Crossed Lines* used an ingenious experiment to examine people's pattern of engagement with dramatic video narratives. Using an interactive video setting, people select the video sequences they are drawn to and in effect generate the narrative thread through their choices. Her work examines the complex ways in which people interact with visual narratives, monitoring their eye movement and times spent on each of the nine interlinked narratives. The suggestion behind this study, which again straddles the boundary between art and empirical enquiry, is that the nature of television viewing contrasts with other scopic regimes, tending: 'to be fractured and distracted as viewers multitask in their home environments and the television is no longer the sole focus of their attention.' Atkinson's work provides potential for narrative investigation which could focus both on the nature of specific narratives, deep structures which cross generic boundaries, and the engagement and use of narratives by different people.

The construction of visual narratives is complex and depends on a negotiation of possible meanings. The 'raw' narratives recorded are often usefully linked to broader regional, national or global narratives. Specific stories gathered within a case reveal a narrative fabric, a sense of lived experience which amplifies and deepens the features of a specific case study. While narratives may be criticised as anecdotal, stage-managed, rehearsed or fictional, this does not suggest they are invalid. The ultimate value of a story rests not on rigorous verification of facts in the narrative, but rather on their communicative validity; building a context in which the telling is meaningful. When David Cameron (Conservative challenger in the 2010 UK elections) used stories in the televised debate before the election, he was roundly ridiculed in the national press for telling stories that were at the best spurious and inconsistent.[5] However, his use of such stories (fabricated or based loosely on real life cases as they appeared to be) was telling in itself as it revealed the areas in which he perceived Conservative policy was weakest. By identifying with certain demographics we might suggest he was attempting to bridge the 'representation gap' between himself (the product of elite private education at Eton, and Oxford University) and 'ordinary' working-class and ethnic minority people.

A powerful example of the visual context of the interview is witnessed in the example (Figure 7) of an Aboriginal community leader. The community he represents is one of the most marginalised and neglected in the western world; the visual impact of the difficult conditions of the camp where the interview took place bring the immediacy of the situation to the audience. In the sequence (Spencer, 2005) the speaker compares the conditions and treatment of the group to a form of 'ethnic cleansing'. His use of this term in the setting of the squalid camp near Darwin city centre reflects the desperate living conditions and noticeable lack of support from the civic services given to other city residents. The point was not to examine his use of this term in any literal fashion as semantically accurate or inaccurate, but as a comment made in the immediate context. In addition, the comment needs to be seen in the broader context of the history of dispossession and constant removal of land. The traditional lands of indigenous Australians which were more fertile were seized by settlers as prime grazing land for sheep and cattle; this often led to the indigenous population suffering banishment to more inhospitable areas at pain of death.[6] Hence the circumstances in which the term 'ethnic cleansing' is used have a long history which needs to be recognised.

In another example of expressive video narrative, a colleague originally from the Caribbean recounted the story of his arrival in the UK from the Caribbean in the early 1960s – his experiences and expressions were strengthened by his articulate presentation on video. In addition, archive film of *Windrush* arriving at Tilbury Docks in 1948 was used to add to the sense of anticipation and hope of the new arrivals from British colonies in the Caribbean, while the narrative expressed the dashed hopes of many who had been expecting 'an open-arms welcome' only to be confronted with the dispiriting experience of inner city racism.

Finally, here is a still from an interview with a younger, second-generation African-Caribbean man, talking about the disintegration of his community in Sheffield. While these visual narratives successfully convey personal experiences, lived conditions and identities, all of these accounts link historically to wider

'I read somewhere during the Bosnian war ... I think ... about 'ethnic cleansing', well I'm beginning to think that that's what's happening here, it must be some kind of ethnic cleansing.' David Timber, Coordinator of the Kumbutjil Association – on conditions in the One Mile Dam community in Darwin, Northern Territory, Australia. From Spencer (2004) *Framing the Fringe Dwellers* (Academic Video, C-SAP)

'I walked the streets evening after evening in the darkness, reading newsagents' windows to see if I could get a new flat, a new room, stuff like that. And sometimes it would say 'blacks, Irish – No Blacks No Irish No dogs', or some times you'd get 'Blacks need not apply' or you know ... but it was firmly saying that you weren't welcome – but and then the more insidious ones I though, was the ones where it didn't say anything but you went and got the door slammed in your face as soon as they saw who it was. Or if you rang and they didn't realise what voice or accent it was and they'd say well come in and you went and then they saw it was you – you got the racist treatment – I think that was probably the worst.' (Malcolm Cumberbatch, Political Sociologist)

From Spencer and Radley (2006) *Under the Skin of Multiculturalism* – Academic video

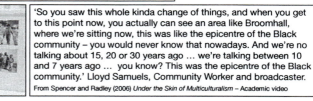

'So you saw this whole kinda change of things, and when you get to this point now, you actually can see an area like Broomhall, where we're sitting now, this was like the epicentre of the Black community – you would never know that nowadays. And we're no talking about 15, 20 or 30 years ago ... we're talking between 10 and 7 years ago ... you know? This was the epicentre of the Black community.' Lloyd Samuels, Community Worker and broadcaster. From Spencer and Radley (2006) *Under the Skin of Multiculturalism* – Academic video

Figure 7 Video narratives. Top: Kumbutjil sign, Pariah website; middle: Windrush Square (public domain image); bottom: Lloyd Samuels (2006).

social and cultural meanings. Indeed, they demonstrate the 'sociological imagination' at work putting the microcosm of the individual's personal milieu into a wider dialectical context, suggesting links beyond the local to other times and other places and resonances within the broader cultural framework.

The power of visual narrative accounts was explored in several video interviews with academics and community members (two of the latter appear in Figure 7) for a video project examining discourses of multiculturalism (Spencer and Radley, 2006) and the resulting video material has been used with students to help illustrate theoretical ideas. Watching the academics talking passionately about their subject areas added drama and life to an account of something which when written in a textbook may be far less engaging and is often couched in language which is constrained by narrow, academic conventions of the disciplines in question. Similarly, watching real people from communities talk about their lived experiences was refreshing to students, as it captures their embodied expressions in context, when, by contrast, written commentaries from 'the community' can seem like abstract truisms.

Participants should be actively involved in the research. Several authors have suggested that this is a negotiated relationship of mutual learning. For Langton (1993) such negotiations are an example of 'intersubjectivity' by which a level of understanding between parties can overcome relations of ingrained prejudice. Within the participants' story may be *epiphanies* or dramatic turning points – 'in the end, the narrative study tells the story of individuals unfolding in a chronology of their experiences, set within their personal, social and *historical context*, and including the important themes in those experiences' (Cresswell, 2007: 57). Reflexively, the research also traces a journey for the researchers as they navigate between their assumptions, theoretical literature and the empirical data uncovered. As Willis and Trondman (2002) suggest, ethnographic research needs to find a balance between raw empirical data and abstract theoretical paradigms, both of which can supply fresh and surprising insights (their 'aha' effect: ibid., 399). Such a balance requires a constant interplay between induction and deduction. Similarly images can be understood as immediate sensory data but their value can be further unlocked as the semiotic processes within are deconstructed, resonating with the wider socio-cultural and political meanings of the society.

In the examples given above it is clear that other forms of visual research could have a role to play: life histories and oral histories may draw inspiration and be punctuated by key images from a family album, and building the historical context of values and beliefs could be enhanced through clusters of archive images. Certainly such accounts could be transcribed and read, but the visual power of these narratives is considerable because of their immediacy, non-verbal emotion and explicitness of context; images build up a feeling of the lived reality of the individual or group in question.

To consider visual ethnography as a collaborative quest, to expose what one might consider oppressive conditions and in some way bring about collective action, may be overly optimistic. Faris (1992) suggests that we are deluding ourselves if we believe that by mere presentation on video or film our audiences will understand the conditions or be roused to take action. In this view film or video (and indeed the project of anthropology itself) is of questionable value because:

> The subject of ethnographic film will always be object, no matter who does the filming, so long as *we* are the viewers. The West is now everywhere, within the West and outside, in structures, minds and technologies.
>
> (Faris, 1992: 178)

This is an important criticism to take into account and one which at the very least suggests that video projects call for careful pre-planning to create a more long-term and collaborative approach (for a discussion of this see Spencer 2006b: 177–178). Nevertheless, the dilemma of ethnographic film could still be argued to be the one Faris identifies as between an implicit us-and-them division in the subjects and audiences of visual ethnographies. Instead of preserving this objectification of 'them', the point is surely to 'obliterate otherness while preserving difference' (Faris, 1992: 174).

However, it seems overly *pessimistic* to judge the 'we' in Faris's argument to be so homogenous; this might be more the case for classic anthropological ethnography but for videos like *Under the Skin* which deal with urban multi-cultural issues the audience are already diverse, and such ethnographies resonate with the debates which inform their everyday lives. With *Framing the Fringe Dwellers*, which focuses on Australian indigenous/white relations, perhaps Faris's contention is more valid; because there is a cultural distance between indigenous and non-indigenous groups – but this is gradually changing. One audience member at a Centre for Sociology, Anthropology and Politics[7] conference where the video was shown suggested after the showing of this video that it could be perceived as dwelling on the plight of urban indigenous people in Darwin and was an example of the 'victimist gaze'. In other words, the video portrays the group in question from a dominant, white, middle-class perspective, and could be seen as another link in the chain of colonial domination – merely affirming the 'other's' place as a subordinated subject and making cultural capital from their condition. Conversely, it could be fairly argued that this video's contribution is to examine and undermine this perception and especially the normative discursive construction and misrecognition of the group as a static, primordial culture.

The complex interplay of methods discussed in this chapter suggests that in reality these approaches are far from being separate trends; frequently they can be used simultaneously. The short video sequences addressing the situation for indigenous Australians (Spencer, 2004, 2006a) are individual narratives discussed with reference to the broader cultural and historical narratives about 'Aborigines' in the mediasphere and semiosphere. While these video interviews do not fulfil all of the traditional criteria for ethnography (there was no long-term immersion in the culture) the insights are certainly both ethnographic and phenomenological as they examine collective experiences of similar phenomena, and in places arguably captured the 'nitty-gritty' of everyday lived realities.

Primarily, of course, case studies tend to look within a narrow time frame and focus on specific communities. However, the changes in cases over longer time periods are often revealing. Cases might be usefully revisited building on the initial study and noting change as well as continuities. Theoretical explanations tended to emerge as the stories, observations and representations of different community groups began to build up, rather than being pre-emptively imposed upon the data. As understanding of the complexity of the case progresses the theoretical models used originally may seem less adequate and other paradigms may be needed to explain what is being observed. It seems there are benefits in a more flexible approach which vacillates between induction and deduction. In other words, an ability to think on one's feet rather than doggedly pursuing a theoretical 'line' may maintain higher validity.

Video production issues

With the advent of portable and affordable digital video cameras and computer-editing software, researchers are increasingly turning to video production as a means of collecting and presenting material. The active use of video ethnography can bring a richer sense of understanding and ownership to issues which may seem fairly remote. Video is an extremely efficient mode of recording and presenting research, and, now that the technology is no longer as bulky and cumbersome as it used to be, becomes a viable means of gathering data.

> Video is not just a useful recording device; it also has distinct advantages as a way of presenting research. Video images presented on a screen come to the viewer directly as perception. Hence, they have an apparent immediacy and realism which is different from that apprehended in the 'interiority' of our thoughts when we read a book.
>
> (Jacka and Petkovic, 2000)

The immediacy of video imagery can provide rich ethnographic material conveying social contexts and people. Firsthand visual ethnographic research is only viable where there is a level of collaboration with the people involved. In addition, the process of producing video requires critical thought about what needs to be conveyed in the limited time available, and which aspects should be highlighted or edited out.

This is an unavoidably political practice which could have a marked impact on both the people depicted and future audiences. This highlights the complex constructed nature of visual texts, and in the case of ethnographic videos there are inevitably issues for ethical reflection and the process of working with other communities and arriving at a transparent and negotiated approach.

Throop suggests that certain techniques like interviewing and questionnaires might move us closer to this empathic understanding – to reveal 'those explicit reflective processes that *tend* to give coherence and definite form to experience – strategies such as the video taping and/or systematic observation of everyday interaction that focuses upon capturing the often pre-reflective, real-time unfolding of social action' (Throop, 2003: 235).

Video may record these authentic, less-rehearsed aspects of social life giving a sense of 'being there' as events occur. These pre-reflective nuances permit a more rounded and coherent sense of people's lived experience. The verbal content combines and strengthens the visual contextual and non-verbal aspects of the exchanges. Before the conscious process of interpretation and theorising, the raw video of people telling their stories often leaves a profound impression. As the different elements of research accumulate and combine we might hope to provide multilayered interactive data which give a fair approximation of the feelings, experiences and intentions and the broader social and political realities of the subjects recorded. In the Darwin case study (Spencer, 2005, 2006a), the contact with the people themselves, though limited, provided a sharper focus for the other archival and popular cultural texts which made up part of the analysis. What became clear was that often the broader cultural attitudes and beliefs could be reached through artefacts, journalism, observations, public events and 'researcher-found' imagery. In a complex case study visual texts may play a vital role in understanding events. This demonstrates a basic tenet of sociological thought in that it shows the importance of seeing the individual local conditions in the light of wider historical and cultural changes.[8]

Representation/reading strategies

It is important to consider video or still images as texts which are encoded and decoded rather than as some form of direct conduit into other cultures, and this raises the issue of how the researcher conveys the produced nature of the text. There was a trend (which still has much to recommend it) of striving for transparency by exposing the process of construction rather than presenting the film as a seamless vision carried out before an open and impartial eye. However, the problem with ethnographic film, as with other media, is that the lack of supporting contextual cues along with the conventional closed structure of the documentary film may render the message overly simple. Too many documentaries offer only portrayals which focus on weird and exotic customs diminishing the complexity of cultures. Just as in wildlife documentaries, 'they' become mere objects of fascination. Some ethnographic film resists this tendency to interpret other cultures through dominant ethnocentric narratives, and attempts to reduce the asymmetry between the observed other and the film maker.

> Fieldwork should be a two-way engagement in which the subjectivity of the 'other' has the opportunity for self-assertion and the political nature of the definition of 'otherness' would be exposed and thereby open to resistance, negotiation and redefinition.
>
> (Warren, 1982)

Examples of this more reflexive approach follow from the work of pioneers like anthropologist/film-maker Jean Rouch (1954, 1959) to more recent examples like Jacka and Petkovic's (2000) study of the 'floating' itinerant population of women in provincial China, in which the authors set out to present a case where a relatively powerless group is given the opportunity to express themselves with little mediation. Active negotiation of cultural viewpoints opens up the possibility of ethnographic video which avoids the 'othering' of its subjects by better embracing an intersubjective approach. Muecke commented on significant theoretical advances in a framework developed by Marcia Langton to address the necessary cultural negotiation needed when attempting to understand and communicate aboriginality in a less one-sided way. Both white Australian and Aboriginal identities are:

> constantly renegotiated according to a triple schema: *One:* Aboriginal people negotiating with each other in the context of Aboriginal cultures; *Two:* the stereotyping and mythologising of Aboriginal people by unknowledgeable whites; *Three:* A dialogue situation in which both Aboriginal and non-Aboriginal people participate in a mutual construction of identities.
>
> (1994: 3)

This active schema encourages consciousness not just about the story-line – the content of the film – but equally importantly the 'narratives about production (what we think we are doing)' (ibid.). Recognising this process of negotiation is of great assistance, not just from the viewpoint of a fairly untutored film-maker, but also the implications it has at the 'receiving end' for the theoretical framework we wish to articulate to audiences of academics, students and other publics, enabling thought about the reflexive nature of video as a medium rather than a static portrayal of ethnicity as a picture of a distant reality. It appears that there may be a strategy developing here which, while more demanding, could be a great deal more rewarding for showing the development and synthesis of cultural identities. Further to this, there is a key issue here drawing a line underneath the positivist views of what constitutes method and the traditional striving for supposedly 'value-free' research. Experience of working with groups as discussed suggests that embracing subjectivity is not only permissible when examining how knowledge is constructed in communities; it is essential.

Awakening vision: developing visual research in sociology

In a paper written a few years ago, Eric Margolis (2004) raises the question of whether there is a sociological look or gaze which envisions the social world through its unique discursive perspective:

> I am asking first if visual sociology constitutes a scientific "paradigm" as Kuhn defined it to: 'include law, theory, application, and instrumentation together and provide models from which spring coherent traditions of scientific research' (Kuhn, 1970: 11). We have instrumentation and application, do we have theories to counter or accommodate the antiocular philosophies? Is visual sociology a mere method like interviewing or counting that contributes data to other paradigms – say, Symbolic Interaction or Critical Theory? Do we have a sociological stare to mimic Foucault's medical gaze? Are we building an application, a language, a spectacle, a simulacrum? Following Foucault, Jay would ask us to consider how visual sociology develops, by the accretion of sense data – facts and images collected by the social scientific eye? Or is visual sociology primarily a conceptual activity that works with verbal and visual images absent 'real verification by sense data'(388–89)?

In other words, is visual sociology a perspective which generates theory? Is it a unique and developing discipline in its own right or just a research 'tool kit' for other theoretical trends to use? Five years later conferences of the IVSA (International Visual Sociological Association) attract hundreds of researchers from all over the world; a growing number of practitioners producing visual studies in sociology, cultural studies and anthropology as well as in the visual arts; this kaleidoscope of studies questions (and sometimes transcends) the disciplinary boundaries of a purely sociological vision. While it is important to embrace the interdisciplinary nature of much visual research, the enduring vision of sociology is open enough to admit the insights from a wide range of disciplines. The 'sociological imagination' (Mills, 1959) frees the individual to see beyond the appurtenances of everyday life in all its trivial details – to observe these aspects of the human world with a transcendent eye; uniting the milieu of the individual with the broader pattern of social and historical processes.

'The sociological imagination enables its possessor to understand the larger historical scene in terms of its meaning for the inner life and the external career of a variety of individuals' (1959: 3–10). C. Wright Mills' famous description of 'the sociological imagination' is perhaps still one of the most useful touchstones; a vision drawing upon ideas of culture, history, economics and psychology.

Often the act of recording data visually stems from a desire to go out and see what is happening, what people think about issues. While finely tuned theoretical arguments are the life-blood of scholarly debate and research, to avoid theoretical abstraction, merely converting one theoretical argument through the lens of another, ideas need to be tested and challenged in current social contexts. Active research helps us to better understand and communicate social issues, effectively lifting them away from abstract secondary analyses removed from real life. This retains the relevance of the sociological project and invests theoretical ideas with renewed vigour, recognising fertile examples in everyday life all around us.

Concerns about consumerism, war, race/racism, the persistence of colonial values, social exclusion and moral panics are the stock in trade of sociology and cultural studies. These were some of the issues for which varied types of visual material were collected. In addition to reinvigorating theoretical concepts, research of this kind breaks through the complicit projection of common sense; rather like one of those pond skaters trapped on the mirrored surface of the water, we can be held by the surface tension of the everyday; it is difficult to break through and understand by defamiliarising that mirrored reality. Seen with different, more sociologically adapted eyes, the everyday surfaces of the cities we live in; the scarred layers of industry, and de-industrialisation yield hidden realities questioning and collapsing the tacit common-sense view of our everyday surroundings. Recently, with the idea of looking at the city we so easily become inured to, it was possible to go deeper and unearth visual signs of social divisions and transitions, paradoxes and surprises within the environs of Sheffield (see Chapter 3).

Walking the city streets with a camera might be considered part of a reflexive process to develop a more critical eye. It certainly illustrated to me that the everyday is extraordinary, and that the visual records of the city provide a marvellous resource for teaching and learning if we only learn to look beyond surfaces.

Roger Brown's (Section II) discussion of photography recognises the importance of '. . . drawing attention to the subtle inter-play of observation and aesthetics in their making. To not only what is being described visually but the manner of their visualisation'. This comment again succinctly emphasises the awareness which needs to be developed about the practice of looking and seeing as a dialectical process.

Ruptures in the surface of this tacit common sense occur all the time; we encounter images which redefine or question the consensual illusion which sometimes appears so stubbornly, seamlessly in place, partly projected by the circulation of media messages. In the case of 'multiculturalism' (Spencer and Radley, 2006) a piece of small-scale research sought to examine the complex definitions of the term held by members of the public and academics, demonstrating the troubled and contradictory values associated with the term: at one moment implying celebration and inclusion, but also fraught with recriminations and fears about separatism, essentialist politics and lack of cohesion. Significantly British National Party members adopted the concept of multicultural identity, as they felt it vindicated their platform as a celebration of difference of separate white British identity.

Beginning to recognise these fracture lines the choices for fruitful research became more clearly defined. So when a wall mural was glimpsed, just a flash of colour as I drove past, it immediately fitted into the developing rationale for the project. The mural (see below), the result of a 1980s community-based arts programme, was indicative of the celebratory discourse about vibrant multiethnic communities, perhaps well meaning, and marking a shift in values from a relatively closed and xenophobic society to one which appears more willing to embrace differences. However, the signs of dereliction in this image mark the failure of the Genesis Project in Upper Hanover Street.[9] This mural in 2006 looked like 'the ghost of multiculturalism past'. The concept of multiculturalism was described in the media and political rhetoric as doomed and tarnished.[10] The image added historical context to the sorts of comments we were recording from

Figure 8 Wall mural, Broomhall, Sheffield (Spencer, 2000).

interviews in the area; narratives about the dispersal of the black community from Broomhall to be fragmented and forced into pockets of impoverishment around the city margins; again such images can act as 'specified generalisations'.

Several facets of research seem to begin to mesh in this rather serendipitous way. Visual approaches open up the exploration of issues; the imagery never stands alone – it is encountered within a framework of community narratives, in this case as a testimony of change. Parallel to these interlaced narratives of identity and change are theoretical ideas and strategies for further exploration. Certain facets of the issue or concept under scrutiny emerge and snowball, suggesting other examples, modes of analysis and criticism. People described their experiences, images and scenarios were used as illustrations to elicit impressions and ideas, and in this way what initially seemed like solitary visions became part of a complex matrix. Indeed, the level of complexity and depth behind the local circumstances transcend the boundaries of the case study, connecting it with national and even global processes of change.

This vacillation between examining the stories contained in images, and theoretical concepts, could be criticised as too selective and speculative (especially from a more positivist viewpoint). Have the images been chosen because they fit a presupposition about theory? If, as examples, they appear to epitomise the phenomena in question, might they be distorted and dangerously unrepresentative examples which give an unrealistic reading of social realities? However, as a bounded case study they are elements within a specific and complex local context, and hence valid insofar as they can be shown to be a trustworthy representation of the case. One solution to this critique of trimming the body of social examples to fit the theoretical cloth is to examine very varied perceptions of the same 'body' and in so doing test and challenge the fit of the 'cloth'.

What constitutes a valid rationale for taking pictures or collating existing images, as forms of data for research? In a recent article, Erica Barbiani (2005) suggests: 'Taking pictures is, of course, an extremely subjective process, but pictures cannot be taken of just anything that is considered connected to the research, as Harper states: "I repeated as a mantra that pictures should be produced with an image in mind"' (Harper, 1988: 54). However, while it is important to develop a practice which guides the eye to be selective, to consider the validity of the chosen data and proposed outcomes, like any mantra this might hypnotise, blinding us to the need for an evolving dialectic between empirical research and theoretical paradigm. Much research of the type described is small-scale, case-based and employs multiple methods to provide a composite picture of the phenomenon in question. So the image in mind which we strive to produce runs parallel and is in a mutually informed relationship with the theoretical journey and the developing ability to interpret the visual array of social life. On the importance of realising that at some level photography is a slow release of meaning, Panizza Allmark states: 'my photography is instinctual. I merely take a photograph because I find the subject interesting. The challenge lies in delving deeper.'

Allmark comments that she has developed a very consciously 'feminist counter-aesthetic of the uncanny' (see Section II). This indicates a refined rationale – a specialised view of the world in which the unsettling, 'unheimlich' presentation of the social world becomes a way to develop special insight about the world which is more often presented as unproblematic and seamless. Allmark goes on to say that for her, she sees 'the camera as a defensive utensil against loss of subjectivity'. In other words, far from being a tool of rational objectivity, tha camera is used to present artful and provocative visions of social reality uniting personal identity with social forces of change.

Ethics and visual research

The above discussion of approaches to using images and video in research has made several points which are implicitly about the ethical stance taken by the researcher. That, in fact, taking images without seeking permission is not only a form of 'outsider arrogance' but actually a distorting approach to research because it sets up an asymmetrical relationship between the researcher and the person or persons 'captured' on film.

Prosser (2000: 120) makes the point that without rapport between the photographer and the subject, any image, however potentially groundbreaking, is a hollow achievement:

> Of course, the most dramatic, even sensational images may be of those not wanting their photo taken, but that is no reason for taking photographs. Such actions are not only dishonest, but also counter-productive to the enhance-ment of sociological knowledge. Ultimately the reason for not taking photographs of participants if they are hostile to the idea is not a matter of privacy or morality but the likelihood of such action compromising rapport – a necessity for any researcher hoping to remain in the field.

Are there circumstances which might make a less transparent 'covert' approach permissible? The BSA (British Sociological Association's code of ethical practice (2002, point 15)) states:

> In some cases, where the public interest dictates otherwise and particularly where power is being abused, obligations of trust and protection may weigh less heavily. Nevertheless, these obligations should not be discarded lightly.

Perhaps where the researcher is witnessing an extreme act of aggression like the beating of protestors at a peaceful demonstration (e.g. the 2009 G20 summit in which a bystander was killed by police action) there is an urgency for such a situation to be exposed. However, in this case, legal constraints could also be applied. From 16 February 2009, Section 76 of the Counter Terrorism Act came into force.

> It permits the arrest of anyone found 'eliciting, publishing or communicating information' relating to members of the armed forces, intelligence services and police officers, which is 'likely to be useful to a person committing or preparing an act of terrorism'. That means anyone taking a picture of one of

those people could face a fine or a prison sentence of up to 10 years, if a link to terrorism is proved.

(Victoria Bone, BBC News, 2009)

The draconian implications of this are obvious. Journalists and social activists might justifiably feel that such legislation has dire consequences for reporting and monitoring police actions. Indeed if someone hadn't managed to record the incident in April 2009 during the G20 summit demonstration when actions of the police led to the death of Ian Tomlinson, a newspaper seller returning home, would any disciplinary action have been taken at all? Of course, this is an extreme context and far removed from the typical uses of video or photographic research. Much research in the social sciences tends to focus on the relatively power*less*, suggesting that a collaborative and transparent approach should be encouraged in the mutual interest of integrity and honesty and in presenting a valid representation of social reality. If the premise behind ethnographic uses of video and photography is that we want to empower individuals, as discussed in these first two chapters, this will be difficult or impossible to achieve by covert means. Such an approach could lead to allegations of duping the people you are portraying. The traditions of ethnography in general attract accusations of being another link in the chain of oppression of perpetuating a 'victimist gaze' by the objectification of disadvantage or 'otherness'.

Recently the ethical dimension has received heightened attention partly because of the raft of legislation which is serving to formalise the ethical issues in an area which has been less certain. Data Protection and Anti-Terrorist legislation impose potentially strong constraints on visual researchers. Wiles, Prosser, Bagnoli *et al.* (2008) and most recently, Wiles, Coffey, Robinson, and Prosser (2010) provide the first framework of its kind, alerting practitioners to the developing ethical and legal framework which should inform practice. These papers reaffirm the well-established criteria for ethical research, namely the importance of protecting dignity, privacy and well-being, insisting on voluntary participation, informed consent and strict confidentiality. These articles go on to examine several thorny issues about applying ethical procedures in visual research including the problem of anonymising place, techniques for obscuring identity in images, negotiating levels of consent in the use of family photos, or photos generated by respondents in research, the storage, security and reuse context of the images and so on. The 2008 article makes several concluding points which bear some thinking about:

Ethical decisions in research should not be made in isolation but in the context of a thought-through and considered framework that accommodates a researcher's moral outlook as well as professional guidelines. In the current climate of increasing ethical regulation it is crucial that researchers are able to understand, articulate and argue the ethical or moral case for the decisions they make about the design of their research and the ethical issues that emerge throughout the research process.

(Wiles, Prosser, Bagnoli *et al.* 2008: 34)[11]

The ethics of visual research lie somewhere between the individual and societal moral framework and the more specific forms of professional ethical standards which are regulated by institutions – like universities.

In Section II of this book, Panizza Allmark discusses her adherence to a personal code of practice, stating:

> I have made a point of not photographing people unless permission is granted and they want their image taken, or cannot be identified easily in the image or alternatively are engaging in a form of public display.

These are just the sorts of strategic decisions which allow creative voices to still be heard with integrity when the constraints may seem insurmountable – a more realistic practice is still possible. Social scientists who are also professional photographers like Panizza Allmark and Roger Brown (see Section II) extend the notion of what photography means as a personal and public practice. In a recent IVSA paper, Brown's summary of the meaning of photographic practice revolved around the meaning of 'care' – a term gleaned from the writings of Hurn and Jay (2007):[12]

> Distilling, condensing, what they felt to be a common characteristic amongst the very many photographers of very different character, intent and moti-vation of their acquaintance at Magnum and elsewhere, and drawing from their own professional photographic lives. That characteristic is they say the Quality of Care. [. . .] By that they mean an existential commitment of Care for the Subject; Care for the photography; Care for the truth to the subject. Care for themselves.
>
> (Roger Brown's transcript of IVSA paper, Carlisle, July 2009)

These are concerns which go much deeper than the challenge of (potentially draconian) state legislation, and instead focus on the very humanity and integrity of the enterprise we are engaged in as social scientists.

Summary

Hopefully this chapter highlights some of the issues which underpin and which help to shape the whole rationale of research. Visual methodologies have pre-viously been the general province of qualitative researchers, but as Hiles (1999) suggests the qualitative/quantitative dichotomy can be misleading and the paradigm does not necessarily constrain the strategies chosen in a narrowly determinist way. The interpretation of social realities is never straightforward. The meaning of a set of local circumstances is often complex and contested. Indigenous Australians (or 'Aborigines') can be portrayed as 'itinerants' or as suggested here as people who have been dispossessed by wave after wave of colonialism. Hence from the outset the ontological choice will have an enormous influence over the type of evidence collected and the way in which this is analysed. Furthermore the politics of naming is itself along with the visual iconography an important element to be exposed.

Visual methods are no more honest, objective or authoritative than traditional language-based approaches and indeed, without language to explain and give context and definition, images are sometimes passed over and their value unrecognised. Care is needed because of the seductive indexicality and explicitness of the image. However, as a research practice, visual sociology or anthropology entails a combination of looking critically and creatively at the mundane, developing a form of internalised dialectical approach to the image, along with a 'care for the subject' which requires an ethical and aesthetic awareness of the use of the visual form.

3   Mapping society
A 'sense of place'

A truer image of the world, I think, is obtained by picturing things as entering into the stream of time from an eternal world outside, than from a view which regards time as the devouring tyrant of all that is.

Bertrand Russell

Not to find one's way in a city may well be uninteresting and banal. It requires ignorance – nothing more. But to lose oneself in a city – as one loses oneself in a forest – that calls for a quite different schooling. Then, signboard and street names, passers-by, roofs, kiosks, or bars must speak to the wanderer like a cracking twig under his feet in the forest.

Walter Benjamin, Cities and City Life

In the next two chapters, 'place' and 'identity', two interlinked concepts central to the understanding of social life, are discussed, highlighting the value of visual approaches to research. One use of visual records of research is to map the physical surroundings, add texture and detail to interview situations and generally provide what has been termed 'extra somatic memory' (Khun, 2007; Prosser, 2008). In terms of the issues of place and identity, images can help to convey the subjective feelings, atmosphere and dynamics of the surrounding cultural and social spaces. The two concepts are closely interrelated; for a location to become a 'place' it accumulates meanings for individuals and takes on an identity. Identity itself is strongly grounded in material belonging to a place/a community/a country. Both concepts can be argued to take place within the matrix of social construction and representation.

Sense of place

The concept of 'place' is one of the most complex (but perhaps least discussed) in the social sciences, and understanding place at a deep level is relatively new. Sense of place can be seen as 'a profound association with places as cornerstones of existence and individual identity' (Relph, 1976: 63). Relph's work for the first time began to ask questions about the meaning of space, a concept which had been taken for granted. Relph's major contribution was to present the case for 'a phenomenology of place'. In simple terms, Relph outlines three attributes of *place identity*:

> the static physical setting, the activities and the meanings – constitute the three basic elements of the identity of places. A moment's reflection suggests that this division, although obvious, is a fundamental one. For example, it is possible to visualise a town as consisting of buildings and physical objects, as is represented in air photographs. A strictly objective observer of the activities of people within this physical context would observe their movements much as an entomologist observes ants, some moving in regular patterns, some consuming objects and so on. But a person experiencing these buildings and activities sees them as far more than this – they are beautiful or ugly, useful or hindrances, home, factory, enjoyable, alienating; in short, they are meaningful.
>
> (Relph, 1976: 47)

Cityscapes, town centres, housing estates, suburbia, villages, 'outdoors', parks, countryside or 'wilderness', indeed all the types of place exist *only* within human discourse; they are always socially mediated and never outside of representation. The concept of 'nature' is a term in a system and relative to those things which are not considered 'natural'; hence it is already a construct, therefore 'real' nature outside of this process is unknowable. 'Nature cannot pre-exist its construction' (Haraway, 1992: 296). This complex and shifting boundary between what is perceived as nature or culture is central when considering how we perceive our environment. For example, traditional divisions between the countryside and the city are not easily drawn as objective categories; each type of space helps construct the other. Some places exist which could be said to be 'negative spaces'. If places have identities and are imbued with meaning, it is also the case that there are non-places. Places like motorways, car parks, supermarkets, cash dispensers, which are only means to another end, waiting rooms to the real event (see Seamon and Sowers, 2008).

The work of a number of influential philosophers and social geographers has presented social space as central to an understanding of everyday life. For example, Henri Lefebvre's *The Production of Space* criticised much modern theory for taking space as a given rather than a highly problematic and under-theorised concept, a concept in need of its own science which might distinguish between and examine its different forms: mental, physical and social.

The social production of space and the contingent relationships or boundaries between concepts we use is apparent in such terms as: the global and the local (Robertson's[1] portmanteau term 'glocal' demonstrates their interdependence) relations of centre to periphery, or rural to urban, are cases which point to the continuous process of social change which has a profound effect on the coordinates of our everyday existence. Understanding space and sense of place brings together philosophical concepts of production and dialectical change (Hegel, Marx and Nietzche) as well as the poetics of space, urbanisation and consumption (Bataille, Benjamin and Bachelard) and the complex interconnectivity of space, identity and global political changes (Castells, Harvey and Latour).

Examples of places and their special significance for specific groups is a theme which is an increasingly important area of research. Those contested areas where boundaries of belief and identity intersect demonstrate that place itself is a significant social player in life and hence in sociological research. For example, Blain and Wallis (2007) explore the complex discursive construction of sacred sites in Britain. Sites like Stonehenge and Avebury stone circles throw contradictory conceptions of belief and being into sharp relief. Tensions between new pagans and the 'official' guardianship of these sites through English Heritage highlight the divergent physical, spiritual and interpretative engagements with these areas, often leading to disputes about who should have access to these areas and how the land should be used and cared for. Visual anthropological research is important for this type of discussion; the vision of the land itself is perceived quite differently depending on how the site is understood from pragmatic land management to more poetic and mystical ways of seeing the 'auratic' landscape.

An example of another contested site was discussed in Chapter 2. One Mile Dam in Northern Australia is a small pocket of land, home to a group of displaced indigenous people to whom it was loaned nearly 40 years ago. In a short video sequence (Spencer, 2004), one member of the community was recorded talking about the dam itself, which appeared to me to be a roughly rectangular, man-made, stagnant pond polluted from the nearby petro-chemical storage tanks. What she said demonstrated to me that the superficial look of a place is not the place at all: 'The government wants this land – they see this dam here but this dam is a dreaming. It's connected from here to Beleuyen and up to the islands.'[2] This was an area full of memories and imbued with special meanings, complex connections of clan and totem to which I had only the vaguest, anecdotal understanding. The process of looking and seeing is in itself motivated and shaped by cultural concerns. While the mechanics of vision have a biological and physiological basis, the way in which we 'see' the world is culturally ascribed, learnt, a process of recognising and separating pre-determined categories and meanings from the visual array before us.

Maps in visual research

One form which reflects different cultural visions of a territory is the map. As a sign, the map is both iconic; mirroring the actual shape and contour of the land it depicts, and symbolic; employing a variety of conventional codes, symbols to indicate landmarks and features of the landscape. The map appears, at least superficially, to be a naturally denotative sign, showing clear correspondence with what it is a map of. But actually maps are highly constructed and partial in their portrayal of the real, depending on historically formulated conventions, many of which have become part of the lexicon of cartography, and are arbitrary; for example, the setting of the Greenwich meridian at 0 degrees. The map has also been a tool denoting possession, ownership and delineating the boundaries between neighbouring states. Maps might be said to strive for increasingly exact represention of the terrain, and it is this which Jorge Luis Borges's famous story about the quest for a perfect map parodies, as well as the endeavours of science more generally:

> In that Empire, the craft of Cartography attained such Perfection that the map of a Single Province covered the space of an entire City, and the Map of the Empire itself an entire Province. In the course of Time, these Extensive maps were found somehow wanting, and so the College of Cartographers evolved a Map of the Empire that was of the same Scale as the Empire and that coincided with it point for point. Less attentive to the Study of Cartography, succeeding Generations came to judge a map of such Magnitude cumbersome, and, not without Irreverence, they abandoned it to the Rigours of sun and Rain. In the western Deserts, tattered Fragments of the Map are still to be found, Sheltering an occasional Beast or beggar; in the whole Nation, no other relic is left of the Discipline of Geography.
>
> (Borges, [1935] 1998)

The fable (which was used by Baudrillard (1983) as an example of the *Precession of Simulacra* – see Glossary: 'Simulation') suggests that the best map would capture the contours of the land exactly, covering inch by inch the entire area, parodying the positivist quest for knowledge. The closer the created version mirrors experience of the real world the more valid and reliable it must be. Indeed the impossible 1:1 scale of this map meant that it would actually stand in for or replace the original. At their best maps are symbolic projections of geological, meteorological, topological or political and social contours and boundaries of the country. They are always partial and often make definitive lines where the situation is far from clear, often for the political purpose of trying to 'fix' the territory. There are hundreds of examples of disputed territories include boundary disputes between: Indonesia and Malaysia, India and Pakistan, Vietnam and Cambodia, Palestine and Israel, Guyana and Venezuela, as well as many others in Africa and Europe. Also there are disputes about the way national maps should be drawn up. The alternative projections to the old Mercator map of the world based on cylindrical rectilinear projection have included the Peter's projection which is based on the sphere and hence presents the land masses as quite differently proportioned and giving the developing southern part of the world far more prominence and mass than Europe which seems to be significantly atrophied.

So maps can be seen to operate as metaphors for our relationship to the world. They have evolved arbitrary conventions to represent the real world. They measure political and economic boundaries as well as physical geographical ones. Furthermore, maps can be used in other ways to encompass ideas as tools of satire, and political resistance as a form of artistic expression about shared identity.

The map of Australia as presented in my school atlas, I recall, showed the routes of the famous Europeans, navigators and explorers who 'discovered' and drew up the state and territory boundaries, and catalogued the indigenous wildlife.

The earliest maps described Australia as Terra Nullius – the empty land – ready to be claimed and colonised. The indigenous peoples of Australia were diverse and spread across the entire continent in a network of hundreds of distinct tribal groupings, with distinct cultures, traditions and languages. Recently David R. Horton produced a map which shows the many tribal groupings and the rough boundaries of their linguistic range.[3] The map shows at least 200 interlocking tribal groups, some with land masses not dissimilar to a European country. Such a map is an example of the importance of visual artifacts like maps for delineating cultural boundaries and contrasting ethnographic differences and power relations. Official maps and the discourses which generate them may appear to 'fix' such boundaries, but actually there is constant movement and often resistance. The contested nature of space can also be conveyed through artistic or poetic uses of maps. Figure 9 is a confronting artwork by an indigenous artist entitled 'Why?' A map is roughly outlined in red against black card and questions are chalked into the black space around the map. Questions are rhetorical – I, the white viewer, cannot speak (for once). The questions posed are written in longhand on a chalk board. Is this a lesson in the complicit silence of white Australian culture? Posing the questions which the school curriculum didn't ask us – as white Australians – which it seems the country is in denial about to this day? The challenging questions re-invoke a vision of the brutal subjugation of colonialism. Recounting those stories which were often part of an oral history and have proved easy to discount by politicians and revisionist historians as a 'Black armband view of history':[4] 'Do you know why there were men, women and children being

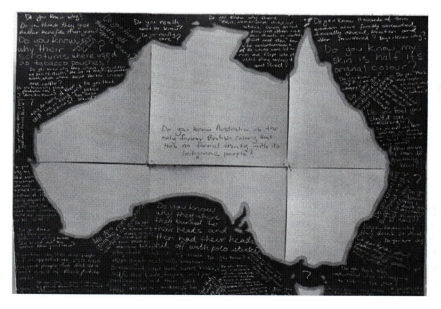

Figure 9 'Why?' by Daniel King.

burned alive and others had their throats or genitals cut and then for the entertainment of the white men were left to run and flap around until they collapsed
and died?' Other questions create an ironic dialogue – 'Are you going to read the
rest of the questions?' or 'Do you feel you should say something?', 'Do you really
want to know?', 'Do you really care?' The map which is like an open wound
floating in a sea filled with unanswered questions was presented at the Bunjilaka
exhibition at the Melbourne Museum in 2004 to 2005. It demonstrates the border
lines between art, social research, politics, history and education.

In contrast, Figure 10 shows a quite different use of mapping to build a sense
of shared cultural identity. This example of a 'Culture Map' of central Carlisle
is part of a community-based arts project (The Carlisle Renaissance) displayed
in a city arcade along with several other art projects seeking to involve people
and encompass the city and its civic identity. People passing by were asked to
add their 'greatest ever cultural experience in Carlisle (with the broadest possible
interpretation)'. These expressions are written or drawn onto a blank postcard
and pinned onto the map in the part of the town of significance to them. Some

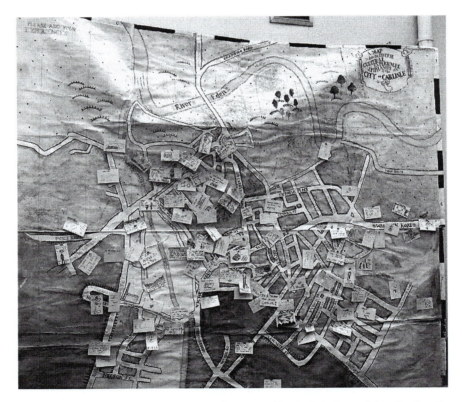

Figure 10 Carlisle 'Renaissance' map project created by Paul Taylor and Sue Stockwell,
2009.

are simple comments of belonging (I lived here for 49 years!); others recommend shops and wares (pictures of pies and sausages), others more personal statements of lived identity, romantic associations (I fell in love here), some appear to show drug use – images of syringes and marijuana, some are about forms of cultural consumption referring to dance, music, and one shows an open book headed 'Poetry Reading'. This scheme, introduced by Paul Taylor and Sue Stockwell in 2009 as part of the West Walls Studio Artists Group, was an attempt to revitalise the city and create an identity and a sense of belonging. Both of these maps are communicating ideas about collective identities in a broadly 'arts' context. Daniel King's Australia map is a sharply political lesson about a divided and silenced space. Waves of colonialism have created a resounding silence about their construction of Aboriginality and the map is like an empty blood-stained canvas in a sea of discourse. In the above, a collective Carlisle emerges through a mosaic of indices of pleasure in the city space.

Similar maps are used by local city wards in Sheffield to involve community residents. Recently a map of Broomhill was used in a sort of road show event where locals pinned different-coloured pins onto the area map and wrote comments relating to the area highlighted – e.g. dangerous crossing areas, areas where cars routinely turn illegally, etc. Maps like this are certainly of value for eliciting responses and gathering clusters of local responses.

Maps are not just useful as a way of orienting and examining over-layered changes and developments in the landscape. They can also be used as research techniques for eliciting data from people about their personal memories and experiences of a specific place. As an exercise in examining the power of place and releasing memories about a time in a person's life, asking people to draw their own maps elicits some vivid recollections and it seems as if the contours of the area are set out, the intersections of streets, paths through parks, fields, woods, other memories associated with these locations are brought back into consciousness.

As a form of auto-ethnography (or should it be auto-cartography?) I tried this with an area I had known well from childhood and had not visited for nearly 30 years: The 'Thicket', a small area of woodland near Maidenhead in Berkshire. I sketched a rough map of the area as I remembered it and labelled certain significant features, as well as indicating where memory was hazy. Inevitably in this process vivid memories were re-invoked despite the passage of time. A skeleton map of memory began to emerge, and recollection put flesh on the half-remembered bones. I was aware that, vivid as these features seemed, they may also be unreliable and part of an immature mind-set. For example, I recalled the man with a gun – but there may have been nothing sinister or particularly 'angry' about this man other than that I knew I was trespassing on private land and the 'gamekeeper' or agricultural worker perhaps used a gun to shoot rabbits or pigeons on that land. The sense of threat on the private land was also present in the carving on a holly tree remembered as 'DEATH' with the carving of a dog's head just above it. I had forgotten all about this until I began to sketch the map. So powerful was this memory that I decided to revisit the area and discretely check and document this

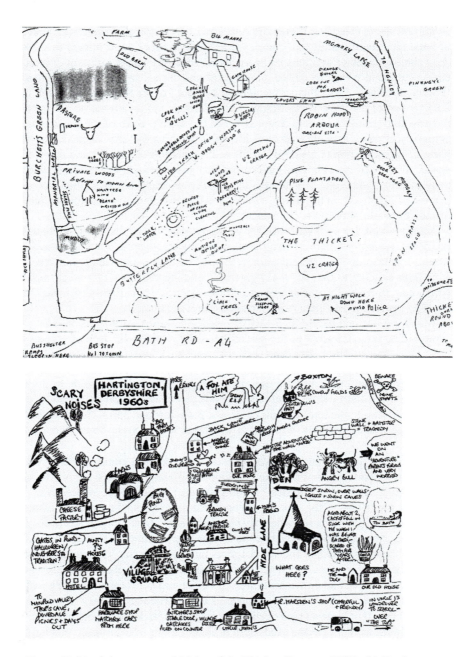

Figure 11 Hand-drawn maps: (a) Map of the Thicket (Spencer, 2009); (b) Hartington Map (Surridge, 2009).

carving and other features recalled from memory (I found the tree in question but the carvings were too indistinct to make out).

The fact that people sometimes camped informally in this area was recalled by the 'Strange bivouaq' and also the indications that there were strange people in the shrubbery, 'tramps' and 'weirdos'. There are historical layers to the area too – the archeological site Robin Hood's Arbour which was formally signed and the remnants of Victorian picnics, stone marmalade jars and antique bottles, ancient rusted kettles and even mouldering shoes hidden in the ivy-covered underbrush. I was led to believe that V2 rockets were the origins of the strange craters which we used to cycle down.

The accuracy or inaccuracy of recall may be superficially tested when a satellite, aerial image is juxtaposed but accuracy is less important that the significance of the area to the individual. The different modes of visual consumption of a landscape suggested by Macnaghten and Urry (listed below) are useful when assessing complex connections to a place.

- **Romantic** – Solitary, Sustained immersion and sense of awe, Gaze involving the sense of the auratic landscape
- **Collective** – Communal activity, Series of shared encounters, Gazing at the familiar with people who are also familiar
- **Spectatorial** – Communal activity, Series of brief encounters, Glancing and the collecting of many different signs of the environment
- **Possessive** – Solitary or paired, Habitual encounters, Scanning over a familiar landscape – as if it could be owned
- **Natural History** – Collective organisation, Sustained didactic, Scanning to survey and inspect nature
- **Anthropological** – Solitary sustained immersion, Scanning and active interpretation of the 'culture'

(Macnaghten and Urry, 1999: 119)

My map is certainly the result of 'romantic', solitary meditation in which the area took on an aura of strangeness. Also, communal activities took place with family and friends, 'spectatorial' ones too. The reading of the personal map also indicates a sense of ownership, solitary reconnaissance and making parts of the area personal and even ostensibly 'private'.

Natural history is recognised in this map; for example, the name adopted for a path – 'Butterfly lane' – where several species were noted over the years being sunny and bordered by tall flowering plants, thistles and foxgloves, flowering creepers, and bracken which seemed to attract them. Deer were seen and noted as special occurrences to be recorded. Trees are recalled as landmarks but also as significant aspects of the natural landscape. Finally the anthropological mode reflected the historical heritage and archaeological aspects of the Robin Hood's Arbour site, as well as the human uses of the area for family picnics, the divisions of the land, between the big estate and the divisions of public and private walkways, and some boundaries going back to feudal times, for example, where ditches at the side of the lane were designated as 'manorial waste' (an ancient concept which permitted public rights over the use of land, for example, to gather firewood).

The reason for this detour into childhood memory is to present a valid way of examining our involvement with the landscape. As an example of auto-ethnography, the above sample provides a unique record of the reflexive perception and uses of landscape. Questions of validity, which are the constant companions of researchers in the social sciences, could be asked about the methodological rigour of such an approach and how 'trustworthy' (the qualitative substitute for reliability) such an approach is. For Delamont (2007) auto-ethnography is essentially lazy, experiential, lacking in analytic rigour, unable to 'fight familiarity' because it, after all, focuses on 'us' rather than a perceived interesting research subject – 'them'.

However, rather than seeing this avenue of research as an indulgently autobiographical practice (interesting as it was to explore) the technique can be built upon and other maps gathered from people. Such maps may form an appealing and human form of evidence, evoking memories and allowing some reappraisal of the landscape in a social context.

Figure 11b is the hand-drawn map of a colleague again recalling an area where he was brought up but with which he had long since lost touch. His reflections on the experience (below) report a similar vivid recall of the features and contours of the village and the vivid recollection of memories. One obvious weakness is illustrated by the relative drawing ability displayed in the two maps – while they are both valid and perhaps honest representations, the Hartington Map's clean, bold and concrete style makes it immediately more comprehensible.

'This map spans the decade from 1960 to 1970, and documents my earliest memories and experiences of growing up in a rural community in north-west Derbyshire. During my childhood, Hartington was a vibrant village boasting a full range of shops run by shopkeepers who my mother knew by name, a hotel, a pub and a petrol station.

The map is a combination of individual events which created a lasting impact and so have remained in my memory, and more vague and intangible feelings. For instance the "scary noises" refer to a regular experience of lying in bed as a very small child and listening to the sound of the herds of cows returning to the farms across the valley for evening milking. At such a young age my imagination conjured up a variety of exotic and dangerous creatures living in those distant hills. Sad events such as the death of my pet rabbit are balanced with recorded situations that still make me smile today; the same rabbit enraged our pensioner neighbour when he escaped from his pen and decimated the old man's cabbage patch.

The process of recalling an event tended to have a snowball effect and led on to related events and feelings. Much of the detail had been completely forgotten during my adult life but the process of drawing the map seemed to unlock my memory. Consequently I made a decision to not be overly concerned about geographic/topographic accuracy, or the artistic quality of my drawing, as I realised that these issues were not key to the process; the important thing was to record this flow of newly remembered material and commit it to paper before these possibly fleeting memories vanished again. However, this has not been the case; since I have committed these experiences to paper they have remained in my conscious memory and have invoked further recollections from my childhood.'

Both of these accounts bear witness to the power of retracing the countours of personal memories of place and the many associations buried there.

Locating the site

Aerial views and the use of tools like Google Earth and Street Level are excellent ways of getting a sense of an area you wish to study. Activating Google Earth and allowing it to begin from the blue 'bowling ball' in space to rotate and home in until the territory is revealed is indispensable when discussing little-known areas of the world which are the object of research interest. I like to show students the process of homing into the area so that they get a sense of 'where in the world'. Nova Scotia looms into view and the vertical strips on the frame indicate where detailed examination is possible, Halifax and environs are recognisable and the cluster of coloured dots indicate the city area, and the dense information available on each site is noticeable as clusters of information 'balloons' giving information and images which have been posted about the various significant landmarks. Finally 'Seaview Dog Park' is sighted – this is what happened to the former township of Africville. Interestingly, new information tags have been added recently, demonstrating that there is still an active protest going on at the site. People's photographs of the area are visibly flagged: snapshots of the Bedford Bridge and the stone sundial which is a commemorative marker for Africville. The use of archive materials and ethnographic accounts then allows a closer, nuanced and historical visual perspective on the area in question (see the latter part of the chapter for a more detailed account of Africville and the use of walking ethnography to capture the lived narratives of the site).

So far this chapter has discussed the construction of place as a vital player in understanding social relations. Maps are artefacts which condense cultural knowledge in different ways. In official Ordnance Survey maps through recognised and precise mapping conventions they provide accurate and reliable guidance to the terrain. In other more individual, hand-drawn maps (like shown in Figure 11) we might elicit special inside knowledge, memories and imagination and personal narratives about places which have strong associations, by asking respondents to create their own maps from memory and perhaps obtaining information which would be much more difficult to access in a conventional purely verbal exchange. Hand-drawn maps are an expressive method for reclaiming the lived experience of place identity through the act of drawing. Using a performative 'hands-on' task allows more active, existential engagement. In a similar vein, David Gauntlett has developed a research approach in which groups use Lego to build three-dimensional visual metaphors of their identities and experiences and then reflect on their creations considering complex social questions. This 'hands-on' approach to research presents a viable visual exploration of complex issues of subjectivity. Gauntlett (2007) emphasises the benefits of using visual channels for an embodied experience as a viable alternative to traditional interviews and focus groups. Such approaches allow a less mediated expression of cultural influence and further demonstrate a form of research which allows personal expression in a concrete and satisfying activity. 'This is a process which takes time and which uses hands and body as well as the mind. The approach is optimistic about people's ability to generate interesting theories themselves' (Gauntlett and Howzarth, 2006). The next section focuses on the city and the complex, often contradictory visions gathered from exploring the city with a camera.

Exploring the city

The city has a special role in sociological thought. It can be argued that the discipline of sociology emerged from a fascination with the chaotic transition to urban life following the French and the Industrial Revolutions (Nisbet, 1967; Karp *et al.*, 1991). The old agrarian order in Europe broke up and was replaced by new, secular forms of urban, industrial life. Nisbet identified five crucial themes stemming from this pivotal transition which were the most evocative for sociology: 'the condition of labor, the transformation of property, the industrial city, technology and the factory system' (1967: 24). In the early twentieth century, Robert Parks and other Chicago school sociologists focused on urban life using qualitative methods; ethnography and life histories to explore patterns of community life.

These themes, and the rapid movement of transition that has changed social life so dramatically, became the core concerns of much of sociology. In the third millennium the technological shifts in production create a constantly changing environment. The early work of Manuel Castells suggested that, essentially, today the urban should primarily be seen as the sphere of collective consumption. He suggests that 'advanced capitalism's central organisation of the metropolitan region diminishes the importance of physical environment in the determination of the system of functional and social relationships, annuls the distinction between "rural" and "urban"; and places in the forefront of the "dynamic" society, the historic meeting place of social relations which form its basis' (1978: 27). This view of the changing dynamic of the city has been very influential. Castells' vision showed that cities should be understood precisely in terms of the complex relation between the state, transitions in modes of production and technology, 'collective consumption', labour, social movements and global networks (see Susser, 2002). With these changing conditions at the heart of the city in mind the following section discusses the visible and multi-sensorial dimensions of a walk through the city, using visual methods to unearth the layers of dialectic change, contradictions and the accumulated meanings built up in popular culture around the lived reality of the city.

Drifting visions and dialectical images: everyday paradoxes in a northern city

As Marcus and Neumann suggest in their introduction to *Visualizing the City*: 'We are all unreliable witnesses caught forever in space and time, our perceptions prescribed, our flight frozen, wings as set as those of an insect in amber in an Egyptian sarcophagus' (2007: 1). The complex existential and evolving reality of urban spaces means that cities exist in many forms and visual depiction is at best partial and fragmentary. The visions of the city which have gone before are part of a flow of meaning; strands of representation add to a growing popular mythology through which the city is known, and gathers reputation and character. Shields (1996) makes the point that cities cannot be understood in any simple close-ended fashion:

> rather than disapprove of representations because of their treacherous selective vision of the city, we need to construct multi-dimensional analyses which, rather than imposing monological coherence and closure, allow parallel and conflicting representations to coexist in analysis . . . leads to a dialogic approach to the spatialisation of the urban.
>
> (Rob Shields in King, 1996: 245)

There are many different ways of seeing and understanding the city. Usually our encounters are short and purposeful ones directed to one form of consumption or another: shopping for items which cannot be had locally, visiting galleries, cinemas or museums, passing through for work, eating out or meeting in a particular pub. So to examine the city as a resource which might enrich the discussion of visual methods meant to see it with different eyes. To achieve this analysis photographs were accumulated from a series of critical, visual forays around Sheffield, a city in South Yorkshire. It was considered useful to record the city visually to generate a series of reflexive resources capturing it from several viewpoints. As Hardy points out: 'Reflexivity involves reflecting on the way in which research is carried out and understanding how the process of doing research shapes its outcomes' (Hardy *et al.*, 2001: 531–560). Adopting a reflexive approach when interpreting visual dimensions of a complex phenomenon like the city is not just flagging up subjectivity to 'cover one's back' methodologically. It is important to recognise that the varied uses, perceptions, and layered representations of the city defy closure, resisting the view of any totalising official ordinance which might present the city as a cohesive, rational space; instead the city can be considered as composed of many lived narratives. Engaging with the city as something new, the images that emerged reflected the dynamic contrasts and contradictions of the city.

As the imagery began to accumulate, the contradictory elements of the city seemed to offer insight into Benjamin's idea of the *dialectical image* – 'that moment produced by the collision of the "objective" forces of nature/culture and our own "subjective" experience as socio-historical beings'(Szekeley, 2006). For Walter Benjamin, images can have a dialectical effect: 'An image is dialectics at a standstill' (Benjamin, 1999: 462). Certain images do seem to have the power to crystallise the dynamics of social change, to capture events which are occurring: 'What has been comes together in a flash with the now to form a constellation' (ibid.). This suggests that images can have the power of catalysts in the process of change. However, it is unclear from Benjamin's work exactly whether such an image is possible; in many ways it would be a paradox – a contradiction in terms. Auerbach (2007) suggests that such an image might be like a Venn diagram making intersecting conceptual fields transparent. Perhaps the inherent paradoxes of a city like Sheffield might provide some examples – concrete realisations of the nature of dialectical images?

'Foot-led' ethnography

One developing approach to an ethnography of place focuses on walking and the routes employed by different walkers for different purposes yielding different and unique readings of the landscape. It has been suggested that the rhythms of walking and the patterns of speech are homologous; they tell stories, they leave traces on the ground and in the memory (Ingold and Vergunst, 2008). For De Certeau (1984: 157) the smallest constituent part of the city is the footsteps in the street. Taking this aspect of the city seriously meant being one narrative among the teeming crowds walking the streets, alleyways, squares and arcades. Because any story 'begins at ground level, with footsteps' (1984: 97). So the intention behind these forays was to begin to understand, perhaps in only a modest way, the everyday practices of people in the city. De Certeau claims that these micro narratives of the city 'elude discipline', remaining invisible (1984: 96).

The aim was to produce a visual record of the walks and a detailed and annotated commentary. These documents were intended to examine the possible modes of seeing the built environment and the relations and constructions of 'nature' and culture. Walks along specific routes (including the River Don and the Sheffield and Tinsley Canal) could build up a sensory map of the sights, sounds and feelings of the walk and meanings. Visual records are used to catalogue the meaningful facets of this landscape and its physical experience. These waterways pass through the industrial heartland of the region and there is a sensation of passing through ingrained layers of industrial change; like the geological strata in a cliff face: the unrelenting 'city of soot' (Fahlman, 2006) beneath the green and recovering landscape, over-layered by a veneer of recent cultural signs; public art, graffiti, signs of surveillance, CCTV cameras, warnings, razor wire and rubbish.

Born in fire and water

The development of cities like Sheffield, rooted in industry, are sometimes visible in these layers of the city; viewed synchronously as a smooth, uninterrupted surface or diachronically as layered with contradictions, always in progress. Phillip Hensher in the *The Northern Clemency* captures the sense of Sheffield as a city forged by natural forces, channelled, contained and directed – with a sense of transformative energy:

The city had been made of fire out of water. And there was the earth too, which Francis did see something of. Around the city, in earthworks and diggings, coal was still heaved to the surface. It was everywhere. The city made its money from steel; it was driven by its waters; it was built of coal.

(Hensher, 2008: 51–52)

The layout of the city reflects relations of production and maps can be drawn to show the manner in which different groups are intentionally separated or are forced into areas due to the competition for resources and the scarcity of social housing. Engels made this observation of slums in Manchester back in 1844:

Owing to the curious lay-out of the town it is quite possible for someone to live for years in Manchester and to travel daily to and from his work without ever seeing a working-class quarter or coming into contact with an artisan. He who visits Manchester simply on business or for pleasure need never see the slums, mainly because the working-class districts and the middle-class districts are quite distinct. This division is due partly to deliberate policy and partly to instinctive and tacit agreement between the two social groups. In those areas where the two social groups happen to come into contact with each other the middle classes sanctimoniously ignore the existence of their less fortunate neighbours.

(Engels, 1845: 54)

A similar mix of intentional planning and tacit agreement along with a logic of the marketplace operates in all cities whether based on occupational groups or patterns of class and ethnicity; the effect is that certain groups are squeezed in or out of specific neighbourhoods, resulting in the unique social patterns of the city. The inherent contradictions of class and ethnicity are part of the divisive function of social division. Cities are powered by inequality; every Fulwood and Ranmoor has its Brightside and Pitsmoor.[5] The 'paradoxes' in this section's title reflect the multiple character of this city, and perhaps all cities. Contradictions are there in the unique forms of the city, but how manifest is the social disunity in Sheffield? One could be forgiven for the view that Sheffield is really two quite distinct enclaves, separated by patterns of affluence and education, housing, health, social capital and occupation. The stark contrasts between the wards of Brightside and Hallam, for example, are among the most polarised in the country. A recent report from the University of Sheffield's Geography Department, appropriately titled *A Tale of Two Cities,* showed that the divisions between the poorest and wealthiest suburbs have only fluctuated a little over the years reflecting changes in government and attempts to try and close the gap. However, with the recession of 2008 came increased unemployment and cuts to public sector funding as well as the prospect of a Conservative government at the next election. The report suggested the city was ominously poised on the brink of a 'perfect storm' (Thomas *et al.*, 2009: 106).

Sheffield is a city which largely came into being because of industry, a town where the infrastructure – schools, hospitals, churches, galleries – was an after-thought spurred by the worldwide success of Sheffield cutlery and a surge in population growth between 1736 and 1801 from 7,000 to 60,000 inhabitants (and by 1901, the population had grown to 451,195). The walls of the Town Hall, first opened in 1897, bear two friezes carved in Derbyshire stone representing images of industry. The two friezes, each 11 metres long, show the moral perception of work from hard labour of mining and forging iron and steel to the work of artisans and architects. All are guided by heraldic female figures; one carries a torch – the light of knowledge and wisdom – and leads the artists and skilled artisans in their endeavours, while on the other frieze a similar figure bearing a cornucopia – a horn of plenty, symbolising the rewards of labour – is followed by smiths, metal workers and miners (Sheffield City Council website).

Multiple meanings, sometimes congruent, sometimes contradictory, are cheek-by-jowl in every street and suburb. There is a sense that, reading between these layers of meaning, cities can be read as historical texts. The shopping centre – Meadowhall, for example – was built on the site of the former Hadfields East Hecla Steel Works. Sweeping deindustrialisation, the result of political and economic changes, affected the livelihoods of whole populations altering the urban settings beyond recognition.

Persistence of memory – holes in the urban imagination

Constant transformation is at work in the urban landscape, a dialectical process of material change, shaping social divisions of class and ethnicity producing residential, regional and sometimes ghettoised boundaries. However, in addition, there are the more subtle discursive and subjective signs which are elusive and fall out of the grasp of any crudely materialist epistemology. Differences of power, resistance, production and consumption; the marketed fantasies and the realities of lived experience. Features of the streets, buildings, shops and parks echo internally and leave their traces on the psyche long after they have been reshaped or demolished. The city also exists in memories and in the constant accretion of popular myths built around the city and its identity. Entrekin describes this internal and external perception of the city as:

> a fusion of space and experience, a space filled with meaning, a source of identity. It is also a specific context for our actions, a configuration of objects and events filled in space, a milieu, as the French say. It is outside and inside us, objective and subjective, universal and particular. We live our lives in place and have a sense of being part of place, but we also view place as separate, something external.
>
> (Entrekin, 1991: 34).

The 'hole in the road' and its disappearance is a concrete example of this speculation about spaces and the complex relationship between objective and subjective meanings. It is an interesting example of the construction of a popular myth around a unique feature, ugly and modernist, as it perhaps was. As a student in the late 1970s I remember seeing the goldfish gasping in the algae-covered aquarium set into the wall of the subway; there was a news-stand and occasionally

Figure 12 Frieze, Sheffield Town Hall (Spencer, 2009).

beggars and buskers. It was a landmark which, having been filled in, seems to have generated a sense of nostalgia, of loss. In a Sheffield Forum discussion one contributor offered pictures of the hole being filled in (see Figure 13b), providing a sense of closure which others appreciated. Jarvis Cocker famously speculated on the fate of those goldfish walled up under the concrete. This concern for the hidden lives beneath the concrete is reminiscent of the Situationist slogan 'under the pavement, a beach', suggesting that beneath the alienating surfaces of the rationalist city lies a mysterious or utopian world. The lyrics to Cocker's song *Wickerman* contain references to the submerged mysteries of the city and its industrial past. Cocker's imagery traces a hidden city which is glimpsed or imagined beneath the everyday surfaces. It is a narrative journey along the mythical river system, peppered with urban myth and the residue of industrial history.

Visual analyses of the city might help to convey an understanding of these dialectical changes; the very gradual and the sudden and catastrophic. Images can be used to explore the relationships and contrasts, offering opportunities to examine the metaphors and tropes of the city which tend to shape and constrain perceptions. De Certeau suggests that 'the everyday has a certain strangeness that does not surface, or whose surface is only its upper limit, outlining itself against the visible' (1993: 154). Beneath the matter-of-fact surfaces of tarmac and concrete are the memories, imaginings and lived experiences invested in those spaces. Rather than approaching the city through a preconceived dissection of its attributes and dimensions, the intention was to allow the disparate rhythms, boundaries, contradictions and multiple meanings to present themselves unbidden – like Debord's concept of the dérive, literally drifting: 'a technique of rapid passage through varied ambiences'(Debord, 1958). This was a notion central to psychogeography – a practice developed by the French situationists who allowed themselves 'to be drawn by the chance attractions and encounters of the urban environment' (Shields, 1996: 244).

Such an approach is not just a piece of feckless flanneurie; sociologically it is important not to disregard the everyday: the collision of the individual perception of milieu with the process of history and large-scale social change distinguishes the sociological approach (Mills, 1959).The commonsense acceptance of the city at face value belies the complex and often contradictory dynamics which are operating beneath the surface. A visual exploration might defamiliarise the everyday surfaces, allow the meanings to emerge. Not only do images have an immediacy, they can also if permitted allow a slow release of meaning. The

Figure 13a The 'hole in the road' in the 1970s (Peter Jones).

Figure 13b The 'hole' being filled in (Sheffield Forum: www.sheffieldforum.co.uk/showthread.php?p=4550571).

resonance of images to 'breathe' (as Marcus Banks suggested in a recent conference) and reveal complex and subtle relationships between the internalised meanings and accumulated poetics of place and the external reality of its changing structures may be close to what Benjamin meant by 'dialectical images'.

The collective identity of the city is created by an informal amalgamation of discussion forums, shared images, anecdotes and poems, popular music, film and documentaries. The 'hole in the road' exists in popular memory through images like those above and through the love/hate relationship expressed in blogs and local history discussion strands. There is even a poem in circulation which captures this almost folk character of the incongruous urban feature. Like the poem there is an abiding sense of fatalistic acceptance for the folly of town planners but also a sense of nostalgia which is unavoidable because at another level these features are imbued with an unavoidable sense of ownership of belonging; the hole and the old town hall (which was demolished), for all their gauche ugliness, were landmarks, part of the lived reality of being in Sheffield.

Ode to hole in the road

When the hole was first thought of it caused such a stir
A hole in the road? Why? How much and where?
The council debate raged to and fro for o'er three year,
Many thought the idea was daft, a bit queer.
But, at last it were decided – an ole we shall 'ave
The Council knows best said t'Mayor, and agreed to the scheme
Madness said some, and so it did seem.
And so in due course, it came to pass, after two further year
The largest bloody hole in the road in the whole of South Yorkshire.
Nobody liked the hole. No decent shops in it, no lavs, no character or sole.
What did thee expect said t' Mayor – its only a hole.
And now, ee you would never guess
They've dug up the hole and moved it to a new address!
Where is it now ? – Nobody knows and nobody cares,
What a terrible, terrible state of affairs.
If they had only left it there where it was – now just think on . . .
they could have dumped the new Town hall in it – that's another thing
    that's gone

                                              Steve Gos

Industrial ruins

Passing along the canal system from Sheffield city centre towards Meadowhall, parallel to the River Don, the route passes through a fossil record of industry. Scanning the decaying facades of the works that line the waterway, rampant vegetation and strung and razor wire barricades festoon the graffiti-daubed and shattered ruins, you get a shock when you pass a working foundry. Men can be seen moving about with red-hot iron, the sound of hammers, Radio 1 and PA systems mix oddly with the birdsong in the surrounding trees.

Tim Edensor (2005) comments on the remains of once vigorous industry as stigmatised landscapes – 'matter out of place'. While popular civic discourse denies the validity of industrial ruins in favour of 'an impossibly seamless urban fabric' Edensor argues that such spaces provide a rejoinder to this desire to eradicate, to commodify, to reduce the signs of obsolescence to bland middle-class aesthetics (in which steelworks become palaces of shopping) and to 'broader tendencies to fix meanings in the service of power'. How should these areas and artefacts be viewed? On the one hand they are monuments to the enormous productive power of capitalist industry and the nostalgic remains of a superseded order which carelessly discards its apparatus: a relentlessly rational process which steamrollers landscapes (and working lives) in its impassive progress. Yet it can be argued that such ruins are not just the follies of grandiose human endeavour (like the romance of the ruins of eternal Greco-Roman architecture so beloved of the Victorians); they could also be read as indices of the fragility of capitalist enterprise.

> The debris of industrial culture teaches us not the necessity of submitting to historical catastrophe, but the fragility of the social order that tells us this catastrophe was necessary. The crumbling of the monuments that were built to signify the immortality of civilisation becomes proof, rather, of its transiency. And the fleetingness of temporal power does not cause sadness; it informs political practice.
>
> (Buck-Morss, 1991: 170)

Walking the Five Weirs route along the banks of the Don in early summer, the variety of plant and bird life is striking. The intensive industry in the region caused the river to become amongst the most polluted in Europe. The rapid de-industrialisation of the city, clean-up campaigns and the preservation of a 'green belt' around the river have improved the situation and salmon have been reported in the river near Doncaster. There are stories that salmon were once very plentiful. 'Once upon a time, the River Don was counted among the most successful salmon fisheries in the land. Rumour has it that young Sheffield apprentices, bored with eating so much salmon, had it written into their contracts that they would only be fed salmon three times a week!' (Waterscape.com).

Along the trail between the alders and willows, fig trees are also to be seen. The story behind them is another dialectical relationship between the history of industry and its long-term consequences. A notice-board at Brightside Weir informs us: 'Fig trees are believed to originate from seeds in sewage, which germinated because the river water was repeatedly heated by steelworks along its banks' (Sheffield City Council and Arcus, 2007).

The divisions at the heart of the city go further than the obvious transition from the rural landscape to the birth and development of mass industry and the rapid growth of urban populations. Cities could be considered to *produce* the idea of 'the natural'; nature as a form of social space to be consumed. This is true insofar

Figure 14 Industrial ruins along the Sheffield and Tinsley Canal: (a) Spencer (2009); (b) Surridge (2009).

as cities provide an inevitable contrast to what is considered 'nature in the raw' (see Short, 2006: 177–80). Yet ironically these river and canal walks are anomalous zones, certainly re-greened but veined with industrial history.

Sections of the Five Weirs Walk were sporadically closed because of anxiety over metal theft from the barricaded factories which still line the river, and one new suspension bridge built for walkers was closed because metal struts had been stolen. Here again, it is useful to examine the ways of looking; there are intersecting discourses, modes of consuming a landscape which is in a state of fluidity in which landscapes shaped by capitalism are later destroyed and superseded at each new crisis (see e.g. Harvey, 1985). Here natural history and romantic, collective or spectatorial aspects of the walking tracks collide with the disciplinary discourses of surveillance, industrial archaeology with observation and protection of private property.

There are the bounded and manicured 'green' areas; green belts which girdle the city, gardens, parks, leafy suburbs, and 'nature strips' (an Australian term for the precious grass verges in residential areas) and the well-trammelled and maintained areas of the Peak District National Park. These are the officially accepted bounded areas but there is also the unplanned irruption of nature within the city's confines: on waste ground and derelict areas, in the cracks and interstices of the city. A city at once deeply seamed with industry and yet the greenest city in England 'It's a surprising fact but it would be hard to find a city with more open green space than Sheffield. Despite its urban location almost three-quarters of the city is taken up by natural vegetation and waterways.'(Live in Sheffield).

Walking back through the city centre an iconic figure captures the anomalous character of the city. A mounted 'botanic' statue in the shape of a steelworker 'Sheffy Stan' is having the last coleus plants fitted in front of the Town Hall (Figure 17). Does this metaphorical image share the elusive qualities of Benjamin's dialectical image? Unifying nature and culture in a historical emblem of the city's past gives botanic man some of the proposed features wherein the cultural becomes assimilated as natural. The suggestion of culture as nature rings alarm bells as it has long been associated with the process of ideology (whereby false consciousness and inverted power relations present a 'natural' order of things) and the highly constructed, from margarine to cosmetic surgery, become naturalised. However, this refusal to reject reification is essential for Benjamin: 'what is historically concrete becomes image – the archetypal image of nature as of what is beyond nature – and conversely nature becomes the figure of something historical' (Adorno, 1992: 226). So instead of an ideological pitfall it is the recognition of important critical relationships. There are profound philosophical concerns which cannot be fully explored here. Images such as these, drawn from the everyday array of sights, have arguably become habitual, a 'natural' or at least an immanent part of our everyday experience of being in the city. The images seem to be part of a taken-for-granted narrative of the city; like Cocker's lyrics about the hidden rivers of industrialisation, they weave and interlace with the lives of people. At Meadowhall, that sparkling palace of consumption, one of the atria houses a group of statues of steelworkers cast in bronze (Figure 18); here

Figure 15
(a) Heron on
Brightside Weir;
(b) information board
telling the story of
the fig trees
(Spencer, 2009).

Figure 16 Warning signs, Sheffield (Spencer, 2009).

Figure 17
'Sheffy Stan' –
botanic steel worker
(Spencer, 2009).

Figure 18 'Teeming'; a sculpture by Robin Bell (1989–90) – Meadowhall Shopping Centre (bronze) (Spencer, 2009).

again is the frozen moment, dialectics at a standstill. The statues remind us that this shopping mall was built on the foundations of a steel foundry.

Signs of diversity – spectres of multiculturalism

Walking around Fitzalan Square, an area I hadn't visited for over 25 years, there were signs of degradation: money lenders, betting shops, amusement and gaming centres, and a hairdresser training centre clustered around a statue of Edward VII. The statue by Alfred Drury (1856–1944) bristled with protective wires to keep pigeons away. Each face of the plinth contained a relief scene in Pre-Raphaelite style. In 'Philanthropy' (Figure 19b) a saintly shrouded Britannia figure is bestowing beneficence on the poor in the form of what appears to be a building, perhaps a hospice (or a workhouse?). The same figure in another relief scene entitled 'Unity' (Figure 19a) selflessly extends imperial power and wisdom uniting the peoples of the world. This sort of colonial legacy can be observed in many British cities and indeed such representations are embedded in the city. Imagery is of subjugation; passive and respectful subjects receiving the bounty of Empire. The subject nations portrayed, interestingly largely through female forms, imploring African and Asian women hold a hand on either side of the impassively merciful and angelic form. These common romantic myths of otherness are deep-seated in cities around Britain.

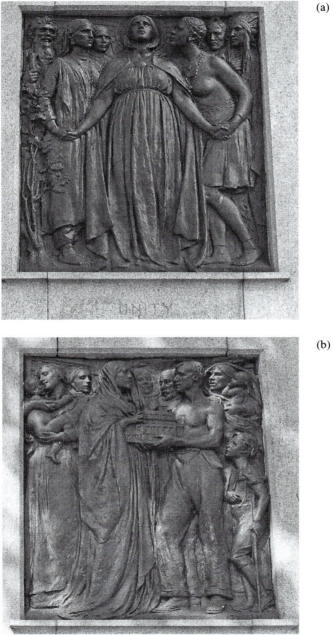

(a)

(b)

Figure 19 Relief panels on a statue of Edward VII, Fitzalan
Square: (a) Unity; (b) 'Philanthropy' (Spencer, 2009).

Seen now, these paternalistic figures remind us that British cities, like Sheffield, depended on the exploitation of colonial resources for their very existence. Charles Lemert (2006) comments: 'In Europe, racism owes more, of course, to its overt colonial past. As America tried to avoid the truth of its racial crimes by the pretense that she was not a colonizer, most European colonizing nations buffered themselves, until of late, from internal racial conflicts by keeping colonial subjects in the remove of distant colonies.'

But as the colonial period came to an end these same colonies:

> were indispensable to the building of its economic power in the capitalist world system. When the colonial system ended, at least officially, Europe was left with the need the colonies fulfilled – cheap labor to mine natural resources and produce the goods and services required of capitalist expansion.

> (ibid.)

Elsewhere in the city one stumbles on more contemporary signs communicating the changing concepts of ethnic incorporation into the city. The 1980s mural glimpsed in Broomhall signifies an idealised community-centred arts project, a sort of cultured rainbow alliance for the once 'vibrant' African-Caribbean community Looking at the dereliction of the area it felt like 'the ghost of multiculturalism past' – faded dreams of multicultural harmony which never came to fruition (discussed in Chapter 2). In the same vein this City Council billboard delivers a very similar message for 2009: 'Sheffield – where Everyone Matters', another celebratory multicultural discourse in which a smiling woman, in colourful traditional dress, demonstrates dance steps to an enthused mixed group (Figure 20).

Hardship and melancholia in the marketplace

Walking on past Primark and descending into the crowded vortex of Castle Markets, a far cry from the glittering celebration of consumption represented by Meadowhall, there are omnipresent signs of poverty. The city in 2009 is awash with signs of economic upheaval; everywhere the clutter of credit and cash converters (Figure 21a, b) and betting shops. The streets bustle with lone traders selling very narrow lines of produce; all indices of financial hardship in a divided city. Sheffield's marked divide is never more obvious than here; within a hundred yards are areas of affluence and high prestige – brand-named shops and the market area for the sale of bargain, generic and second-hand produce.

The cluttered shelves of a charity shop (Figure 23) caught my attention with their disparate array of bric-a-brac. Should they be dismissed as tat or junk, the terminal moraine of an exhausted culture, or objects being retired from their serviceable life in the domestic domain, to gain a new lease of life as desirable retro, pieces of kitsch? Amongst the endlessly varied ceramics and floral patterned plates, bowls and pots there, I notice later a saucer commemorating the royal wedding of Prince Andrew and Sarah Ferguson from 1986. In the foreground is a rather naïve depiction of a golliwog in an armchair alongside two

Figure 20
Signs of
multiculturalism,
Sheffield
(Spencer, 2009).

chicken figures of indeterminate purpose. Do they highlight the everyday and mundane nature of racism and the working class's misplaced loyalty to the royals? Could they be seen as uniquely British signs of 'postcolonial melancholia' (Gilroy, 2006) demonstrating false consciousness at work in the pervasive remnants of a changing culture? Alternatively, are they just random detritus – empty signifiers, misplaced objects of a culture longing for comfort? So easily dismissed, but potentially the sign system of a complex and divided culture. Certainly the golliwog figure is seen as an offensive racist icon, but perhaps such objects demonstrate the unthinking nature of such values, 'everyday racism' (Stratton, 1998; Essed, 2002; Spencer, 2007) deeply embedded in the lives and domestic heart of the household. Edensor captures the startling dialectical quality of these unconsidered trifles:

> other spaces such as charity shops, jumble sales and car boot sales, unex-
> pected shocks from the past – discarded fashions, crazes and trends – remind

Figure 21(a, b)
Traders near Castle Markets,
Sheffield: (a) Surridge;
(b) Spencer (both 2009).

Figure 22
Signs of recession
(Surridge, 2009).

Figure 23 Bric-a-brac in a charity shop (Spencer, 2009).

us of forgotten sensations, reawakening our own ghostly pasts. Office styles, calendars, wallpaper, advertisements, packaging, posters and machinery, and the artefacts produced suddenly seem absurd or kitsch.

(Edensor, 2002)

Returning from the industrial hinterlands of the canal and the river, we cross under the Blonk Street Bridge – the prows of giant modernist corporate con-structions, offices and apartments to let, loom over the derelict remains of the venue for an infamously poor car boot sale (Figure 24). The cycles of production and consumption are visible in these spectral remainders; they appear, as Edensor claims, to be part of a narrative, 'talking back' to, and showing the ruptures in, official rationalist discourses about the city. Mitigating against the vision of smooth urban retail cycles and neatly ordered spaces, these are the cluttered informal and derelict spaces which exist in nooks and crannies around the city disturbing the rational sweep of planning.

These examples demonstrate that the city exudes dialectical imagery, at least to the extent that such images expose the restless processes of transformation. There are dialectical images everywhere when the mind and eye are attuned to the inherent paradoxes and the multiple social realities which stir between the crumbling, over-layered facades and the sleek seamless surfaces of the city. The city is a didactic, visual (in fact multi-sensorial) resource, and while we might be

Figure 24 Venue for a car boot sale (Spencer, 2009).

'unreliable witnesses' we are not sealed in tombs of our time, but we need to learn to see beyond the surfaces of the everyday and recognise the complex strands of representation which taken together create the accumulated mythology of our culture.

This section is largely reproduced from an article which first appeared in *Illumina*, e-journal, Edith Cowan University, Issue 3, December 2009 (with kind permission from the editors).

Video ethnography: walking with a camera

This account has attempted to mirror the meandering progress made through the industrial hinterlands and the city streets with a camera to capture errant visions and punctuate thoughts. The result is a series of disorderly observations stumbled upon in the course of walking through areas of a city and trying to see them in a different, less familiar light.

There appears to be a relationship between the physical movement and rhythms of walking and the telling of stories, recounting of memories, tracing a community's pathways and folkways. On the face of it such a connection might seem tenuous and folksy, hard to substantiate. However, a piece of video research which we embarked upon in 2007 demonstrated that for some forms of research there is no substitute for walking through the area in question (in this case the former site of Africville near Halifax in Nova Scotia) with a respondent who has stories and life experiences about the area.

The writings of Ingold and Vergust (2006) give credence to there being fruitful interconnections between walking and storytelling; narrative trails, footsteps and tracks are like the words on a page. They argue that: 'Walking is a profoundly social activity: in their timings, rhythms and inflections the feet respond as much as does the voice to the presence and activity of others. Social relations, we maintain, are not enacted *in situ* but are paced out along the ground' (2007: 1). 'Walking around is fundamental to the everyday practice of social life' and 'to much anthropological fieldwork' (2006: 67). They further discuss how walking reveals the nature of the places and associations created by routes which people use. This understanding of 'the routes and mobilities of others' (2007: 68) has been taken up effectively by several other practitioners of visual methods including Sarah Pink.

In 2007 research in Nova Scotia led us to a meeting with Irvine Carvery who along with his brothers and the Africville Genealogical Association has been spearheading the movement for proper reparations to those who were removed from their homes when the township was destroyed between 1964 and 1967.

Images from the 1960s show the stark division between the city of Halifax and Africville. Bob Brooks' (Figure 23) picture shows the way the city kept the community at 'arms' length' at the periphery of the official built and finished environment, separated by areas of rough scrub, and the end of the sealed road which stopped just short of the community. Other services were also not extended to the 400 or so people of Africville – sewers, running water, electricity, garbage collection, fire or police protection – even though taxes were levied on the inhabitants. In addition to these forms of exclusion the community was subjected to degradation of their land and resources by the proliferation of numerous unhealthy and downright toxic and dangerous industries and waste dumps. From 1850 to the mid 1960s there was a gradual accumulation of unwanted, dirty and dangerous facilities, including: around 1850 a train line which bisected the community (with no crossings or warnings), 1853, Rock Head Prison, 1870, a Hospital for Infectious Diseases, two slaughterhouses, a depository for fecal waste from nearby Russellville, a tar factory, stone- and coal-crushing plants, an oil plant – storage complex, two fertiliser manufacturing plants, numerous waste dumps and incinerators, sewage run-off from the city and the city dump – relocated here in 1958 (as seen as too close to the city) and later even toxic waste-disposal pits for PCBs (highly toxic, persistent organic pollutants compounds which have now been banned).

Certainly the location of these industries follows a pattern of callous disregard for 'Africvillians'. It is easier of course to locate such facilities where there is a marginalised minority community who have been effectively disenfranchised and are outside of the voting constituency of the city. Thus a stigmatised and displaced area becomes the plausible site for damaging waste. This form of environmental injustice/racism has been discussed in many similar situations. It demonstrates Michel de Certeau's concept of 'spatial purification' in action:

> In this site (the city) organised by 'speculative' and classifying operations, management combines with *elimination*: on the one hand, we have the differentiation and redistribution of the parts and function of the city through inversions, movements, accumulations, etc., and, on the other hand, we have the rejection of whatever is not treatable and that, thus, constitutes *the garbage of a functionalist administration* (abnormality, deviance, sickness, death, etc).
>
> (1985: 122–45)

The experience of walking through the site was rendered especially meaningful as the backdrop to Irvine's narrative; I felt I could almost 'see' the houses, the children and the community's church, where now there were only people with so many dogs (the area is designated officially as Seaview Dog Park).

Certainly the route that we traversed did not correspond to the original Africville roads and tracks, but for Irvine and others the area is laden with meaning and only a veneer overlaying the original site and its rich history of solidarity against the humiliation and neglect at the hands of the City of Halifax.

In the context of Africville this traumatic experience of place, or loss of place, has produced a persistent legacy of injustice. The facts of the area's degradation through what appears to be a history of neglect and environmental racism for the people of Africville (treating them, as Irvine suggested, as 'sub-human') are stark and well documented. However, the more positive aspects of living in this village, which was certainly an independent, resourceful and tightly knit community,

Figure 25 Africville. Image by Bob Brooks, 1960s.

survive in oral reports and in a few photographs (for example, those of Bob Brooks). Two opposing discourses begin to emerge here. First, the discourse of 'blaming the victims' and legitimating the dispersal of the community and its destruction. Second, there is also a powerful affirming discourse of Africville as a proudly independent group of some 400 people who had triumphed over adversity and carved out something for themselves, through resourceful use of the available materials, hard work and communal support.

How far can video ethnography capture and realign this sense of Africville as an important symbolic centre for African-Canadians with deep roots in the province? This remains to be seen, but as a first attempt the video narrative which was recorded with Irvine Carvery (whose family have strong roots in the village) raises questions about the role of visual texts to promote and recover the historical legacies of place. The recording made was crude and partial but did allow a glimpse of the importance of going to the place and *walking* through the site, allowing Irvine to recount memories and events in context. There are landmarks, traces, coordinates which are no longer visible, they are part of a mental map of Africvillians. Effectively there are layers of meaning and reading of a landscape which depend on lived experience. Might this knowledge of the land be conveyed more vividly on foot – as the coordinates of the land hold captive the memories of the generations that lived there?

> So too, walkers have to lift their feet between steps. But the writer does not cease to write on lifting the pen, nor does the walker cease to walk on lifting each foot, alternately, from the ground. Nor, for that matter, does the singer or storyteller cease his recitation every time he pauses for breath. 'Stories walk', writes John Berger, 'like animals and men. And their steps are not only between narrated events but between each sentence, sometimes each word. Every step is a stride over something not said.'
>
> (Berger 1982: 284–85, in Ingold and Vergust, 2006)

In the sequence below the walk and interview/narrative was recorded on location in Seaview Dog Park. Irvine invited us to meet up there and the resulting video record gives a unique insight into this contested space and the strength of such recollections especially when they are taking place in context, to re-create a sense of place and evoke the experience of those who lived in the area which was lost when the bulldozers finished their work in 1967, having taken out one house at a time with little warning, it is claimed, about whose house was next in line.

How are sites like Africville remembered? As discussed, there are oral traditions by which collective ideas of place are nurtured and passed on; of course they can become distorted and embellished over time, just as my mind map of the 'Thicket' area may be prone to inaccuracies and hazy spaces. There are films and photographs which serve as a record of the existence of the site and there are writings, drawings and artefacts which record the lived experiences of people raised there.

During our walk it became clear that Irvine believed that walking on the land in question was important for their case and implied a sort of performative knowledge, a sort of knowing through tracing the steps of the community, sharing the landmarks that situated their lives. Recounting an important turning point in the quest for proper recognition of what had been done to the people of Africville, he had contacted Doudou Diène, one of the UN rapporteurs for the G7, which was held in Halifax in March 2004, suggesting that he should come out to the site to make his own mind up about the case: 'I said you have to come with me to Africville, you need to walk the land, you need to feel it. Right? Because he was African, and I said well, I know this man will understand what I'm talking about. So I brought him out here and we walked and talked, and then when he gave his report back his recommendation was that the people of Africville be compensated . . . first of all given an apology and compensated.'

"you need to walk the land, you need to feel it."

Figure 26 Stills from a short video walk in Africville in 2007 (Samuels and Spencer, 2007).

The recounting of these stories of the struggle for reparation seemed especially poignant as we walked through the area which was now an unremarkable green space where many dogs were being walked or were running together between the trees. The little tracks criss-crossed; past and present, an entanglement of lines mirroring the complex discourses which had led to the fate of the town. There is some evidence that public opinion had been in favour of the move to relocate the Africvillians, as a long overdue righting of a terrible wrong, after a history of neglect; treating people as invisible, as less than human. Richard Bobier (1995: 164) cites *Time* magazine of the day as heralding it as a: 'determined, if belated, effort. . . to right an historical wrong.' He argues that the public tended to support the relocation as a symbol of civic progress, but that by the end of the 1960s this attitude had changed, and the protracted move was transformed 'to a symbol of Black consciousness and white racism' (ibid.). This clash of discourses highlights the complex entangled construction of place. On the one hand the town was portrayed as a stigmatised site, a symbol of otherness, 'beyond the pale', a repository for the unwanted waste of the city, an example of environmental racism, but it also stood as a shaming and living example of injustice on the boundaries of an affluent, supposedly liberal-minded city.

> Africville was located at the north-eastern most corner of the Halifax peninsula, overlooking the Bedford Basin. Its most obvious features were the tracks of the old intercolonial railway that ran east to west bisecting the community, and the city dump that lay to the west. Less monumental than these signs of Halifax's encroachment were the eighty 'shacks' that housed the four hundred residents of Africville.

These dilapidated and aging homes had been almost entirely bypassed by any modernizing influence. Ranging from sturdy but modest bungalows to 'rude shacks made of tin sheets and boards, held together by tarpaper and paint,' the salt air had caused paint to peel leaving the houses mottled yellows, blues, reds and greens. Piped sewage and water were unavailable; electricity was absent; the sole road was unpaved; and city services such as fire and police protection were not extended to this part of the city.

(Bobier, 1995: 165)

But these constructions of Africville as a run-down shanty town or slum are only one side of the picture, an outsider's view which has been argued to be functional for the commercial interests which were intent on reclaiming the land for road and housing development. Such degraded descriptions have been strongly contested. Denise Allen, whose family originated in Africville, believes that there was a rich and picturesque community and that describing Africville as an abject slum was propagandist when in fact it could be compared favourably to the housing available today. Indeed in an interview in 2007 she described the township thus:

The community of Africville was beautiful, it was more beautiful than Peggy's Cove[6] at the time it was destroyed . . . at the time it was destroyed – but what do they like to depict? They like to depict sides of Africville that weren't very charming to the eye, weren't very attractive: they didn't see the roses, they didn't see the blueberry bushes, they didn't see the strawberries. They didn't see the fact that we had homes that looked better than the homes I'm living in right now – that I paid hundreds of thousands of dollars for.

(Spencer and Samuels, 2008)

In fact although some of the families wished to be relocated, many did not, and one factor in their decision to stay appears to be their feelings of pride and autonomy in the sense of community which had a long history. Some of the accounts of Africville residents argue against the dysfunctional and delinquent associations heaped on their community and present it instead as a bastion of independence and enterprise in the midst of the harsh racism of the city. Many of the houses were free-standing and of a good size and some were very well built.

Institutional discourses which arose in the urban renewal projects in other parts of Canada set the agenda in the local situation and set the process of destruction in motion, generating pictures of Africville as a slum, a health hazard, a disgraceful example of neglect and division. New Left thinking and more militant black politics in the late 1960s and sociological interest in the events and the space added further layers of meaning.

In her visual ethnographic research into the Slow City movement in the UK (Cittàslow) Sarah Pink (2008a) examines the importance of audio-visual media in the evolving development of place, arguing that people's 'routes and mobilities are both invested in, and produce, local visual cultures'. Furthermore she suggests a visual ethnography of routes and mobilities 'can inform academic knowledge of how local urban issues are articulated and contested' (2008: 1).

This is particularly true when an area has such strong traumatic entanglements with people's lives, memories and future expectations. The current research is only one of several other initiatives that tell the story of Africville: several documentaries, a new, multilayered map produced by the Africville Genealogical Society[7] which juxtaposes the history and heritage of the site with the current land use and topography; there is also an annual protest at the site, and several recent artworks give a sense of the past and present, keeping memories of the community alive.[8] In addition, a full-length film (*Africville: Can't Stop Now*) is in production, exploring the biography of the three Carvery brothers and their different forms of protest around the loss of Africville. There is even an animation set to hardcore metal track – Bucket Truck's A Nourishment by Neglect – which shows a bulldozer destroying houses and the church (the Seaview African United Baptist Church) as residents stand anxiously by, and shady officials shake hands exchanging money and documents behind the scenes.[9] In many ways the lost town has become a cause célèbre and focal point for local black historians and academics embodying the past and present experience of struggle and identity politics in the region.

So in this case the meaning of Africville is partly created through the sharing of the walk through the site with the research team and the telling of the stories there in the places they happened; the fact that these stories and landmarks have been part of a video recording 'creates' the place in several ways as Pink (2008b) suggests: 'in a phenomenological sense during the research encounter; in the form of the video representation of that encounter; and again through the subjectivity of the viewer of that video.'

The resulting video material links several stories together in a complementary fashion, adding to the wide range of multisensorial representations of the place, as mentioned above.

So far this chapter has demonstrated how visual research, the use of video and still images, electronic satellite-generated imaging, maps and archive material can be used to begin to construct a sense of place. It becomes clear that place is a complex, *intersubjective* construction negotiated with those who live in and understand the area, along with the vast array of popular cultural resources; those numerous discourses which intersect in film, popular media, narrative histories and historical visual records of the area.

Discussions of place in which residents (or past residents) actively collaborate to tell their story are obviously different from the early twentieth-century accounts in which ethnographers and anthropologists strove to collect the authentic remains of what were sometimes perceived as 'doomed' or threatened cultures. The social Darwinist approach to Aborigines in central Australia was touched upon briefly in Chapter 1. Such groups were viewed as having lost the competitive struggle for survival and were of interest as doomed specimens. Margaret Mead commented that: 'The recognition that forms of human behaviour still extant will inevitably disappear has been part of our whole scientific and humanistic heritage.

There have never been enough workers to collect the remnants of these worlds' (in Hockings, 1995: 3).

This endeavour came to be known as 'salvage ethnography' and arguably still continues in documentaries about fragile and marginal indigenous groups threatened by encroaching industry (especially logging) or indeed by adventure tourism which is irrevocably changing cultural practices.

In contrast, another innovative piece of collaborative visual research may be seen in Brogan Bunt's interactive video record of the life of a rural Turkish town – Halfeti. This video record is an interesting case in point as it challenges the notion of what 'place' means. Halfeti no longer exists (at least in its original coordinates or condition). This small township was flooded as part of a big hydroelectric scheme. Bunt has produced an interactive documentary, a video map of the town before it was inundated. The CD-Rom includes a navigable record of the streets, buildings and businesses which once existed there, and conversations with the inhabitants. He created his own software including cursors which allow right and left turns through sequences of still images of the town in different seasons, including ambient sound recordings and short video conversations with shop owners and other townspeople. Pictured below (Figure 27) are a teashop owner and a navigable map of the township. The map may be explored and entered from different locations, giving the sensation of travelling along the streets at different times of the day and in different weather conditions.

In a recent communiqué about his work Bunt said: 'Halfeti was both a specific documentary work and also a generic engine for putting together spatial-navigable projects. It was designed to be low tech and accessible – just a matter of choreographing sets of digital images, sound files and video. The technical system is way out of date now. These days it should be possible to develop a system that works effectively in a broadband web context.'

This collaborative project which has 'salvaged' the way of life of a small rural town on the Euphrates questions the boundaries of real and imagined constructs of place. A 'new Halfeti' was built for the people of the soon-to-be-flooded town

Figure 27 Halfeti: 'Only the Fish Shall Visit' (Bunt, 2001).

– but Bunt's interactive site is the only way that the place in its antediluvian form can ever be visited.[10]

Perhaps Maria Tumarkin's concept of 'traumascape' is a possible way to capture the collective experience of such sites as Africville, One Mile Dam or Halfeti. They are similar in that each place seems to demonstrate the vulnerability of the inhabitants to the schemes of government to sacrifice the small community in the interests of business and commerce; in the case of Africville and One Mile Dam there is the added legacy of historical exclusion and environmental racism as well as dispossession. Tumarkin argues that places exert a deep influence upon their human inhabitants. The landscape transformed by tragedy becomes a repository of collective feelings; the legacies of the trauma linger in the stones of the roads and houses.

> In the world we inhabit, traumascapes are everywhere. They are the physical sites of terror attacks, natural and industrial catastrophes, genocide, exile, ecological degradation, and communal loss of heart. Yet far from being mere backdrops to cataclysms, traumascapes are a distinctive category of place, transformed physically and psychically by suffering. They are part of a scar tissue that stretches across the world, from Hiroshima to Auschwitz, Dresden to Srebrenica, Sarajevo to New York, Bali, London, Jerusalem, and New Orleans.
>
> (Tumarkin, 2005)

However, traumascapes seem an unwieldy category; uniting such radically different traumatic sites as Port Arthur or Lockerbie, Belsen or Bali – just because many (perhaps even most places) have traumatic histories; does this constitute a special category? However, Tumarkin makes an important point about the land not being merely the passive recipient of trauma but in fact an active mediating force in social events. The legacy of traumatic sites and their accumulated meanings for those people who live there keeps on radiating through the ground. Interestingly the reverse side of some of these traumatic landscapes is that they are also imbued with hope and longing; the promise of renewal that change could brings is also a uniting feature encouraging collective protest around contested sites.

Before moving on to the next area of concern it seems important to at least mention an aspect of place which is the source of growing interest and which may mark a radical departure from the older, more rooted notion of place. This is the increasing experience of interaction within the web of the internet, through avatars in Multi User Domains, and virtual spaces in computer games, social networking and other parallel realms of electronic hyperreality.

Writing about the experience of virtual reality, Katherine Hayles (2002) suggests that there is a shift from presence and absence foregrounding instead of pattern and randomness. The liminal spaces which the individual enters in virtual reality offer a paradox. 'Questions about presence and absence do not yield much leverage in this situation, for the avatar both is and is not present, just as the user is and is not inside the screen' (p. 154).

To an extent, the examples already discussed are themselves complex and ethereal. Africville exists as memories and dreams, an imagined community; Halfeti lives on, albeit in a strange, dislocated fashion in Bunt's virtual cartography. Even Sheffield, very much a tangible city, exhibits complex multilayered aspects which belies its concreteness.

Recently, virtual ethnography has received interest from visual sociologists and anthropologists (e.g. Hine, 2000; Murdoch and Pink, 2005) wishing to explore the complex entanglement of electronic signals with material bodies and the creation of entire worlds of interaction opened up by Web 2 applications such as Second Life (see e.g. Boellstorff, 2008).

From the well-trodden streets of what was once a 'city of soot – now the greenest city in England', to the stigmatised yet proud legacy of Africville, still breathing beneath the bland surface of a park and the minaret of Halfeti jutting surreally from the Euphrates, the examples discussed in this chapter have demonstrated that 'place' is a complex, mercurial concept. Visual methods have an important role to communicate this restless weave of physical location, entanglement of routes and roots, legacy of memories, oral histories and heartfelt beliefs, and the proliferation of representations.

4   Visualising identity

The sense of identity commonly conceived in Western thought is as a set of central, distinctive and enduring characteristics that typify a person or a group. But these distinctive features are not closed-ended. Identity can also be seen as fluid open-ended and always a process of becoming:

> Identity is a work in progress, a negotiated space between ourselves and others; constantly being re-appraised and very much linked to the circulation of cultural meanings in a society. Furthermore identity is intensely political. There are constant efforts to escape, fix or perpetuate images and meanings of others. These transformations are apparent in every domain, and the relationships between these constructions reflect and reinforce power relations.
>
> (Taylor and Spencer, 2004: 4)

Identity has taken its place amongst the key concepts of social science, becoming central to discussions of culture and the theorising of change, especially the shift from modernity to post-modernity; one key feature being the fragmentation of mass movements often argued to be due to 'identity politics'[1] and an emphasis on difference. Recently, discussion of multiculturalism reached fever pitch and national identity became a burning issue with political and media rhetoric full of impassioned proclamations from both ends of the political spectrum.

This chapter is about how this ubiquitous concept in sociology and cultural studies might be examined through the lens of visual research. Because much 'identity work' occurs within representation, it ought to be possible to capture some manifestations of identity in visual form.

Social identity is central to our sense of self, but how easily can these aspects of social being be visually examined and revealed? The representation of different groups in society contributes significantly to the manner in which identity is constructed. Boundaries are those markers of difference which delineate the contours of our sense of identity, between self and others, between us and them. Some boundaries are drawn socially and controlled by the state, such as retirement age, citizenship, immigration status or the legal status of families (see Best, 2005). What divides us may not always be such Manichean divisions, but more subtle differences. Indeed, boundaries are constantly being drawn and re-drawn, demonstrating that people are not easily divided into bounded units, but, rather as Barth suggests, fundamentally 'open and disordered', composed of 'overlapping social networks with crosscutting boundaries' (Kuper, 1992: 7). These complex aspects of identity, belonging and difference are expressed and acted upon at the individual level, but also mediated and regulated discursively through key social institutions and media. While boundaries can be hard-edged geographical or political lines drawn on a map to delineate territories and states, they are also part of an internal landscape: 'Boundaries define the borders of nations and territories as well as the imaginations of minds and communities' (Cottle, 2000: 2). Identity is defined by societal boundaries – social divisions both external to the person and internalised and hegemonic.

Visual culture can be a powerful dimension for affirming personal as well as collective identity. From the child's first existential moment of ego awareness when looking in a mirror, to the mass identification which occurs in advertising, sport and other forms of popular culture, recognition of self and identification with others and with the values of society is frequently mediated through an array of visual signs. There are studies which focus particularly on sign systems deployed to demonstrate or encourage nationalist sentiments (Allmark, 2007; Jenkins, 2007; Madriaga, 2007) especially in relation to the concept of 'banal nationalism' (Billig, 1995) where flags or other everyday representations are used to build an imagined sense of national solidarity and belonging. The researcher may choose to use visual means to record manifestations of social identities; apart from flags and nationalist symbolism, the constant struggle for symbolic dominance in sport and politics, trade and other international arenas creates strong, often visible, emotive rhetoric of national identity. The flag is a symbol of the nation and flying the flag or for that matter desecrating it can have enormous significance (many countries have penalties for public destruction of the nation's flag).

The diagram in Figure 28 helps us to recognise identity as part of a complex matrix of social processes which produce and circulate meanings. Stuart Hall argues that we should think of cultural identity as 'a production which is never complete, always in process, and always constituted *within not outside, repre-sentation*' (1990: 222). The model suggests that the process of identity formation is continuous and links to the material cycle of production and consumption (including both tangible products and artefacts and intangible messages and values) and their representation through language, media and other cultural signs.

Visions of identity

Some photographers have developed a practice which deals with the poetics of the image, and through creative juxtaposition of images capture the implicit contradictions of everyday life. In this context see Panizza Allmark's work (Section II) which seeks the implicit contradictions brought into being by selected instances of duality, as two seemingly incompatible elements collide and create 'the third effect'.[2] These juxtapositions are, it seems, to be expected in a society

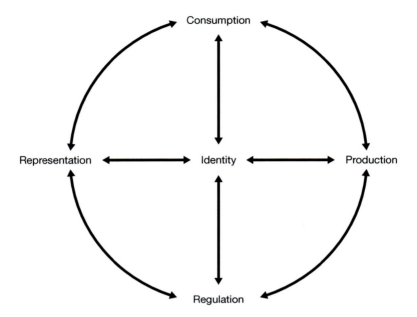

Figure 28 Matrix of cultural identity (Spencer, 2006a).

which as postmodern theory suggests is an array of signifiers without depth (dislocated from their signifieds and from the deeper meanings of modernity), a pastiche. Sarah Atkinson (Section II) develops Foucault's suggestion that we are living in 'an epoch of simultaneity: we are in the epoch of juxtaposition, the epoch of near and far, of the side-by-side, of the dispersed' (Foucault, 1967). The practice of capturing this reality through the creative alignment of objects, images, narratives and contexts can be used to suggest the ironies and paradoxes of our place in this divided world.

As already suggested, the elements which make up identity (at least those that can be expressed and communicated) are shaped *within* representation, or within the codes of the society in which we live. While it is evident that the visual manifestations of identity are useful as part of a broader set of methodologies, the analysis of visual signs, symbols and the outward trappings of identity is very revealing, exposing attempts to forge identity, to show one's 'true colours', to position with or against others, show solidarity or resistance and derision.

To sum up then, aspects of social identity are collectively maintained and regulated through cultural communication. There are competing discourses of national, ethnic and gendered identities, as well as cross-cutting forms of socio-economic identity which may conform to traditional class-based values or be more associated with consumer identity. Some social identities are invested in traditional meanings, others break with tradition and question these values. Only a small part of this is visually displayed; for example, via the popular iconography

Figure 29
Ray Egan –
a John Bull-style
protest (Spencer,
2000).

of nation, particularly in relation to flags and other insignia of the nation in question. As discussed, Billig's use of the term 'banal nationalism' is valuable 'to cover the ideological habits which enable the established nations of the West to be reproduced. It is argued that these habits are not removed from everyday life, as some observers have supposed. Daily, the nation is indicated, or "flagged", in the lives of its citizenry. Nationalism, far from being an intermittent mood in established nations, is the endemic condition' (1995: 6).

This suggests that the meanings of nationalism become deeply embedded in social practices and are not merely the province of marginal extremists but only dormant and ready to be mobilised in the wake of events which warrant such displays. The protestor in Figure 29 has adopted the traditional 'John Bull' character to personify Britishness in his one-man demonstrations in defence of the pound and other British icons. He has become a familiar sight, protesting at sites of corporate takeovers (BMW takeover of Rover and more recently Kraft's manoeuvring for Cadburys).

Social divisions can be subtle and transitory in nature. Sometimes evidence is apparent only when the historical processes are better understood; for example, when considering ripples caused by colonialism. The diaspora (for example) has political, social and cultural meanings: individuals of 'mixed race' in the Caribbean are the 'evidence' of European domination, and the internalised meaning of lighter skin which is still prevalent in countries like Jamaica is a visible reminder of the iniquitous power of colonialism. Thus societal perceptions of these boundaries can be visualised and reflect a colonial history based on colour-coded power relations which maintain hegemonic influence post colonially in those nations, as well as among the diasporic communities in European and American cities.

Using visual approaches to examine social divisions allows the researcher to explore the context by which social disadvantage and discrimination lead to unequal life chances. Available to the researcher are dominant forms of representation of difference which may affect the individual's social identity. Visual methods allow the critical appraisal of not only social contexts like cities, institutions and public spaces, but also of human subjectivities. This section considers social identities, suggesting some uses of visual analysis which reveal the implicit meanings by which we make sense of identities.

When examining age, gender, sexuality or ethnicity there is a profusion of signs which have acquired the status of Barthes' myth. These are ingrained and embedded cultural signs which are part of the habitualised culture of our lives; they are disguised, 'exnominated' and presented as benign and obvious. A good example is age and the embedded conventional values which are associated with belonging to a particular age group. Age is a biological fact but also a social category – age appears to be a 'natural' or commonsense division, yet the way our ideas of age stages are culturally marked across the continuum of the biological life cycle provides insight into how different divisions along this lifeline are understood culturally, and how these meanings and values change over time.

In addition, boundaries vary markedly between cultures. Childhood, youth, old age; how the boundaries between them are drawn, and the meanings and emphases attributed to these stages, are in a state of flux and depend on cultural, social and economic aspects of the life course. The 'teenager', for example, arguably only came into existence in Western culture after the Second World War, and the attitudes and values ascribed to teenagers, and the ways in which *they* are represented, have changed depending on the broader processes of social change. However, it is arguably, a frequently problematic life stage as it is a time between boundaries: what anthropologist Edmund Leach called an 'anomalous' zone. The problems of being between stages – the disparity between societal legitimacy, ages of consent, voting age etc., and physical and mental maturity are a matter of popular knowledge.

An interesting example is given below (Figure 30a). My grandmother's Empire Diary (1938) was apparently used by the family to gather recipes, tips for household economies, newspaper cuttings and pressed flowers. This cutting was found in its pages and creates an ironic contrast. On the one hand the dour 'lest

Figure 30
(a) Construction
of the teenager;
(b) *The Gap: A Book
to Bridge the Dangerous
Years* (Wordley and
Blake, 1959).

we forget' deceased figures, exemplars of wartime patriotism and masculinity: the late King and Earls Haig and Jellicoe, and opposite struts a very different American teenage image of masculinity in a cutting from later in the 1940s or early 1950s. This demonstrates how the accidental juxtaposition of images and artefacts can give an impression of the changing values of wider society.

Researchers may use such archive material to demonstrate the prevalent value system. One document might yield rich examples of the pivotal issues of the time. For instance, Figure 30b and Figure 31 show illustrations from a 1950s pamphlet *The Gap* (1959) about juvenile delinquency. This document is revealing of the moral values of the time; fears of the in-between stage and influences which might corrupt moral values. Familiar anxieties around 'sex and drugs and rock and roll' are presented as a contagion among the middle classes. The booklet 'contains a series of 'moral' tales from key figures of authority in the community: the South Australian Police Commissioner, a police sergeant, the mother and one of the disgraced teenage girls, others from religious and business leaders. This type of document illustrates some of the processes proposed by Stanley Cohen (1972) by which moral panics are said to unfold:

- someone or something is defined as a threat to values or interests;
- this threat is depicted in an easily recognisable form by the media;
- there is a rapid buildup of public concern;
- there is a response from authorities or opinion makers.

In the example given in Figure 31 the fear is one of a descent into moral turpitude. In the 'Doors to Delinquency', Sgt Gollan outlines the viral spread of the bodgie and widgie[3] cult and its affects on the culture of Adelaide (City of Churches): 'In Sydney and Melbourne the cult had been responsible for outbreaks

Figure 31 Scenes from *'The Gap'* – a 'moral panic' (Wordley and Blake, 1959).

of violence with gangs beating up people but in Adelaide its early form of attack was sexual – our sexual record became very bad.'

One of the features of a moral panic is that it mobilises the forces of authority, police chiefs, judges and other lawmakers, priests (especially in the 'City of Churches'), sportsmen and women, and mothers (who have special moral authority in this instance). What other group highlights so vividly the sense of moral outrage as the icon of 1950s motherhood (Figure 31, below right)? Indeed, the iconic nature of these civic leaders and guardians is clearly transcendent and approaches what Roland Barthes has called 'myth'. For example, there is the myth of fallen innocence of girlhood evoked in the 'Story of a Girl': 'The Past Doesn't Just Die' (Figure 31, above right).

Other commentaries examine the erosion of traditional values through the advent of rock and roll:

> When Elvis grinds out 'Hound Dog' or confesses he's 'Gonna sit right down and Cry' it is, no doubt, partly because he feels miserable, but it's as plain as a Presley purple pikestaff that he hasn't got anything better to do. And neither have the boys and girls who swoon exhausted around the gramophone, consistently listening to him in a smoke-smothered haze. If only they had been taught to play their own banjo . . . Nervously drained after playing 'Chicken', juvenile delinquents could not know the satisfying, healthy exhaustion of a Saturday afternoon's tussle of football, hockey or life-saving.
>
> (Blake, 1959: 17)

These images and the melodramatic titles indicate a desire to retain the illusion of an innocent world. It is reminiscent of the American small-town genre; picket fences, brightly scrubbed, and civic-minded youngsters fishing or delivering newspapers. A world before the fall – that hasn't fully shed the protective cotton wool of infancy. This is the world of small-town America so effectively parodied by film director David Lynch in his 1986 *Blue Velvet*. 'It's like saying that once you've discovered there are heroin addicts in the world and they're murdering people to get money, can you be happy? It's a tricky question. Real ignorance is bliss. That's what Blue Velvet is about'(David Lynch, in Coughlin, 2003).

While these expressions emanate from a sign system with roots in a different era with a different construction of youth, in which teenage experimentation was not seen as permissible, it is likely that the portrayal of youth prevalent in current media, for example, news stories concerning 'hoodies',[4] are destined to appear similarly outlandish. Recent concerns about asylum seekers, foreign workers and paedophiles, as well as the perennial interest in different youth groups and the unemployed are often prone to be portrayed in similar terms. The evidence is partly drawn from media texts and images and also from documents and artefacts derived from narratives which are mobilised around fears of crime, lack of control, and moral outrage, often amplified by media out of all proportion to the phenomenon. The visual aspect of these 'moral tales' is a small, but influential, component. Visual research plays a role in showing how media and other sources are mobilised and legitimate certain readings of culture. The richness of such documents demonstrates that ethnographic study can include the dimension of representations of popular culture: Kelly (recorded in Coover, 2009) affirms this: 'some of us are now involved in doing ethnography through popular entertainment: employing popular entertainment as a way of showcasing a culture, providing knowledge about a culture, gaining access to that culture by being drawn into a narrative style' (p. 237).

As discussed earlier (Chapter 2) the examination of media, fictional narratives and propaganda (of which *The Gap* pamphlet could be considered an example) are viable forms of ethnography. Such material links our analyses of cultural identities to the meanings of identity which are circulating at a given time and allow patterns of continuity to be recognised in the form of these narratives. The visual component of these samples plays a significant role, characterising the style and context of the times; for example, what counted as a moral panic or the tabloid expression of outrage at the time. Some of these images are direct records of people and places and in some instances they are also examples of institutional documents which incite a proliferation of discourse. Moral panics are more than mere sensationalism to sell newspapers, they appear to serve in some cases as a touchstone for public awareness about changes in the society and the culture, highlighting the fracture points between the old and new aspects of culture and the shifting ability of the social order to contain and control social meaning.

Dorothy Smith recognised the importance of texts like this in her development of an institutional ethnography, using them to 'hook you up beyond the local; they are not contained within the local setting. And the more I began to explore that the more I began to see how important that was in the whole development of what I have come to conceptualise as the "the living relations"' (Widerberg, 2004).

What Smith is suggesting here is that some texts play a constitutive role in linking individual identity to broader societal discourses mediated through institutional forms. Dorothy Smith's approach stands as a critique of sociology's claim to be able to see the social world from a high vantage point without ever having to humble itself by asking the people how things look at ground level: 'It is as if the society could be understood in its totality and from above, from the gaze of God, or rather, from the view of a bird but without the bird' (Widerberg, 2007: 21). This suggests that a ground-level empirical approach is important and that a form of ethnography is needed that will listen rather than be drawn to grand spectacles and theorising which disguises rather than reveals the lived experiences of people: 'Institutional ethnography recognises the authority of the experiencer to inform the ethnographer's ignorance' (Smith, 2005: 138).

'Institutional ethnography' is an approach to empirical inquiry combining theory and method, making connections amongst the sites and situations of everyday life, professional practice and policy-making. Smith coined the phrase 'textually-mediated social organization' to discuss this interconnection between texts and institutional practices and policies, and the shaping of identity and behaviour through these. Drawing on the Foucaultian concept of discourse,[5] as the 'controlling, positioning and productive capacities of signifying practices' (Threadgold, 1997: 58) whereby: 'Individuals come to speak as particular kinds of subjects – to speak themselves into being – through speaking the discourses that enable the particular institution' (Lee and Poynton, 2000: 5). So discourses can be seen as structured sets of meanings which construct aspects of an individual's identity; as Vivien Burr suggests, our identities are fabricated from the available discourses in a culture through 'a subtle interweaving of many different "threads"' (Burr, 1999: 51). There are discursive structures which shape our experience of age, gender, education, sexuality, work, etc. The range of discourses for some of these identities is much broader and more complex than others. Burr sites sexuality as being the result of a 'restricted menu' offered by society (p. 52). Images, objects, outward appearances, clothes, interior design, can all be read as 'texts' through which discourse is manifest.

The teenager, as discussed in the context of 1950s Australia, can be seen as similarly woven from a range of complex discourses: trends in music, cinema, notoriety of subcultural trends which reflected a new state of independence (partly fuelled by growing post-war youth consumerism) contributed to the repertoire of styles, attitudes to authority, differences in dress and recreational use of drugs, alcohol, dance and music trends. Subcultural groups use the distinctive trappings of style to symbolise their divergence from dominant culture. The following section explores some examples of symbolism as expression of collective identities.

Collective identities

Collective symbols become embedded through the process of 'habituation' as discussed by Berger and Luckmann (1966: 51–55):

> All human activity is subject to habitualization. Any action that is repeated frequently becomes cast into a pattern, which can then be reproduced with an economy of effort and which, ipso facto, is apprehended by its performer as that pattern. Habitualization further implies that the action in question may be performed again in the future in the same manner and with the same economical effort.

In Section II, Roger Canals discusses one such example in the form of the 'nomadic image' of María Lionza in Venezuela. The sign, which may derive from narrative folklore, a charismatic character, an animal, uniform, flag or colours, which gradually through convention come to represent something to groups, whether they are national, ethnic, religious, political or sporting.

Collective images of regional or national identity often draw on popular cultural figures. These shorthand symbols may come to represent deeply held values of a culture. National colours, flags and emblems, or in charismatic individuals who are seen to embody something inviolable about the nation – the gathering and presentation of these symbols begin to reveal the complex interwoven fields from which cultural identities are composed and through which individual local identities are negotiated.

There are several useful ways to understand the fluidity of cultural identities: Berger and Luckmann (1966) see everyday life as a social construction. Hall (1997) and others have emphasised the circulation of social meanings and current studies in phenomenology of the city and nation, using photographs of urban landscapes to examine the collective symbols of the city (several examples are mentioned in this volume: e.g. Allmark, Section II, and Spencer, 2009). A study in images, whether they are photographs, films, maps of social spaces, buildings, or other features of everyday social context is increasingly recognised as a less filtered phenomenological study. However, the social context and motive behind the production and consumption of these cultural forms is very important, and one must be careful to steer between a naively realist view of images as reaching into an untainted vision of social reality or conversely become overly dismissive of visual representations as highly contrived as 'almost purely arbitrary constructions' (Pauwels, 2010: 572). Symbols, however, are at the arbitrary end of the semiotic continuum, often sharing little with the entity they denote and dependent on cultural knowledge of the associations and connotations to which they refer. Hence subcultural symbols can seem arcane; a secret language into which acolytes are inducted.

As Anthony Cohen (1985: 18) points out:

> Symbols are often defined as things 'standing for' other things. But they do not represent these 'other things' unambiguously . . . if they did so they would be superfluous and redundant. Rather, they 'express' other things in ways which allow their common form to be retained and shared among members of a group, whilst not imposing upon these people the constraints of uniform meaning.

Furthermore, symbols are not often visual: 'Most symbols do not have visual or physical expression but are, rather, ideas. This may make their meanings even more elusive' (ibid.). This elusiveness is evident in the example of the Mexican Charro figure. Certainly it is a sign which goes to the heart of Mexican culture, but at the same time it is one which demonstrates the fluidity of the concept and its ability to meander between meanings being appropriated variously for different social and political identities.

El Charro – Mexican iconography

El Charro is a complex symbolic expression of Mexican identity typically denoted by a cowboy with a bandolier and a large hat. This is a figure associated with the land, peasantry and resistance long argued to represent Mexican culture and identity (see e.g. Nájera-Ramírez, 1994). The image reached a particular realisation in General Emiliano Zapata, a Mestizo of Nahua Indian and Spanish ancestry. Zapata was a respected horseman who dressed in the flamboyant clothes of the Mexican Charro. Zapata fought for the rights of the landless peasants in the state of Morelos, first establishing via ancient title deeds their claims to disputed land, and finally taking up arms when progress was too slow. He was a key figure in the Mexican revolution, along with Pancho Villa, who led the army of liberation in the North, while Zapata became Commander of the Ejército Libertador del Sur (Liberation Army of the South).

Figure 32 shows five depictions of the Zapata figure. First (top right), from Mexico City's underground train station, 'Zapata' bearing the iconic representation of General Emilliano Zapata. Second (top left), during the emergence of an astonishing rural indigenous uprising in Chiapas Zapata became an emblem for the Zapatistas (pictured here on a banner in San Cristobal de las Casas in 1991). Possibly Zapata's Mayan origins and his struggle for land ownership for peasant farmers made him an attractive figure also for the Zapatista movement. In the bottom row two portraits of Zapata obtained in Mexico City. One (bottom left) was sold as a keepsake and features the classic Zapata image stuck on to a piece of card. Bottom right – Zapata leads the massed hats of rural peasantry under the banner 'Tierra y Libertad' (land and freedom), shoulder to shoulder with industrial workers, in a detail from Diego Rivera's mural on the walls of the National Palace in Mexico City. The poster (bottom centre) is based on an image by Garcia Bustos and depicts the figure of Zapata representing the Popular

Figure 32 El Charro: Zapata figures as a collective symbol – poster and public art in collection of author.

Socialist Party, taken during a demonstration in Mexico City (1991). The hat is a potent symbol of the worker and the revolutionary peasantry, for example, in Tina Modotti's famous image El Machete (1924) published by the Communist Party, which used Modotti's photographs. Jonathan Jones discusses the photograph as elements in a radical iconography:

> **Distinguishing features**: We do not need to see their faces. They are not individuals; they are the proletariat. The future does not belong to the bourgeois self. The future is collective. Their hats form an abstract composition of circles within circles, intensified by the hot monochrome sun, wheeling in darkness, like bright stellar phenomena. The light sublimely picks out the wrinkled, landscape-ridged surface of the newspaper. Almost at the very centre of the composition is the hammer and sickle, a black icon.
>
> The hats are agrarian, and evoke the romantic guerrilla heroes of the Mexican revolution that began in 1910. The light on the hats is intense, the absence of the men's faces glaring, the arrangement startlingly geometric. The hats suggest, with their circles within circles, the cogs of industry, the wheels of progress, the industrial rather than rural proletariat, a symbolic transformation of reality into Marxist myth similar to that violently carried out in the Soviet Union during this period.
>
> (*Guardian*, 15 February 2003)

The symbol of Zapata is adopted across the political spectrum as a powerful national symbol. The El Charro image and name have been appropriated commercially for advertising tequila, boots, bags, restaurants and cars. These are examples of 'ritual condensation': a process (as discussed earlier) whereby abstract ideas are transmitted into material objects and often imbued with special significance.

Richard Jenkins makes the point that images or ideas can become potent symbols of community. Symbols like the charro or the hat itself as a synecdoche (a part that stands for the whole) allow a degree of openness and accommodation to quite varied users – although, arguably, core concepts of the rebel and the land are behind the power of such symbols to mobilise feelings around foundation myths of the Mexican nation and its independent spirit.

> Whether we are talking about symbols *of* community or community *as* a symbol, the power of the notions and the images thus mobilised depends on the capacity of symbols to encompass and condense a range of, not necessarily harmonious or congruent meanings. By definition symbols are abstract to a degree, imprecise to a degree, always multifaceted, and frequently implicit or taken-for-granted in their definition. As a consequence, people can to some degree bestow their own meanings on and in symbols; they can say and do the 'same' things without saying or doing the same things at all.
>
> (Jenkins, 2004: 112)

Hence the nomadic and fluid meanings of the Zapata or charro figures, or of flags or other symbols; the degree of openness allows them to be adapted to different uses. This is a feature explored in Roger Canals' work (see Section II) which shows how spiritual values associated with the folk goddess María Lionza are worked into cultural representations; figurines and paintings, dances or acted out in spirit possessions or by dance troupes and actors to be appreciated by audiences. The varied representations of the figure meet the symbolic needs of the diverse communities which adopt the goddess cult.

Accessories in the environment

Forms of individual expression are selective signs of cultural identities, tastes and at the same time signs of internalised societal structures. The internal and external are aspects of identity which are part of an ongoing individual dialogue which negotiates meanings and expressions of identity. 'The society "in our heads" and the society "out there" which we have to cope with somehow, are aspects of the same thing and not, finally, more or less real than one another'(Watkins, 1975: 31). For the individual wishing to express aspects of self-identity there is, as Jenkins reminds us, the possibility of individuals drawing upon 'a wide palette of accessories in the human world'(2004: 49) to express their identities. What follows is a short discussion of the sort of visual evidence which might be collected to enhance, or in some cases become the central focus of research.

Body projects

For an increasing number of people the body itself, as well as being an instrument of our identity experience, and indeed the embodiment of our identity, is an arena upon which cultural messages can be inscribed – it is a communicative text. During an interview a local tattoo artist commented: 'It's your own house, the only thing you'll ever really own' (Dave Murray interview, 2000). Making ideas flesh is an increasing preoccupation as people seek to increase their social or cultural capital, through implants, cosmetic surgery, gym work, tattooing, piercing and even branding. Such forms of body modification are an expressive form of consumption which draws boundaries between the self and others and allows the individual to project themselves on to a broader canvas. Social science has long presented such 'body projects' (Shilling, 1993) as signs of deviance in which the tattoo serves as 'a badge of dislocated, ostracised, and disenfranchised communities'(Atkinson, 2004). However, the recent upsurge in popularity of tattooing and piercing indicates a much more complex use of body markings as forms of individual and social identity. Rather than narrow and gang-related signs of some compulsory collective belonging, research is showing that tattoos and piercings are viewed as 'voluntary auto-biographical resources for personal identities constructed around values of individuality, difference and authenticity' (Ferreira, 2009: Abstract).

The tattooed subject (Figure 33a) suggested that tattoos were an expensive and aesthetic commodity for the discerning professional, and rejected the working-class stereotypes associated with the practice, making the point that tattoos such as his were not the province of the working classes, but distinctive, individualistic and requiring a middle-class income and outlook; in his words: 'Tattoos historically are actually status symbols – they're not the working class, sailor type "jack tars". The people who can afford the sort of work Dave does are generally

Figure 33 The body as a project:
(a) tattoos as personal expression;
(b) 'the world's most pierced woman', with permission of Elaine Davidson.

quite professional people.' The subject's personal project was a private odyssey defining and developing a personal narrative subsuming and reflecting new expressions and revising earlier icons of taste: 'my tattoos are fairly dark and strange – that's a reflection of me, it goes back to something Dave said earlier, you know, people will actually wear their personalities on the outside without realising it – it's not the British way to share that much' (unpublished interview with tattoo artist Dave Murray, 2000 and a long-term client). For this person, year by year, these visual forms gradually extended and changed along with his self-perceptions.

Sometimes it seems the 'project' can become a major facet of the person's life and identity rather than simply a fashion statement. Elaine Davidson (Figure 33b) has suggested that she feels happy and fulfilled with her thousands of body piercings. At this level of adornment the individual crosses from private narratives of expressions of identity to public exhibition and a form of celebrity. Indeed, Elaine is the official world record holder for body piercing and as of February 2009 her piercings total 6,005.

> The former nurse from Brazil first broke the record in May 2000, when a Guinness World Records official examined her and found 462 piercings on various parts of her body, including 192 on her facial area alone. 'People often just want to look at me or touch me – some even want to kiss me' Elaine says.
>
> Elaine never removes the rings and studs, which she estimates weigh a total of three kilos. She insists there is no pain involved in piercing and sleeps soundly with all of her piercing ornaments in place.
>
> A lady of many talents, Elaine also sleeps on a bed of nails, walks on fire and lays on broken glass, and holds a black belt in Judo which she earned in Japan.
>
> Elaine does not drink, take drugs or smoke cigarettes and she wants people to know this. In some ways this is because she sees her position in the Guinness Book of Records as a responsibility as much as a dedication. However, Elaine does have a soft spot for Coca-Cola.
>
> (www.elainedavidson.co.uk/)

It is well known that status recognition is frequently bound up with 'conspicuous consumption' – a concept first developed by Thorstein Veblen, and perhaps body projects are one conspicuous form of status symbol. However, they have a more personal and less easily assigned status value than those branded products like cars or fashion items and many tattoos are designed to be only discreetly visible in more intimate settings rather than overt signs of wealth or dominance.

Expressive adornment is a form of negotiated use of accessories for increasingly personal motives, a decision based on aesthetics, style and personal taste. As Veblen noted over a hundred years ago:

> This growth of punctilious discrimination as to qualitative excellence in eating, drinking, etc., presently affects not only the manner of life, but also

the training and intellectual activity of the gentleman of leisure. He is no longer simply the successful, aggressive male–the man of strength, resource, and intrepidity. In order to avoid stultification he must also cultivate his tastes, for it now becomes incumbent on him to discriminate with some nicety between the noble and the ignoble in consumable goods. He becomes a connoisseur. . . . High-bred manners and ways of living are items of conformity to the norm of conspicuous leisure and conspicuous consumption.

(Veblen, 2008: 53)

Purchases can be aspirational and display facets of our identity, of the 'face' we wish to present (see Lury, 1999). Even rebelliousness or resistance to consumer trends can be commodified and caught in the web of representation. For example, subcultural styles have created niche markets through which the icons of style and rebellion can be regulated and 'clawed back' into the material processes of capitalism, a process which has perhaps led to youth subcultures now being considered as 'post-subcultures'. This suggests that identities may be recognised as more fluid, fragmented and based on consumption rather than easily or strongly identified with traditional working-class cultures.

Certainly the display of taste can be seen as recognition of social status; consumption provides us with opportunities to display our status and largesse to legitimate and give evidence of our social position. Commodities are symbols of identity and status in society. Different people surround themselves with different constellations of products cementing their social identity or creating distinctions between themselves and others. Bourdieu (1986) made a study of these overlapping maps of distinction amongst the French middle classes and their cultural consumption in 1960s Paris. Films, literature, painting, music and cuisine are forms of cultural capital especially associated with taste. It could be argued that categories such as lifestyle, taste and fashion have 'become the key sources of social differentiation, displacing class and political affiliation' (Waters, 1995: 140).

Bourdieu's mapping of cultural capital in *Distinction* (1986) shows how patterns of taste cluster along axes of high or low economic and cultural capital. For example, in the quadrant in which economic capital is predominant rather

Figure 34 Visual markers of class and taste (McCarter, 1999).

than cultural capital, and overall capital is low, we see a cluster of taste indicators: TV, football and rugby, Brigit Bardot, lard, vin rouge ordinaire, potatoes and accordion music in a cluster around employees on lowest to mid-low incomes. In the diagonally opposite quadrant where cultural capital predominates and spending power is highest, the top cadre of professionals like university lecturers appear to surround themselves with opera and avant-garde music like Boulez and Xenakis, they visit art galleries, and have an appreciation of the pop artist Andy Warhol. It was the first study of its kind to correlate cultural consumption and social and economic position. Bourdieu's concept of habitus has been highly influential. In simple terms individuals and social groups have a 'habitus' – a generative principle which tends to reproduce hegemonic cultural and economic relations and which develops as an internalised shaper of dispositions in the individual resulting from their material conditions. The individual consumer makes distinctions between products based on an unconscious classification system which reflects in-built habitus. This system of classification relates to structural oppositions between high/low, masculine/feminine, white/black, distinguished/vulgar, good/bad (see Lury, 1999: 86).

If the material practice of consumption delineates individual and group identities, could a visual portrayal of those things be instructive and be used to present profiles of individuals? The problem is that Bourdieu's concepts were not without opponents. The definition of habitus is vague and contradictory (see Jenkins, 1992, and Glossary for discussion of habitus). Habitus as a unitary formation in which attributes, tastes, codes and cultural knowledge all tend to cluster around an individual's position in society may seem hard to support. Bennett (2009) cites Bernard Lahire's (2001) work which showed empirically that people often have 'dissonant' cultural tastes which straddle the boundaries that Bourdieu had drawn. However, the notion that identity might be positioned through economic and cultural location seems to be an obvious extension of materialist cultural views of society. It is quite clear that educational level *does* largely determine cultural literacy, and access to certain forms of literature and the avant-garde in art is the province of an elite. Moreover, the education system tends to reproduce these inequalities, and tastes remain segregated. Status, cultural capital and patterns of consumption are key aspects of identity. The relationship of consumerism to identity formation can be examined through analyses of media advertising and product promotion which have long been concerned with tailoring promotional messages and product attributes to target specific demographic and deeper psychographic features of consumer identity and personality. To the extent that representations of identity are marketed, it could be suggested that advertising is partly about selling us back images of ourselves, but these images are frequently distorted, idealised and aspirational. However, for all the obvious power of the market to distract and seduce the consumer, there is much about these complex processes which is less overt and much more personal. In Chapter 1 the special importance of objects to people was discussed; aside from the intentional sales messages of advertising and promotions, individuals develop strong relationships with consumption which may be subtle and idiosyncratic. Some advertising campaigns, however, purport to bring about change in attitudes through use of hard-hitting and emotive visual messages.

> With the road toll in Victoria at nearly 1000 a year the brief for this campaign was to 'upset, outrage and appal'. The first TAC commercial, which aired on December 10th 1989, told the story of a young man whose drunk driving had led to his girlfriend being admitted to hospital with serious injuries. A Charge Nurse at Royal Melbourne Hospital, describes the impression she has of drink driving casualties 'you have to learn to cope with the sheer human waste, the stench of alcohol', 'they hurt themselves and the people they're supposed to care about', culminating in the phrase which became the memorable logo for the posters and other forms which span off from this ad: 'If you drink, then drive, you're a bloody idiot'.

The advertising campaign shown in Figure 35 by Grey Advertising of Melbourne presented a range of hard-hitting visual images on large posters located strategically on billboards around the city. The image was taken from a TV advert

If you drink, then drive, you're a bloody idiot.

Figure 35 The TAC advertising campaign of 1989. With permission of James Branagan (actor) and Grey Advertising, Australia.

for the Transport Accident Commission in Victoria by Grey Advertising in 1989, which produced a harrowing TV advertisement to shock audiences out of drink driving. The young man portrayed is anguished at the death of his girlfriend caused by his drunken driving, and the shame and guilt he suffers is embodied in this still from the ad., along with the hard-hitting slogan beneath. When the image was used in poster campaigns along the highways in Melbourne, the agency had designed the impact to be similar to the visual awareness of brand recognition in the case of the McDonald's logo which would have an immediate consequence – i.e. feel hungry and seek the drive-in entrance for McDonald's – or in the case of the drink-driving ad – ease off the accelerator and think of the consequences. Hence the influence of the video had served as a form of operant conditioning and the response to their 'brand' would be the impulse to slow down and avoid the guilt and trauma. Drawing the analogy between the McDonald's logo as a stimulus to trigger buyer behaviour, Grey's TAC account executive Greg Harper stated:

> Road safety is an impulse decision that requires constant, high, top of mind product promotion to penetrate and motivate behaviour. It's more like buying a McDonald's hamburger. You need to be reminded of who McDonald's is, and what they sell, every day of the year. The same top-of-mind awareness is required for the road safety message to remain effective.
>
> (Grey Advertising, 1989: 36)

In this instance the agency has manipulated imagery which triggers strong emotions of empathic abhorrence and guilt and triggers a reduction in speed – perhaps almost subconsciously an easing off on the accelerator.[6] Much has been made in the past of the power of subliminal images and messages, images which have a latent content subconsciously perceived: concealed sexual images and words airbrushed into ice-cubes or clouds. However, although inevitably advertisers will try and exploit the ambiguity and arousal factor in images, there may be little need to use such so-called 'hidden persuaders'[7] because images are already operating at a sub-threshold level; there is no need to posit hidden imagery, as by their very nature images link to powerful intertextual connotations evoking strong emotional responses. From the discussion so far it becomes apparent that consumer goods are packaged and branded to target certain features of the product, or the promise of the product which will be seen as significant to the individual consumer (sometimes these are concrete entities, such as fridges or computers, sometimes abstract ones, such as road safety or safe sex). In late capitalism brands are said to have personalities which resonate with groups of consumers and their aspirations, dreams and desires, as well as their fears and anxieties.

Visual identity and product attributes

Levi-Strauss derived the meaning of bricolage from the 'bricoleur' – someone who does odd jobs, making and mending things from bits and pieces which have been left over from previous jobs. It provides a 'science of the concrete' by which the world is ordered in minute ways. Jean-Marie Floch (2000) in *Visual Identities* uses this concept to discuss the way in which visual identities are created through a process of bricolage, implying both continuity and difference in the manipulation of signs. These identities have become a central part of life in our material consumerist culture. Floch gives well-known global examples of Apple and IBM as well as more characteristic French ones like the Opinel knife which has developed a rich Gaelic peasant mythology, including esoteric terms like the 'coup de Savoyard' (which is the little tap the user gives the knife to release the blade), and the multi-sensorial world of Chanel. These are the dramatis personae of Floch's portraits. These detailed analyses of the visual identities of consumer objects include their design, the 'value systems of consumption' and the 'ideologies of advertising', relationships between form and design, and market position. Floch shows that a great deal is revealed from a micro-semiotics of the consumer system in later capitalism which breathes life into branded objects.

Judith Williamson (in her 1978 book *Decoding Advertisements*) uses the term 'bricolage' to explain the way in which advertisers exploit fragments of pre-existing ideological thinking to construct social meanings and identification for products. The linking of many different reference systems such as interlinked meanings of celebrities (what Richard Dyer (2003) has termed the Star System) and the values which they have come to represent. For example, Catherine Deneuve's association with sophistication and chic fashion became linked to Chanel No. 5 (see e.g. Dyer, 1982). In some cases the personification of the brand (the so-called 'brand personality') enmeshed as it is with the public perception of the celebrities in question can become problematic if the image of the star in question becomes tarnished or they become involved in scandal; for example, the association of Michael Jackson with Pepsi, or recently Tiger Woods with Gillette. As revelations unfolded about the troubled personal life of these stars they lost their viability to embody the supposed virtues of the brand. The desire to possess products which appear to have been imbued with these sought-after human qualities of excellence, triumphant strength and skill, youthful energy, rugged individuality or sensual allure arguably sustains and reproduces a market-driven system:

> The power of purchase – taking home a new thing, the anticipation of unwrapping – seems to drink up the desire for something new, the rest-lessness and unease that must be engendered in a society where so many have so little active power, other than to withdraw the labour which produces its prizes. These objects which become the aims of our passions are also shored up to protect us from them, the bricks of a dam held together by the very force it restrains. Passion is a longing that breaks beyond the present, a drive to the future, and yet it must be satisfied in the forms of the past.
>
> (Williamson, 1987: 13)

The quote from Williamson captures nicely the paradox of consumerism; we, like the bricks in the dam, are harnessed into a system of production and consumption, an unbroken chain held together by our very desires to break out. The term 'desire economy' is coming into popular parlance – a recognition that we are in a new period in our social and economic identity in which the aspirational has replaced the merely utilitarian and functional, brand identity replaces use value, identity politics and consumer sector cleavages are the new markers of identity. In the same way that Kress and Hodge's (1988) 'ideological complexes' give a distorted false consciousness from both positions of dominance and solidarity in resistance, consumption seems to do the very same thing: products and their imagery seem to contain a promise, of escape, recognition, luxury, esteem and attractiveness, but at the same time through their purchase the system of dominance is perpetuated.

This chapter has tried to demonstrate the visual and textual resources (accessories in the environment) through which identity can be expressed and represented and hence recorded and mapped visually and via documents and artefacts. The examples given here suggest that powerful symbols of death, danger or pleasure and escape can trigger responses (often non-rational and less conscious). Identity can be a personal expression drawing from expressive repertoires in the environment, but it appears that it might also be channelled and regulated by advertisers and other media within the matrix of cultural messages. Attempts to trace and record expressive symbols of identity through visual research are an important way of revealing these processes at work.

Are visual methods really essential to discern identity and delineate boundaries of social identity? Not at all, but they can, nevertheless, be an integral part of the way we mediate our own identities, and hence the visual dimension of identity is a viable focus for social research.

5 Visual analysis

The approach taken in this book has been one which seeks to encourage and develop personal research practice, embracing a reflexive yet critical empiricism. The focus has been on visual research as an interpretive craft which understands meaning as the result of complex construction and mediation. Rather than enumerating instances and attempting to generalise to larger populations, the type of research highlighted here has focused on small-scale case studies and detailed 'thick descriptions' derived from visual narratives of individuals, groups, relationships and events. It has also been suggested that the 'craft' of visual research requires a balance between inductive forces – allowing the collected data to speak for itself, and deductive forces – structuring, ordering principles derived from theoretical models and concepts.

Analysis is not an end point (despite the placing of this chapter), a precursor to summing up and concluding; it is central to the process of research from the outset, beginning with the preplanning stage, conceiving valid questions, considering valid methodology and theoretical explanations. In addition, as well as agreeing with Geertz's famous statement that the analysis of culture is 'not an experimental science in search of law but an interpretive one in search of meaning' (Geertz, 1973: 5). The approach pursued here has been founded on active fieldwork and researcher-generated images, and developing a critical 'sociological eye' to the study of broader cultural representations of issues and phenomena. All of these actions are purposeful and analytical, and suggest an interplay between theoretical paradigms, methodological concerns and the data itself.

Typically, how information about the world is presented and understood is based on the paradigm of thought which underpins the study. If, as in the example case studies cited in this book, an interpretivist approach to the study is embraced, then the object of study cannot be distanced and separated from the research; it is as Banks suggests: 'ontologically constituted through the act of study' (2007: 37).

The analysis of imagery has already been discussed in simple terms. The diagram in Chapter 1 (p. 22) utilises Shannon and Weaver's information model as a reminder that communication problems can occur at many different stages in the process of encoding, transmission and interpretation. In addition to more physical barriers to reception, the danger of misinterpretation of the intended meaning is often a concern. Images are open to interpretation, they can be understood from different viewpoints (the producer, the audience or the image itself). However, the relationships and narratives which images can display are complex, and we are already dealing with legacies of interpretative systems. This is the 'double hermeneutic' at work; Giddens' concept which implies that not only are societal meanings already interpreted by social actors but the 'responsible speech' of sociology which creates critical distance from everyday behaviours and commonsense definitions itself becomes the currency of popular parlance (e.g. terms like 'class', 'norm', 'moral panic', 'self-fulfilling prophecy' are commonly used).

However, the boundaries to the image; the choices of subjects, editing, framing, filters, timing, angle, point of view, etc. act as elements in a story or headline. So, even though different audiences will interpret differently they are viewing a narrative which is already partial, necessarily restricted, bounded and mediated.

The discussion which has taken place so far about images and objects and their roles in the circulation and construction of cultural meanings suggests that much of the analytical framing is done in the initial choice or construction of the image. However, often the significance of visual materials collected emerges in the later stages of the research. As more in-depth analysis proceeds, the relationships within and between images, media and archive documents, fieldwork interviews and so on begin to become clearer.

This chapter sets out to examine different levels of organisation of data and review some forms of analysis. This is far from exhaustive and focuses mainly on some suitable approaches to understanding the complex meanings implicit in visual texts, in particular those of semiotics and forms of discourse analysis. These are approaches which claim to expose the underlying ideological bases of texts, their links to institutional systems of power and knowledge and constructions of 'truth'. Analysis, as previously stated, does not start, or stop, at a point in a linear research sequence. The process of research is necessarily self-referential; much analysis begins with the ideas and beliefs which underpin the approach, the question and the research strategy chosen. However, there is also a more gradual unfolding of the meanings and the relationships between the images and other forms of data collected, and the following section addresses the complex relationships which can be discerned between images.

Building relationships between images

How far is it possible to show visually the continuous relationships between levels of meaning? C. Wright Mills' (1959: 8) conception of the 'sociological imagination' is one in which the subjective 'personal troubles of milieu' are illuminated by looking more broadly to 'public issues', their history and the bigger social picture. Are there examples of imagery which might demonstrate these dimensions of social life? Might complex relationships between images and their social contexts be examined to provide a broader basis for a visual ethnography within a particular case? The diagram in Model 2 draws on Ritzer and Goodman's (2003: 486–87) model of 'Major Levels of Analysis' which attempts to integrate micro and macro phenomena with their objective and subjective dimensions, insisting that the sociologist must focus on the dialectical interrelationship among these combinations. For example, the Macro-Objective quadrant includes concepts of 'society', 'law' and 'language', whereas at the opposite end, the Micro-Subjective includes examples of 'perceptions' and 'beliefs'.

The idea was to juxtapose images from a case and draw out macro and micro contextual issues and the relationships between relative objective and subjective sources which help to shape and constitute them. In this way the dynamics of the case are thrown into sharper relief and the incommensurability of certain representations is starkly revealed.

In the top left, a postcard depicts Australian 'Aborigines', effectively reducing 'them' to static, historical, romantic and passivised images; a familiar tourist discourse, and indeed the image many tourists might associate with Aborigines. The timeless quality of such imagery presents a highly romanticised discourse to, in one sweep, encompass the enormous cultural variety of indigenous Australians. Furthermore, this is very like the Barthesian 'myth' (see Glossary) as it could be argued to be actively disguising the reality that many indigenous people have been displaced from their homelands and are 'fringe dwellers' – un-picturesque reminders of the colonial legacy of conquest and dispossession are transformed into a montage depicting an encompassing naturalised harmony.

Narrowing the focus, but still at this level of public representations of 'otherness' is the newspaper headline from the *Northern Territory News* 'Permits for Aborigines' (top right). This is a message which could certainly be seen as controversial and likely to be strongly contended nationally, but apparently permissible in the more isolated, rural culture of Northern Territory. One function of news stories is arguably to construct an issue with some authority (a veneer, at least, of objectivity) for its 'ideal audience'. This is a very local issue – the story is about troublesome 'itinerants' (a euphemism for Aborigines) in the centre of Darwin whose presence is said to be a nuisance, especially to foreign tourists. Focusing down to a specific local context (bottom left) a cluster of ethnographic images, video stills and an aerial image (from Google Earth) begin to pick out a specific case example from the broad context which is alluded to in the bigger pictures above. Here the conditions at One Mile Dam are documented through the scenes witnessed there: everyday sleeping and cooking areas depicting the lack of facilities and vulnerability of the group. While the representations in the upper cells were certainly selected by the researcher they are aspects of popular culture which are available to all. The imagery in the lower cells, however, is specific to the researcher's chosen focus and restricted access to the community who had agreed to the documentation of their conditions.

Finally, from public discourse, to community to individual; an image of David Timber, who assumed the role of leader in the group's struggle to resist the group's eviction from this small pocket of land, a home (which they had been granted more than 30 years previously). The narrative from Timber and others

MACROSCOPIC

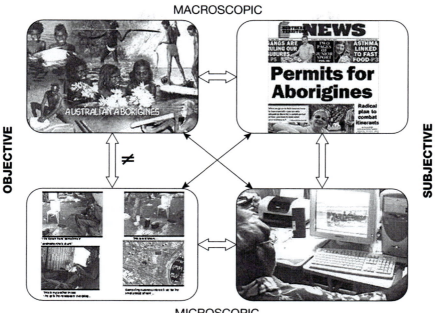

OBJECTIVE

SUBJECTIVE

MICROSCOPIC

Model 2 Micro and macro relationships

constitutes a specific individual commentary within the narrow local confines of the situation in Darwin. Nevertheless the local situation interrelates to all of the other frames. Indeed, for each of the levels of representation and reportage indicated in these cells there is an important link to the other levels of analysis. There is a movement between one level of relative objectivity to one of relative subjectivity (although neither is objective in the foundational sense) – the audience and the focus of research is both wider and narrower, more national and more local, an area of collective or of personal experience. Considering these different types of image or visual events, there is a clear divide between the societal representations which operate at an entirely different level to the research-based imagery. The media forms assume a preferred (hegemonic and narrow) reading of 'aboriginality'. They are a long way from exhausting the meaning of 'Aborigines' in Australia but they re-invoke certain well-worn discourses: romantic and racist, implicit cultural readings which connect the meaning of Aborigines to a specific relationship between nature and culture. The research recordings are also part of a discourse, although it is not so well understood, and does not sit comfortably with the tourist imagining or the tabloid discourse of 'race' and criminality (although research certainly *could* reproduce dominant values), it is too specific and reports realities which are marginal or largely ignored in Australian popular culture.

The importance of examining the dialogic relationship between specific visual examples and the social system that produces it is obvious. In this example both macro and micro cases inform one another. At the level of objective and subjective analysis, Mills' concept of individual 'milieu' and 'biography' is contrasted to the bigger narratives of historical change (or the apparent lack of it). The local and the personal are seen within the wider social portrayals reflected in the local media; the proposal for permits (which was quickly abandoned, perhaps because of its uneasy similarity to South African apartheid pass laws) was aired in the media and fuelled the sense of indigenous people (euphemistically referred to as 'itinerants') as threatening outsiders. Looking at the specific context of groups who are pushed to the boundaries who never have enough space in the city area, One Mile Dam is a paradigm case and visually these documents from the camp highlight the total lack of correspondence between popular media depictions of indigenous groups and their everyday lives. This example (which is articulated more fully in Spencer (2004, 2006a) and in both text and video pieces) suggests some of the different levels at which research can shift its focus and how case material may be at once specific and tied to a bounded example but also relevant to the wider social realities on public and national discourses.

While this diagram shows arrows between the portrayal in media and the people themselves at the level of representation this is a relationship where there is a total disconnect. On one side the portrayal of timeless bush settings compared to inner city deprivation, on the other a headline which proposes a 'radical plan to combat itinerants' and the leader of the Kumbutjil Association[1] whose family and community is on the receiving end of local government plans to restrict indigenous people (euphemistically 'itinerants') from the city centre.

The specific dynamics of a case with all its historical influences and geographical circumstances is at once unique and contained while at the same time resonating with broader societal imagery in the wider region and nationally, if not globally. This layering and creation of dialogues highlights links and associations; the conditions on the ground are partly shaped by the dominant discursive structures in the public sphere, which in turn are a response to perceived threats to the economic or moral order. Looking at the dynamic relationships between images (both still and video) the competing terms of reference, relations of power and broad ways of thinking, it is patently obvious that discourses are at work constituting the regimes of representation and lived conditions. Similarly, in the visual research process itself, other discourses are at work selecting images and sequences, piecing together events, even before the actual editing, to conform to the analytical discourses of certain academic disciplines.

Using stills to capture an 'instance in action'

The time and resources needed to make a film (even an amateur version) can be prohibitive. Using stills retains some of the dramatic immediacy of film and allows accessible visual stimuli which aid understanding. Still images are able to capture elements of a narrative and illustrate the themes (see the examples given below). Of course, still imagery entails a very different form of signification; static images, from which copies can be made and pondered over, have the advantage of being less transient in our perception, while the analogical flow of film/video fades rapidly from memory. Still images are synchronous and can take on a significance quite removed from the context from which the image was taken. Visual imagery can capture 'an instance in action' – a case in point from the flow of continuous observations, giving time to ponder the 'rhetoric of the image' (Barthes, 1982).

The complex cognitive process which occurs as we perceive an image means that, in Barthes' words: 'the denoted image naturalises the symbolic message, it innocents the semantic artifice of connotation' (ibid.: 45). This suggests that although read as 'innocent', representations are highly constructed. Ethnographic film stills may seem far less contrived than the more obviously constructed images used in newspapers or on postcards, but inevitably they have been selected to foreground certain values, meanings and 'preferred readings'. An example (Figure 36, image 7) captures a moment in which a number of contexts collide: tourism, masculinity, Australian myths, attitudes to drinking, Aboriginal commodification (the production of Aboriginal art and artefacts like didgeridoos and boomerangs). The image extracted from the flow of video is able to breathe and expand its contextual significance as we reflect upon it. Rather than operating in some potentially ideological way the image has in fact exposed an unspoken norm of everyday life in this part of the world. The issue of public drinking, which is so demonised when indigenous people do it, is here shown to be legitimate and commonplace for white Australians or tourists. To focus for a moment on this one theme other images were found showing that the derogatory stereotypes of Aborigines and drinking are deep-seated and historical. As a theme emerges and comes into clearer focus it can lead the researcher to look for historical and anthropological precedents and create a richly detailed contextual description which informs the interpretation of behaviour.

Combined methods: 'thick description' in a case approach

A particular photograph in a newspaper or magazine, a postcard or a poster might have caught your attention. This may provide the impetus for research, the beginnings of a case study of similar or contrastive portrayals, or suggest to you that in this form of representation a particular discourse or 'regime of truth' has been chosen; perhaps there are ideological reasons why the image has been chosen in its current form: what are the underlying messages implicit in this image? There is often this level of serendipity in the development of a research trajectory; however, of course, such 'discoveries' are not so accidental; they are often the result of a gradually developed critical viewpoint – so that material which was previously ignored suddenly becomes laden with relevant meanings.

To briefly demonstrate one piece of research where visual aspects played a key role, see the linked items in Figure 36 which became the elements in the short video piece about indigenous Australians. One of the first pieces of visual evidence was (1) the headline of the *Northern Territory News* in 2003 showing a group of indigenous Australians sitting around on a patch of grass with several green cans (recognisable as Victoria Bitter) visible in the image, underneath a banner headline 'GO HOME': 'Itinerants told by their own people to go home.' This imagery sparked my interest and led to several lines of enquiry into the situation in Darwin and also to some examination of relevant archive materials, including caricatures dating from the 1860s picturing indigenous Australians as drunken or unable to adapt to 'civilised' lifestyles (2). Images from postcards which were on sale in Darwin in 2004 (3) by contrast presented a tourist-friendly image of 'Aborigines' as unchanging, homogeneous, traditional groups. Fieldwork in Darwin included an invitation to visit an informal indigenous camp where conditions were far removed from the idyllic postcard images, and quantities of beer were clearly being drunk (4), although such imagery could be misleading as statistically white Australians have a higher rate of consumption.[2] However, because they are generally not permitted to enter pubs or hotels, those indigenous people who do drink tend to be conspicuous in parks and other public places. By contrast, beer cans are used to build boats (5) at the annual Beer Can Regatta which is an event attended almost exclusively by white Australians and public drinking is commonplace (7) although should indigenous people be seen they are likely to be taken away in police vans. Images 4–7 are stills from a short video (Spencer, 2005). There is the suggestion (supported by anthropologists in the field) that the 'regatta' is presented as 'organised and purposeful' drinking – much beer is apparently consumed so that these boats can be built. By contrast, indigenous drinking behaviour is seen as disorderly and chaotic (see Day, 2001). Following developments in this case I noticed another image published in 2007 online (8) (PARIAH, 2007) which further demonstrates the government's affirmation of this riotous and negative image of indigenous Australians. In what could be seen as a further sign of the local government's cynical paternalism a sign was erected at the entrance to the community warning of the penalties for bringing alcohol or pornography into the community. These actions appeared to offer no amelioration of the negative intervention policy put in place by the previous Howard government which targeted all Aboriginal communities as potentially dysfunctional and prone to child abuse and violence on an epidemic scale.

As forms of representation, 1 and 8, 2 and 3 (respectively: found images collected in the research context, historical and societal representations) each in different ways highlights and contrasts historical and social discourses about the 'other' as unable to assimilate into white Australian culture. There are assumptions about the inherent nature of indigenous people, where they belong and how they can be out of place if they emulate Western mores. Their apparently static material culture (1) allows them to be presented as 'noble savages' – at home in nature, held to have preserved ancient traditions which do not permit any real social or technological change. Images 4–7 are researcher-created visual data – stills from a short video piece (Spencer, 2005). Image 6 shows one of the two toilets which are available for (sometimes over a hundred) people in the community. Using still and video images of this sort might be criticised as perpetuating a 'victimist gaze', because while it clearly provides contrasting imagery to challenge the stereotype of unchanging 'Aboriginality', there is frequently a tendency to highlight only relentlessly negative images of marginal groups; further, it is arguably only a small step towards blaming the people for their conditions.[3]

Beginning to draw out the narratives and relationships between these images and their implications for analysing a complex situation demonstrates the multiple layers of evidence and treats the phenomenon in question as 'thick descriptions'. To comprehend the relationships and current attitudes which inform policies towards 'Aborigines' it appears that contextual and historical factors still operate to affirm stereotypes. Video ethnography was only one source of qualitative data

Figure 36 Eight images from a case study (Spencer, 2010):

1 Front page *Northern Territory News*, 2003. With permission of Newspix.
2 'Nature/ Civilization', *Queensland Figaro*, 6 August 1887. With permission of Ross Woodrow, University of Newcastle, Australia.
3 'Postcard – Australian Aborigines', Visit Merchandise Pty Ltd.
4–7 Stills from a video, *Framing the Fringe Dwellers* (Spencer, 2005).
8 Sign outside One Mile Dam, retrieved from Pariah.com (2007).

used; others included: interviews with indigenous academics, representations of the indigenous groups in the local and national media, historical imagery, secondary anthropological material and the accumulated popular cultural discourses which were gaining mainstream recognition at the time (e.g. *Rabbit-Proof Fence*, 2004).

Encounters with different groups never occur in a vacuum. The diagram suggests that ethnographic data are usefully contextualised by attention to the proliferation of representational data. Harper (2005: 748) suggests that 'one can argue that these cultural studies are ethnographic in an indirect manner; they are based on the analysis of the visual culture writ large'. The diagram demonstrates the unfolding visual data clustered around the focus of a particular case study and the ethnographic detail which was gained. Focus on a small community (a camp where different indigenous people lived a few minutes from a major Australian city) yielded a series of interviews and video depictions of daily life. As the case study progressed and the degree of intersubjective discussion and collaboration deepened, the understanding of the context and history of the case expanded and benefited from other forms of visual research, from the local context and outwards to the broader socio-historical and political representations of the phenomenon. While this kind of mixed method approach cannot close the gap between the ethnographer and those people's lives being studied, it helps to develop the context for the case and permits the examination of issues from several different popular viewpoints.

However, simply adding different forms of data does not automatically confer validity. Using multiple methods is not the same as 'triangulation' – a term which suggests that if two or more forms of data lead to the same conclusion the conclusion can be upheld with more confidence. Yet the conclusion itself may, in the nature of ethnographic cases, be complex and tentative. Also, even if there seems to be consistency in the results, this is no assurance that the inferences drawn from the data sources are correct. As Hammersley and Atkinson (1997: 232–33) point out: 'It may be that all the inferences are invalid, that as a result of systematic or even random error they lead to the same, incorrect, conclusion.'

This layering of different image types implies a purposeful and constant process of steering towards validity, and negotiating the reefs of misinterpretation. Using multiple methods does not seek to hammer home the 'truth' (there are different possible readings, different possible truths) but rather to explore the complex interwoven, historical, social and cultural associations by which the ways of life in question are delineated. The relationship between ethnographic interviews and observations and 'indirect' ethnographic images provides a link to broader contextual cues. This does not compromise the integrity of the bounded case but actually strengthens the narrative setting the specific dynamics of that case within the wider circuit of cultural discourses.

The idea that a piece of work is either valid or not should be reconsidered; instead of conceiving of a 'state of validity' as the starting point it is more useful to be engaged with a process of 'validating'. As Kvale suggests it is never an either/or situation: 'The quest for absolute certain knowledge is replaced by a

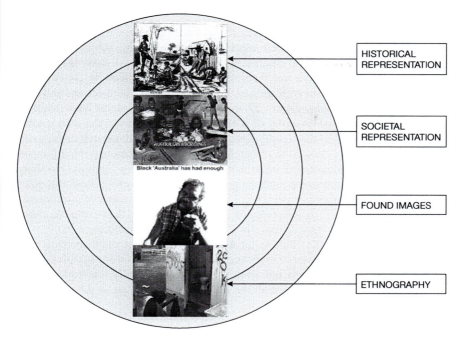

HISTORICAL
REPRESENTATION

SOCIETAL
REPRESENTATION

FOUND IMAGES

ETHNOGRAPHY

Model 3 Levels of visual ethnographic research.

conception of defensible knowledge claims' (Kvale, 1995: 19–40). The well-rounded approach which employs visual evidence in places as a complement to other forms of knowledge certainly provides a more trustworthy understanding of a complex situation. The use of images in this way encourages a carefully analytical and collaborative practice. Weaving together the elements in a complex case is akin to developing skill in a craft (Barbour, 2007; Rose, 2007) and validation might be seen as a measure of the quality of craftsmanship in research (Polkinghorne, 1983).

Finally in the types of study under discussion here, in which identities and complex cultural meanings are the object of study, understanding is always positioned and subjective. Therefore it can be seen that the knowledge produced by research, through the visual researcher's collection and interpretation of data is socially constructed. Hence only by pursuing a reflexive approach, in which a rigorous analysis of motives behind the interpretative path chosen, takes place, might a tentative sense of validity be achieved. Central to this view is the process by which social and cultural meanings (including interpretative paradigms) are mediated within and between the wider cultural sphere (semiosphere), and the mediasphere within which public discourses and individual micro-subjective viewpoints are in a constantly dynamic and negotiated relationship (see Figure 46 in Glossary under 'Mediasphere'). The language, texts, institutional and disciplinary discourses which shape our interpretations must be revealed if validity is to be strengthened.

As a case study unfolds, in the way this example has been shown to, connections and interrelations between areas of social meaning, subjectivities and theoretical structures begin to emerge. A key strength of a case study is its ability to explore causal pathways and theoretical ideas. In the example above, some visual facets of the case have permitted discussion of these connections and their links to theoretical ideas. Figure 37 and 38 give an example of how this case might demonstrate the features of a theoretical paradigm – the well-known concept in sociology of the 'moral panic'. This sequence demonstrates the value of reflective analysis *during* the research process. As the project (which focused on the growing concern and mobilisation of resources in Darwin, Northern Australia, around a perceived problem group – 'itinerants') progressed, it seemed evident that the sequence of events in Darwin had the hallmarks of a traditional 'moral panic'. In this instance plenty of examples presented themselves to match the classic stages of a 'moral panic' in Cohen's (1972) conception.

However, this example could suggest a tendency to allow the theoretical concepts to shape the collection of evidence, raiding the material for samples which fit the theoretical model, although in this instance there really was a plethora of diverse evidence suggesting that all the features of a moral panic were there.

1. This image was produced by local Indi media site PARIAH.COM and bore the title 'Why were these people moved on from the city centre? For breathing while being black.'

Initially a threat to the social, moral order might be identified, especially as tourism became increasingly profitable in the Northern Territory, and as a portion of the revenue is linked to a burgeoning interest in indigenous art, bush sites, traditional crafts and areas in the central Australian areas of the NT, such as Katherine Gorge, The Olgas, Uluru. The vision of homeless destitute urban indigenous people was seen as a threat to the city's image, exposing the few concessions which the state has made to the majority of urban Aborigines in Darwin.

2. Typically, the causes for perceived problems associated with the threatening group are simplified. In this case, one simple cause cited is alcohol (and in particular public drinking – a spectacle which is seen as shameful for Aboriginal people – who are renowned for their inability to remain sober). Thus stigmatised through the 'constant dripping' of media portrayals like the ones shown here – as bad, dirty, drunks, 'losing it' and becoming violent. Interestingly, the fact of indigenous people's dislocation from their traditional lands and the sense of dispossession, the lack of facilities and investment in those areas, the loss of native title on pastoral leases, and an entire history of dispossession are not seen as causes of people becoming 'itinerants'.

3, 4, and 5. As the panic builds, the inflammatory rhetoric increases and presents a degrading image of Aboriginal people (3) which in turn stirs up outrage (4) and

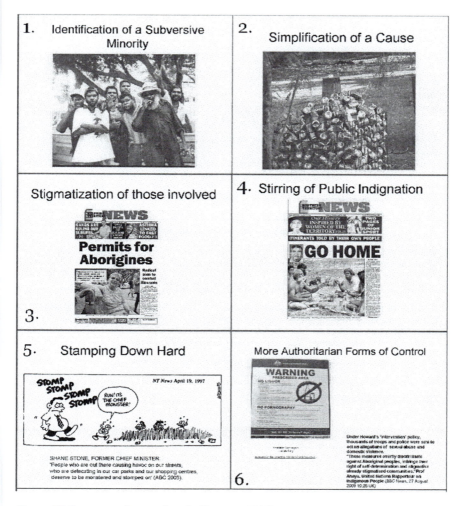

Figure 37 Sequence of a moral panic (Spencer, 2010).

begins to mobilise a stiff show of authority (5). One example a few years earlier occurred in the form of pronouncements by an outspoken Chief Minister (this indicates that moral panics surfaced on the same issues periodically). Finally, and as a result of a more generalised perception nationally (within the Howard government) of a crisis of 'dysfunctional communities' in which violence and child abuse was endemic, Federal Intervention programmes are unrolled to all Aboriginal communities and Australian Defence Force soldiers were sent in to communities (6) in June 2007 as part of the previous administration's 'Intervention' programme which was intent on banning alcohol and pornography, as a means of stamping out what was believed to be widespread child sex abuse fuelled

The Genealogy of Moral Panics

IDENTIFICATION OF A SUBVERSIVE MINORITY
'The few who spoil the enjoyment of millions.' Focus on subcultural styles; dress, behaviours, language, music – past, etc.: football hooligans, 'new age' travellers, rap and hip hop cultures, etc.
SIMPLIFICATION OF A CAUSE
'Dumbing down', lack of discipline, loss of moral standards, TV culture, alcohol and drugs, etc.
STIGMATISATION OF THOSE INVOLVED
Media portrayals of group as a mob, out of control, violent, depraved, animals, morons, etc.
STIRRING OF PUBLIC INDIGNATION
Media campaigns call for action, 'naming and shaming', outrage over 'soft penalties', 'political correctness gone mad', evoke 'national shame'.
STAMPING DOWN HARD
Constant sensationalist media coverage – leads to mobilisation of government and public authorities, police, social workers, anti-hooligan legislation.
MORE AUTHORITARIAN FORMS OF CONTROL
Send in police, army, draconian legislation, ASBOs for under-12s, etc.

Figure 38 Genealogy of a moral panic.

by chronic alcoholism. In the view of James Anaya, who is the first UN Rapporteur on Indigenous People to visit Aboriginal communities: 'These measures overtly discriminate against aboriginal peoples, infringe their right of self-determination and stigmatise already stigmatised communities' (BBC News, 27 August 2009).

This initial examination of the dynamic relations between images has been shown to yield important formal and theoretical correlations which demonstrate the continuity within social contexts and make important links between the local and the extra-local. Another tool for examining texts of all kinds is semiotic analysis (or semiology). Semiotics is a loose amalgam of analytical procedures which aims to uncover the deep structure, societal connotations and myth beneath the denotative surface of the images. First, a brief discussion and examples of some key concepts.

Modes of analysis – semiotics

The rationale behind semiotics is that language and other sign systems are arbitrary and conventional codes. Swiss linguist Ferdinand de Saussure demonstrated that the sign had a duality, it was composed of both a 'signifier' – the (sensory) form which the sign takes (word, image, smoke signal, etc.) – and the 'signified' – the meaning or the concept the signifier represents. Figure 39 gives a simple demonstration of the semiotic process by which news headlines could be analysed. Every 'text' is a combination of structured elements drawn from a field of choices and put together in a specific order. These choices and chains can be seen in the composition of imagery in popular culture just as they can be recognised in the language of news stories or advertising. The choices (paradigms) made in communication and the chains (syntagms) in which they are sequenced can be analysed and the ideological content can be more easily recognised. In *Language as Ideology*, Kress and Hodge (1979) recognise that surface structures of language have undergone transformations from a deep structure form. For example, the sentence 'The police shot dead five demonstrators on Monday' might convey the basic facts of an event; however, after processing through journalistic filters and political toning this may be rendered as

PARADIGMS

Agent	Action	Affected	
POLICE	SHOT DEAD	RIOTERS	DEMONSTRATION
FORCES OF LAW AND ORDER	KILLED	HOWLING MOB	STREET BATTLE
AGENT PROVOCATEURS	MURDERED	PROTESTORS	RIOT
PIGS	SLAUGHTER	DEMONSTRATORS	PEACEFUL PROTEST
RIOT SQUAD	DIE	CROWD	BRAWL

SYNTAGMS

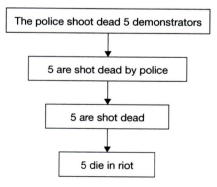

Figure 39 Paradigms and syntagms.

'five die in riot'. Not only has the agent been deleted and the syntax been changed to passivise the event but the word 'riot' is used which has an in-built negativity (connotations of civil unrest and disorder). This makes the reading of their deaths almost acceptable as we might now view them as active participants in a violent affray. So every word chosen in the resulting sequence indicates a choice (either conscious – as in propaganda, or less so, in the nature of professional codes of practice to which the journalist may become inured). The use of emotionally toned words can change the perceived meaning dramatically (e.g. 'five terror suspects die in street battle with police'). The implication of this set of words is markedly different and may appear to justify the death of the five (even though they were only suspected of terrorism). Fiske and Hartley (2003) argue that 'the meaning of what was chosen is determined by the meaning of what was not'. The choice of paradigms is based on factors such as code, connotation and style.

Paradigms and syntagms

De Saussure organised signs into codes: paradigms and syntagms. The dimensions of paradigms and syntagms are often presented as axes, where the vertical axis is paradigmatic and the horizontal axis syntagmatic. Paradigms are choices from a lexicon or cultural repertoire of words, images or other sign vehicles. Syntagms are the sequences which are put together from these elements, giving a sentence, a video sequence, a dance or a stand-up comedy routine. A photograph is also a syntagm in that it is the result of a combination of choices (angles, lighting, framing, timing –shutter speed, effects, etc.) coming together synchronously. The examples below are linguistic but it is not difficult to envisage how the scenario could equally be scripted for a video piece or a series of photographs.

Note how successive transformations in the four examples (passivisation, agent deletion and deletion of active verb) completely alter the possible reading of the event. In *Language as Ideology* (1979: 15) Kress and Hodge define ideology thus: 'ideology involves a systematically organised presentation of reality'. They argue that we must describe the truth and show how an ideology reorders the presentation to expose its operation. They offer several examples of this strategic ordering of words: 'Demonstrators confront police', or 'Police confront demonstrators'. The choice indicates a clear preference for and interpretation of events. The choice of the question 'Has the garbage been emptied?' leads to the angry retort: 'You know bloody well I've been out all day – how could I have emptied it?' The first statement strategically changes the direct question 'Have you emptied the garbage?' to a more euphemistic form in order to try and influence the person without exposing the intention. They also show how the process of nominalisation disguises the agency of the original: 'strikers picket the factory' becomes 'picketing'.

In a very similar way the elements in a picture can be manipulated to project a particular reading. Police can be portrayed sympathetically or as brutal enforcers of unjust laws; protestors can be presented as ordinary people exercising their right to make public protest or as violent radicals intent on causing damage.

The problem is that the social reality of mass demonstrations (like most situa-tions) is complex and there may be choices to selectively portray the event from what appears to be one unequivocal point of view or another quite opposed view. This issue of point of view and the ease with which images can be manipulated to give a 'preferred reading' has been discussed in earlier chapters. Semiotic approaches offer ways of discussing the choices and transformations which have led to the particular reading we are confronted with. However, this is an approach which is prone to forms of hyper-positivism at one extreme and elitist sub-jectivism at the other. So it is important to pursue a semiotic approach which is grounded in evidence of material social phenomena.

Semiotic analyses might uncover something of the intentional arrangement of an image, the manipulation of conventional codes privileging a certain 'reading' of the image, but can all of the elements in an image be reduced to these codes and categories, or is there more going on within the image?

Rhetorical images

Barthes' famous essay 'Rhetoric of the image' (1973) addresses this question directly and shows how conventional codes and the processes of multilayered signification do not exhaust the image. Barthes explores the process and movement of meaning in an example from advertising. He chose an advertising image because its intention is overt, and shows how the interplay of conventional codes creates an accessible narrative around the pictured products and the Panzani brand.

Barthes uses the advertising image of the shopping bag of Panzani produce (spaghetti, salsa, Parmesan and the raw ingredients for an Italian dish) to discuss the construction of Italian culture. The products are presented as authentic ingredients central to the Italian lifestyle. The advert invites the consumer to participate in the carefree vibrancy of Italy through an implied narrative of a trip to an outdoor market in a provincial Italian town, bringing home the produce suggested by the casual open string bag on the kitchen table. The consumer can step into this world of warm promise, a cultural romance contained in the brand (the Panzani colours themselves are those of the Italian flag). It is the creation, Barthes suggests, of 'Italianicity': a mythical construction of Italy. In this dis-cussion of the complex interrelated processes of signification which can be identified in the advertising image, Barthes also discusses the difficulties of pinning down the meanings of the connotative sign. At the level of denotation the signifier (word, sound-image) is interpreted in a literal way (the word 'rose', for example, designates a rose in the real world or the meaning of the word in a dictionary), whereas a connotation is the cultural association of the word – in this case it could stand for romance, passion, chivalry etc. Connotations are many and varied and cannot be easily contained as they also depend on which interpretations are possible to a reader at a particular point in time. Barthes asks: 'How are the signifieds of connotation to be named?' (1973: 47). He imagines a task worthy of a Borges story in which a massive inventory of all systems of connotation is produced; these being essences at the deep level of the sign which are singular and condensed ideological constructs like Barthes' invented term 'Italianicity' – 'the condensed essence of everything that could be Italian from spaghetti to painting' (p. 48). However, even if such an inventory could be produced, there are still elements which are not transformed into 'connotators'. Indeed, as Barthes suggests: 'there always remaining in the discourse a certain denotation without which, precisely, the discourse would not be possible'(p. 50). The function of these syntagmatic denotative elements is to naturalise the ideological to present the ideological as innocent and elusively commonplace, when in fact (sometimes) an intentional construct has been chosen and juxtaposed precisely to make the strongest impact on the 'reader', whether this has the propagandist function of political messages or social control in policy documents, or of stimulating desire and consumption in advertising or other commercial media.

More recently the cabinet encountered in a chain hotel (Figure 40) was also intent upon creating the essence of Italy. Two cabinets were found in a hotel lobby, each containing an array of Italian products – brands and signs chosen to create an ambience of Italy in a hotel in Carlisle. The attempt to create a portable constellation of Italianness in a city which is anything but Mediterranean is an interesting project. The disparate cultural references used include: tiles and product packaging with rustic rural imagery – fruit trees, flowers, shells, chickens, culinary products, and well-known evocative brands of spaghetti, lasagne, Spumanti, Martini, Barolo, etc.; signs of classical antiquity – a ticket for the Rome Olympics for 1960 with the Ponte Vecchio in Florence and statue of Athena, Venetian gondolas, romantic and rococo Italian imagery, tourist posters from the 1950s of Viarregio and Cervinia, and odd memorabilia such as ticket stubs and coins, and even a Juventus badge.

These examples are very different. On the one hand the product itself is part of Italian culture and lifestyle; its invitation is easily accessible to the consumer with its narrative of the good life. The cabinet of things Italian seems much more remote and slightly surreal in a hotel lobby in Carlisle. Its ability to generate Italy in the north of England by scavenging cultural forms seems doomed to failure – it becomes nothing more than window dressing, a museum cabinet containing souvenirs of an imagined Italian vacation, evoking nostalgia for facets of an alien culture, like the bullfight poster and castanets of a Spanish holiday gathering dust in an English suburban semi. The hotel located in a budget quarter of the city might feel the need to promote its international character to lift it away from the plethora of other chain hotels. Obviously this would not be a concern if the hotel was located in a more glamorous holiday location – like the one at Roma Tor Vergata (we cannot imagine them trying to capture the romance of northern England with a cabinet of postcards from Cumbria, Hadrian's Wall or Carlisle Castle).

Critical semiotic approaches

One useful application of semiotic analysis is for uncovering the processes of signification exposing latent meanings of ideologies and myth[4] beneath the

Figure 40 Italianicity revisited, 2009 – themed cabinets in a Carlisle hotel (Spencer, 2010; Ibis Publicity).

surfaces of everyday and commonsense meanings. However, certain strands of semiotics, in particular some of Barthes' theorising, must be recognised as problematic. Semiotics (or semiology) in the Barthesian tradition, as Strinati (1996: 123–128) suggests, is hard to validate empirically; meanings do vary hugely depending on the context. However, it seems reasonable to suggest that certain signs are employed and evoke dominant (preferred) and traditional values, although clearly these values may be disputed, negotiated or rejected as suggested by discussion of Hall's 'reading positions' (1973). Barthes' groundbreaking 1957 book *Mythologies* created a platform for the sardonic, witty intellectual to deconstruct the shibboleths of his or her times, and many others have followed this lead. The problem is that the approach became associated on the one hand with a form of arid structural formalism which stifled any aesthetic response, and on the other with a relatively haphazard set of critical tactics which at times bordered on theoretical arrogance (see Hayward 1996).

Barthes does suggest that signs are potentially polysemic, but also that there are dominant values and meanings which are foregrounded in certain texts. However, mainstream semiotics makes assumptions that the highlighted meaning of a text is self-evident and can be arrived at through a mechanical procedure, when in fact the openness of the sign may make the semiotician's reading only one of many such possible readings. Chandler (1994) sums up the collective criticisms of semiotics, suggesting that although some have rejected a purely structuralist semiotics this does not exhaust its scope. The movement towards a 'social semiotics' recognises the social context and the complexity by which semiotic systems operate in real social situations (the work of Gunther Kress and Robert Hodge (1988) has been significant here). It is this political and context-specific sense of semiotics which may prove most valuable for the social researcher.

Semiotic approaches, despite these cautionary critiques, are an important tool for conveying a sense of the complex construction and mediation of cultural values. A case in point is the invisibility of 'whiteness'. This can be shown to be a contingent construction of otherness – those who are visibly different to a 'white standard' are constantly treated differently in their portrayal in popular representations, demonstrating that an unspoken (what Barthes calls an 'exnominated') set of values is at work. The role played by mass media is crucial in affirming a habitual sense of what is 'normal'. By performing what Fiske and Hartley term a 'bardic' role, the media carries cultural values and broadcasts events like the travelling bard or minstrel of old. This mediation foregrounds one set of values and by habitual reference renders the stereotypical representation of others as natural and invisible.

Also, semiotic processes and signification take place in a historical context and do not rely merely on speculative analyses but can lend support to these with more empirical data (a range of both quantitative and qualitative evidence can be marshalled, e.g. in the discussion of indigenous Australians, statistics and media imagery demonstrate the prevalent white Australian mindset about Aborigines). The value of such analyses, in this case, is to expose the material consequences of the construction of difference, and how such differences are constantly presented as 'natural' categories.

> 'Mainstream semiotics' emphasises structures and codes, at the expense of functions and social uses of semiotic systems, the complex interrelations of semiotic systems in social practice, all of the factors which provide their motivation, their origins and destinations, their form and substance. It stresses system and product, rather than speakers and writers or other participants in

semiotic activity as connected and inter*acting* in a variety of ways in concrete social contexts.

(Kress and Hodge, 1988: 1)

In other words, semiotics needs to be practical and relate to an account of how the process of meaning construction is linked to views of social reality. So as a form of analysis, semiotics can provide insights but needs to be anchored to social realities and perhaps used in conjunction with other methods rather than relying on the privileged subjective voice of the 'expert' ethnographer or semiotician:

> Unless semiotics confronts this relationship, it can have no relevance to the world of practical affairs with its confident assumptions about 'reality', and it cannot account for the role of semiotic systems in that world.

(ibid.: 23)

The researcher might use what Prosser (2006) described as 'researcher found' images. These are valuable not only for adding contextual detail and thick description to a specific study but also for allowing discussion of the underlying ethos which produced them; they can be good material for honing skills of critical analysis. One way of grounding the analysis of culture in material production is through the analysis of interlinked popular imagery from historical to more recent signs showing the formation of dominant discourses.

Figure 41 gives two simple demonstrations of the semiotic process by which images and texts could be analysed. Every 'text' is a combination of structured

Figure 41 'Nature/Civilization', *Queensland Figaro*, 6 August 1887. With permission of Ross Woodrow, University of Newcastle, Australia.

elements drawn from a field of choices and put together in a specific order. These choices and chains can be seen in the composition of imagery in popular culture just as they can be recognised in language.

This nineteenth-century caricature depicts Aborigines as 'noble savages' in a bush setting but rendered as dissolute parodies of white respectability by 'civilisation'. In many ways the image of the 'noble savage' is still prevalent and contrasts sharply with the true urban condition of many Aborigines. Such imagery proved instructive for understanding the conditions under which Aboriginal people live today and the prevalent attitudes which still exist about them. The caricature is from an 1887 edition of the *Queensland Figaro* and could be considered as a moral homily about the nature of indigenous people. The condition of indigenous people at this time was evidently one of dispersal and separation from kinship groups, loss of land and the ability to provide through hunting and fishing as trees were felled and ground was levelled for pasture and stock. The actual situation for many indigenous people then was of slavery or at best bonded labour; this was the case especially in more remote settlements. 'Aborigines commonly regarded by whites as ferea natura, "vermin to be trampled on", or if conceded to be human, "little above the level of a working animal", were placed like pariahs beneath contempt – at the nadir of any scale of honor' (Saunders, 1984: 202).

The ability of white Australians to take the moral high ground in these portraits of apparently destitute 'modern Aborigines' is cruelly apparent. However, institutionally and legally Aboriginal people were prevented from any upliftment (by European standards). When the Aborigines Protection and Restriction of the Sale of Opium Bill was reviewed in 1897, 'A clause allowing blacks to purchase land was peremptorily deleted. . . . As Patterson points out in defining the legal form of slavery: "It is not because the slave becomes a form or object of property relations, but because he is denied all possibility of being a *subject* of property relations, a proprietor, that property is so important in the transformation of slavery"' (ibid. p. 200).

Thus the image by itself reveals some, but not by any means all, of the discursive apparatus through which Aboriginality has been constructed. We might, at face value, examine the image in terms of the operation of binary terms which are embedded in the culture. Levi Strauss, and more recently, media analyst and critic John Fiske (e.g. 1989) have demonstrated that Western culture, and indeed all cultures, divide the array of cultural phenomena in this way. Here the divide between NATURE and CIVILISATION creates a diptych and further binaries are suggested: country/city, naked/clothed, healthy/sick, sober/intoxicated, noble/ignoble. Intertextually it could easily be seen as reminiscent of Hogarth's moral caricatures as well as loaded with mythical values about the Australian bush and Aboriginal connections with it.

However, a closer look at the historical records and the legal and social relations between white Australians and indigenous peoples, evidence from the social context of the time, as we have seen, reveals further depth and poignancy to this portrayal. Quoting again from Saunders' (1984) discussion of the conditions of Aborigines in the colonial period:

[I]n most instances, the relentlessness of European reactions overrode any resistance attempts. As A. Turnbull commented from Burketown in 1896, '. . . even now . . . a rebellious nigger loses the number of his mess [i.e. is killed] in a remarkably short time (and no questions asked).' Ultimately as the threat of physical death hung continually over the heads of the colonised Aborigines, their situation was reduced to that of a form of social death. 'For even while their physical lives may have been spared, their social lives in a society which both despised them and fully endorsed the master's coercive controls were not.'

(Saunders, 1984: 203)

Images reveal their secrets as part of a broader research process and the dictum that they can be interpreted as they stand is fallible, as all interpretation is dependent on understanding and reviewing the codes through which the image has been constructed and positioned, historically, socially and culturally.

The advert shown in Figure 42 for the Australian Advertising Industry Council appeared in Australian papers in the 1980s. It suggests that our relative affluence and amount of consumer choice is directly related to the commercial activity of advertisers. The text underneath informs us:

And they don't have all those boring, repetitive commercials interrupting their favourite programmes.

And they don't have all those different newspapers, magazines, television and radio stations bombarding them with information.

And they don't have all those unnecessary products taking up valuable space in their homes.

No. In some countries they've got nothing to complain about.

Advertising. You'd probably notice it more if it wasn't there.

How might an image like this be interpreted semiotically? There are several basic procedures which examine the image in terms of its combined elements (syntagms) and the choices that are made in each of its constituent elements (paradigms).

1. First, the *context* should be noted, i.e. daily national broadsheet newspaper circa 1984. *The Australian* (conservative Murdoch flagship). Source of advert: Australian Advertising Industry Council.
2. Begin by examining the obvious *textual features* – this is the level of *Denotation*. In this example the image is a grainy black and white photograph. The arrangement of the scene shows stark lighting and protective body language of the family creating a sense of insecurity and vulnerability.
3. Our reading of the scene will depend on our repertoire of *intertextual references* (e.g. the bare, unshaded light bulb, minimalist décor, choice of

Figure 42 'In some countries. . .': advert from *The Australian* newspaper c. 1983 (Australian Advertising Standards).

realist font (Courier)). These features recall other genres and other uses of the same visual codes. They are the visual tropes which emotionally tone the meanings of the image.

4. *Anchorage of text and image*: what is the effect of the linguistic and visual elements together? (i.e. in this case, the bulletin reportage style suggests this is a news story 'from the front line' – a connotation of hard-hitting, gritty realism).

5. *Level of connotation*: 'some countries' clearly not *our* country, Australia. The text and image together suggest that without advertising there is no choice. There are also clearly 'cold war' associations we might – particularly at the time this paper was printed – consider the cheerless and repressive conditions often alluded to in Eastern bloc countries. The message could therefore be read as: 'Advertising, capitalism and free market economy give choice and freedom.'

Faced with this stark image, the implications are clear – our lifestyle comes with a price tag. In some ways we could argue that this advertisement is a plea for capitalism itself. The bleak alternative suggested by the ad's reference to 'some countries' is clearly a reference to the Soviet bloc. The grainy black and white image, the huddled family group, the absence of any adornment and the iconic use of the bare bulb, even down to the pairing of the image and the Courier script used for the text, all deliver the impression of vulnerability and hard-edged realism.

Clearly the suggestion is that capitalism and the necessary nuisances of advertising and commercial activity by which it is underpinned are the mechanisms by which our lives are enriched by product choices and diversity of information. The alternative is the unthinkably stark and Spartan existence symbolised by this image: a life devoid of luxuries, of excess, a life where 'utility' is still important and 'brand identity' has no place. The same structure of argument is illustrated in Barthes' essay entitled 'Operation Margarine' (1974). To introduce this concept he states: 'To instil into the Established Order the complacent portrayal of its drawbacks has nowadays become a paradoxical but incontrovertible means of exalting it' (1984: 41). Barthes recognises that this inoculation against consumer culture comes in many forms, but margarine in this essay is the paradigm example:

> It is found in the publicity for *Astra* margarine. The episode always begins with a cry of indignation against margarine. 'A mousse? Made with margarine? Unthinkable!' 'Margarine? Your uncle will be furious!' And then one's eyes are opened, one's conscience becomes more pliable, and margarine is a delicious food, tasty, digestible, economical, useful in all circumstances. The moral at the end is well known: 'Here you are, rid of a prejudice which cost you dearly!'
>
> (ibid.)

Capitalism and advertising are presented in just the same way here. We have the luxury of our prejudices about advertising – but the alternative would be nothing to complain about because there would be no choice of products at all. The apparently reasonable, non-coercive nature of marketing, providing choice and upholding the ethos of a free market economy away from state control, was generated by and helped to rationalise the capitalist orthodoxy in the post-war era. These images of the limitless abundance of capitalist production were a strong ideological weapon during the cold war years. The Soviet State was frequently represented as one in which choice was not permitted. Indeed, the yearning for the forbidden fruits of capitalism is often cited as a key element in the undermining of communism – the so-called ''velvet revolutions' in Czechoslovakia, Hungary and Poland.

> If I think about the advantages of Western democracy, I come up with one word – hope. Communism ground up people with ideology that did not allow a different view; with its equalization, its stupidity, and especially in the initial phase, its brutality. A liberal society brainwashes people in a more refined way – the myth of success, the diktat of consumerism. Communism was about life without hope. An open society provides an escape route. It is not so little, what democracy brings.
>
> (Mejstrik, 1999)

Mejstrik reminds us that Western democracy (despite our concerns about the perpetuation of the hallowed myths of success and consumerism which keep us in thrall) is preferable to the grinding despair of Soviet communism. This analysis of the image and language in the Australian Advertising Industry Council advert is suggesting another level of signification which Barthes has called myth.

6. *Level of myth*: the elements discussed above could be argued to combine to create a sign which in turn is the signifier in a higher order of signification – that of myth. The terms in the first system at the level of coded elements in a language transform into a *metalanguage* (see glossary for more detailed explanation). Arguably in this case the sharp contrast that could once be drawn between Western culture and the Eastern bloc countries is no longer possible, yet neither is it necessary; if living alternatives are not available, the question no longer has a locus. Perhaps the 'vaccination' is no longer needed – we are all immune now to the call of other ways of being, because the alternatives have been subsumed within the central marketing framework. The advert serves to signify this other sign: the unrivalled triumph of a capitalist system and the demise of the 'deluded' system which sought to challenge the desires of consumer society, with the embedded inequalities this inevitably entails (see discussion of 'Myth' in Glossary).

Discussing another interesting facet of semiotic unravelling of the image, Barthes suggested that aside from the all-too-obvious in visual texts, there might also be an 'obtuse' meaning, element(s) in the image which disrupt the easy reading of the text and point to potentially subversive meanings which undermine the intended meaning.

'Punctum' – the subversive focal point

Further interrogation of the image in popular culture led Barthes to make the distinction between the *obvious* and the *obtuse* meanings in photography and film.

In *Camera Lucida* (1982) he suggests that images are routinely observed through the *studium* – a superficial and less acute mental state in which one peruses the symbolism of an image – the background interest. Figure 43, for example, might be observed in the state of studium as a document of ethnographic interest. Barthes contrasts this background with the *punctum* – the point which disrupts this easy apparent symbolism. Details of the image may rupture what at the level of the *studium* is an easy conventional reading and hint at other meanings which are difficult to properly pin down. The 'punctum,' Barthes says, 'rises from the scene, shoots out of it like an arrow, and pierces me' (1982: 26).

Looking at Figure 43, it might be possible to detect other, possibly subversive readings, and these subsequent meanings undermine the intended or preferred reading of the image. The punctum could be the face of the woman in the centre (enlarged detail, left). Her sidelong glance at the photographer seems to question the context in which the image is set. Hammerton's depiction of this as a 'pleasant rural scene' seems especially dubious alongside the figures of these women: their oppressively heavy, Victorian garb, their exhausted and toil-worn faces. The face of the woman to the right of the turning woman looks bruised and swollen (enlarged detail above right), her clothes torn and her mouth set (we might even believe she is pregnant or suffering from an illness). Hammerton goes on to discuss this image as an example of a willing peasantry in contrast to the slavery which ended, he assures us, in 1834. This image begins to stand out, the faces of the women seem suddenly more 'real' in that they seem to show complex, nuanced personal gestures and challenge the easy glance which catalogues this as another standard posed, genre photograph.

Figure 43 'Negro women tending young sugar canes' (Hammerton, 1933). This is an extension of a discussion which featured in Spencer (2006: 18–20).

The details punctuate, disturb and may transgress the studium – that conscious investment in the image, a very wide field of unconcerned desire, of inconsequential taste: 'a kind of general, enthusiastic commitment, of course, but without special acuity' (Barthes, 1982: 26). In some pictures, then, the eye is drawn to a feature or features which rupture the easy assurances of the text. In this case, Hammerton's voyeuristic compendium of colonial others, with its facile assurance of benevolence, is undermined and as the first weevil is spotted in the bread we notice it is infested with others; other meanings begin to multiply and overturn the bland assurances and closure of the commentary. The problem with a detailed examination of specific images like this which focuses on their internal dynamics is that the analyst could be accused of elevating a subjective response to the level of serious analysis. This is, as discussed above, the constant refrain:

> Semiology wants to demonstrate that the meanings uncovered by its approach are systematic in that they possess a comprehensive structural form and are prevalent within the society in which myth is found. However, if the analysis is confined to the sign itself and the problem of empirical validation is ignored; it is difficult to see how this claim can be substantiated.
>
> (Strinati, 1996: 124)

Nevertheless, it can be seen that images have a great deal to contribute – there are hidden depths which may be worth exploring – but we must guard against aberrant decoding. The best way to do this is to anchor the analysis to other forms of historical and social evidence to make the analysis less speculative. In the context of a much more thorough and finely tuned semiotic analysis, Daniel Chandler (1994) has identified over 50 semiotic procedures in the form of a DIY Semiotic Analysis – a comprehensive guide and checklist.

The procedures discussed so far are forms of 'hermeneutic' analysis. Hermeneutics is a word which originated from its uses to interpret and reveal the meanings of ancient texts and knowledge – particularly biblical. The word stems from Hermes, the heavenly messenger: a go-between or translator of wisdom from above into earthly language. Research is about the interpretation of systems of knowledge and truth – revealing their latent meaning in social exchanges and in the currency of everyday life. Techniques of semiotic analysis, although they vary, are more fine-grained and text-based, whereas the concept of discourse analysis, as discussed in several places throughout this book, is an approach examining the relationships between language, texts, knowledge, power and truth, and their manifestations in social life, institutions, laws, schemes of representation, and in bodies.

Forms of discourse analysis

The problem with discourse analysis is that there are a baffling number of different forms covering a broad canon of thought about language, power, structure and agency and social context, and all come with a legacy of particular schools of thought. Critical Discourse Analysis (CDA), for example, as articulated by Fairclough (e.g. 1995), has a focus on language use as a social practice; it happens in context, in institutions and within structures which condition and shape how it is articulated.

For Fairclough, the processes of text production and consumption include institutional routines and editorial procedures, and how texts are consumed and fit into household routines (e.g. TV is watched at certain times by different people fitted around their work and family times). Discourse processes can also mean in the narrower sense of the transformations which texts go through in production and consumption. Discourse practice, then, for Fairclough, is seen as mediating between textual and social/cultural practice. [5]

When examining institutions and their shaping and controlling of knowledge and people's lives and their very bodies, it is considered by some that power is always a vestige of direct coercive power. Foucault suggests that *power has materiality*. It's not a matter of there being a form of power which derives from force, coercion and violence and the antithesis of that is some sort of ideological perception of power. The idea that the *truth* can be revealed by systematically exposing the distortions and lies and ideologies of the state is for Foucault a lost cause. 'The state is superstructural in relation to a whole series of power networks that invest the body, sexuality, the family, kinship, knowledge, technology and so forth' (Foucault, 1980: 122).

Discourse in Foucault's conception is the web of correspondences through which power is constituted, a radical departure from the notion of power as a possession installed and wielded by (for example) an all-powerful authoritarian state. Foucault instead recognised power as the result of the association of various disciplinary practices and knowledges and resistances to these. There are varieties of forms of power; some of those crystallise and accrue to institutions. Discourse as defined by Foucault refers to:

> ways of constituting knowledge, together with the social practices, forms of subjectivity and power relations which inhere in such knowledges and relations between them. Discourses are more than ways of thinking and producing meaning. They constitute the 'nature' of the body, unconscious and conscious mind and emotional life of the subjects they seek to govern.
> (Weedon, 1987: 108)

Foucault's analyses trace the origins of the asylum (*Madness and Civilization*), the prison and regimes of punishment, incarceration and surveillance (*Discipline and Punish*) and the different social formations around sexualities (*History of Sexuality I, II, III*). In this sense discourses are those broad patterns of institutional thought, or as Foucault suggested, 'regimes of truth' which define and limit what can be said about a specific topic. In addition to this institutional 'apparatus', discourse is also articulated through finely detailed 'technologies'; the practical manifestations of these conceptions of power/knowledge.

To trace the genealogy of certain influential discourses, it is necessary to recognise the way in which social relations are constituted – as in the example shown in Figure 44. While the concept of an underlying truth is problematic, such an approach might at least allow a more critical response to essentialist and commonsense assertions about the nature of social reality and in particular show the way that visual 'technologies' serve the practices of power/knowledge articulated through institutions and the discourses which constitute them. Discourses seem to have the eerie ability to breathe life into subjects, constructing them through a matrix of associations of power and knowledge.

Gillian Rose (2007) suggests that discourse analysis can be usefully separated into two analytical processes if one wishes to examine phenomena in terms of their discursive structure. Discourse Analysis I and Discourse Analysis II attempt to mirror two different emphases in Michel Foucault's work. Rose suggests that the division can be made thus: Discourse Analysis I 'tends to pay rather more attention to the notion of discourse as articulated through various kinds of visual images and verbal texts than it does to practices entailed by specific discourses. ... It is most concerned with discourse, discursive formations and their productivity.' While Discourse Analysis II 'tends to pay more attention to the practices of institutions than it does to visual images and verbal texts. Its method-ology is usually left implicit. It tends to be more explicitly concerned with issues of power, regimes of truth, institutions and technologies' (Rose, 2007: 146). This distinction is a useful one, similar to the Saussaurean division between 'parole' and 'langue' (just as a sample of language differs from the abstract system which made the utterance possible).

The postcard (Figure 44) is an artefact in which the self-conscious rhetorical organisation of elements can be considered in terms of the process of semiosis: the denotative and connotative levels implicit in the images which make it up. The central title which anchors representations of disparate peoples under a blanket term – their boundaries blurred in this montage and semantically by their inclusion under this category.

Diverse images are melded into a diorama of 'aboriginality'. The visual elements here can be seen to serve the discursive function of the language to, in

Figure 44 Available discourses – 'Australian Aborigines', Darwin, 2005.

Gary Foley's words, 'in an instant, disembowel the vast 100,000 year histories and culture of about five hundred different peoples in Australia by naming us "Aborigines"' (Foley, 1997). The sense of discourse which might be derived from this image perhaps constitutes the sense of discourse as reproducing canons of received knowledge, affirming the narrow ways which exist in mainstream society and popular culture to define 'aboriginality'.

The use of a visual example, like the above, can serve several purposes in research. First, it allows consideration of the manner in which elements in an image or other text are arranged at a micro level – looking at the combination of elements – the choices and chains (paradigms and syntagms) through which meaning is encoded. Secondly, considering the manner in which such artefacts are produced to present a narrow articulation of a people and their relationship to knowledge and power reveals the discursive boundaries used in mainstream culture. Muecke's (1982) article 'Available discourses on Aborigines' suggested that white Australians were limited to ways of speaking about Aborigines by four influential discourses: anthropological, romantic, literary and racist. In this case, a further 'tourist' discourse might be added to Muecke's discourses. The extraordinary influx of tourism to Australia in the last 25 years highlights how the dominant discursive structures which have shaped understandings of 'aboriginality' have become a resource for promoting the country. Tourism is recognised to entail the pursuit of *authenticity* (McCannell, 1999) via romantic, primordial experiences of 'nature in the raw'. Such desires resonate with the historic portrayals of indigenous Australians. As a result of this interplay of discourses this type of imagery is pointedly appealing – part of the industry of manufacturing authentic cultural experiences.

In terms of how these institutional relations of power/knowledge are put into practice, such images may seem benign, but they are only one surface manifestation of a discourse which operates to regulate behaviour – and has the coercive force of the state behind it. For example, during fieldwork in Australia (Spencer, 2006: 145), I interviewed an indigenous lecturer and Head of Indigenous Studies on the issues of conceptions of 'aboriginality':

> Some of the legislation is so draconian. To satisfy a land claim you've got to have lived a lifestyle that occurred before 1788 – of course we've changed a lot since 1788! – But the legislation doesn't recognise it – the government doesn't recognise that cultures change, and also we have to change if we want to survive. They look at indigenous culture as static – they don't look at any other culture – but they certainly see indigenous culture as it has to be static which we're certainly not.
>
> (Sonia Smallacombe in Spencer, 2005)

This demonstrated that such images are part of a broader institutional framework which has material power effects. In today's social context, the 'tourist' discourse reprises and rejuvenates these primordial views of the indigenous 'other'. While such semiotic treatments of images could be claimed to be subjective interpretations of a potentially open text, the choice of imagery and the prevailing social and political climate needs to be understood to demonstrate a valid knowledge of the construction of 'aboriginality'. Visual representations like this then are rich texts which expose the ideological biases of the dominant culture, and allow students/researchers to critically engage with the context and content as well as the processes of analytical research.

In the above image looking through the lens of Discourse Analysis I, we might note the arrangement of the elements themselves; the manner in which they have been chosen from paradigms of similar pictures and their logic of combination, the syntagmatic relations between them like the arrangement of words in a sentence. There is the all-encompassing use of the written element 'Australian Aborigines' to centrally unite the perhaps unrelated vignettes of indigenous people. This image and many like it could be subject to various forms of analysis based on the immediate elements and their arrangement and the features of the people: are they smiling or are they engaged in typical forms of material culture – hunting, fishing, tool making, ritual performances? These elements form patterns which reveal the discursive structure of the images – the habitual rhetoric which produces such forms. Potter has used the term 'interpretative repertoires' for the apparently systematic terms which underpin the combination of these elements, forming a sort of grammatical structure (Wetherell and Potter, 1988). These constitutive semiotic elements are arranged by the broader principles of discourse, for example, those identified by Muecke as 'available discourses': the romantic, anthropological and racist discourses. Muecke adopted the approach of discourse analyst Michel Pecheux who perceived grammar, discourse and ideology 'to be related theoretically in a hierarchy of materialization':

> one should conceive of the discursive as one of the material aspects of what we have called ideological materiality. In other words, the discursive *species* belongs, according to us, to the ideological *genre*.
>
> (Pecheux in Muecke, 1982: 98)

This is an important point and suggests that ideological apparatuses generate discourses[6] which consequently produce the 'meaning effects' that 'make coherent classifications of the institutional structures and the behaviour of individuals within them'(p. 99). In other words Muecke following Pecheux takes discourse (or discursive processes) as the underlying source which is manifest in the space of language, the grammar and syntactic forms of texts, institutional documents. From the implicit constraints apparent in the language used about 'the other' we can see the reflection of discourses operating through the institutional framework. Aboriginal people are lumped together as one undifferentiated group and the means of address identifies the positions of us and 'them' (the term used by white Australians which distances and disallows real contact from the start). Much of this can be deduced from the elements in the card or dozens of similar images (see Spencer, 2006a).

Looking again at the postcard example, if we were to take Rose's Discourse II approach, the point is to transcend the actual cultural form and to examine the institutional practices which might generate this type of image. These tend to be quite specific to particular social institutions. For example, in the context of Darwin in the Northern Territory of Australia (where the card was purchased) the 'Community Harmony Strategy' was a Northern Territory government initiative also supported by ATSIC (Aboriginal and Torres Strait Islander Commission) for dealing with 'the itinerant problem'. As this record of the 2005 report indicates, the association of several authorities with complex motives, health, antisocial behaviour, substance abuse and mental illness, are mobilised and the policy appears non-coercive and humanitarian. However, the rationalisation of how to deal with homeless indigenous people who arrive in Darwin is what underpins the necessity for such documents. 'Aborigines' might be seen as out of place, transgressive elements not conforming to the dominant (though mythical) image reinforced by popular culture and tourist representations.

> The Community Harmony Strategy arose from concerns regarding the health, well-being and behaviour of 'itinerants' in the Northern Territory. A research project was conducted by the Northern Territory Government and ATSIC into the situation of 'itinerants' in Darwin and Palmerston. In June 2003, the NT Government allocated (AUD) $5.25M to create a Territory-wide Community Harmony Strategy.

> The strategy's two key aims are to reduce antisocial behaviour of 'itinerants' and to provide infrastructure and services that support the needs of 'itinerant' groups. Strategies to achieve this include proactive intervention, provision of infrastructure and the expansion of health and treatment programs. These steps are designed to provide pathways that allow 'itinerants' to return home or settle in towns. The Community Harmony Strategy will also focus on providing services for 'itinerants' suffering from substance abuse or mental illness.

The language displayed in this and other reports displays a euphemistic way of talking about the concern of homeless indigenous people in the city. There is recognition that to name the group directly can invoke criticism, while at the same time 'they' seem to be the specific targets of derogatory rhetoric by the tabloid press. These manifestations presenting static, romanticised and passive representations are the result of several discourses which can be shown to have developed historically. Hence a variety of discourses combine from different institutions to produce documents which will provide an apparently measured civic tone – while in practice the reality of dealing with 'itinerants' may mean removing them forcibly in police wagons and unceremoniously dumping them at the informal and heavily burdened settlements (like One Mile Dam) outside of the city centre. Discourses may appear eminently reasonable and in the public interest, but they may have serious, material impacts upon those who are their object. Such consequences may not seem pejorative because they are the result of complex discursive forces which produce and regulate values and beliefs, constructing some groups (itinerants, the homeless, 'aborigines') as outside of the framework for normal social relations. This is a view reinforced through our major institutions and hence strongly interwoven into the culture.

Using new technologies

It would be remiss, in a text which is discussing visual research, not to make some mention of trends in using technologies. There are plenty of manuals which set out guiding principles of video and photography production, and the latest hardware and software is arguably more flexible and easier to use than in the past. Cameras which can give basic recordings are now available cheaply or come as additional extras added to phones and other devices (to the dismay of some more traditionally-minded photographers who see the approach as adding to an avalanche of poor quality and thoughtlessly produced materials) (see Jean Rouch's dismayed reaction to the digital revolution on p. 39).

So while many of us have become self-taught in some of the principles of making, editing and presenting visual work, it goes without saying that ignorance of the technical aspects of lighting, sound, appropriate framing and composition will inevitably impact on the depth and validity of the work and more importantly shows an inappropriate lack of 'care for the subject'. However, much of the anxiety about the flood of images triggered by the ever-increasing capacity of digital technologies may be unfounded. Certainly an individual can now take several hundred images rather than a dozen or so, but does this imply that he or she has any less discernment for what makes a 'good' image? Why should such a critical faculty be only the province of the professional, the 'auteur'?

One developing and robust digital technology entails systems which might allow more complex appreciation of the relationships between images, texts, sound and other data. Digital Replay System (DRS) is designed for people who want to bring together disparate forms of digital media. These might include video, transcriptions, log files, audio and more. DRS is a next generation Computer Aided Qualitative Data AnalysiS (CAQDAS) tool. There are a range of potential uses for this system, which might effectively be considered a means of combining qualitative and quantitative data. The system can organise, replay, annotate, code, represent and analyse data. The system which is available as freeware allows researchers to present digitised data in simultaneous relationships along a common timeline. This facility could allow subtle and complex relations between a range of visual, textual and other features of the context to be recognised when juxtaposed in this way.

One demonstration was given of subjects who were on a fairground ride. Video of their faces (from a head cam worn by the subject), audio recordings of their voices, and records from a heart monitor worn by the subject were streamed simultaneously, giving a multi-sensorial impact. In addition, the audio output had been transcribed. The system permits all such digitised information to be played synchronously using a common timeline. Potential for these sorts of innovations

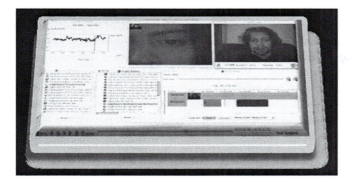

Figure 45 Digital Replay System, reproduced with permission of Nottingham University.

has yet to be fully recognised, but one important feature is the system's ability to select marked themes within a video and to play back only those selected themes. Hence the same raw visual data could be viewed in separate strands or sequences along with selected transcripts, or other digital information. This could be remarkably useful for comparative analyses of video sequences and enable the presentation of common patterns which can be a compelling form of evidence. The fact that all of these data appear on the screen gives a great deal of experiential information in a very convenient format, and allows visual and verbal information to be interwoven in a way which promises to allow some detailed analyses which have not been possible before.

One suggestion made by the Nottingham team concerns the insight gained from simultaneous playback of verbal transcripts and nonverbal signs – permitting some micro-observations of the complex relationships between gesture and speech (for example, the connections between verbal and non-verbal signs when people are telling lies):

> for many interaction researchers, it is the complex *interactions* between dialogue, non-verbal behaviour and system activity that are of most interest. There has been an increasing interest in the relationship between certain nonverbal behaviours and the linguistic context in which they occur as researchers recognise that they can be tightly synchronised in natural language (e.g. to convey shared meanings, Bavelas and Chovil, 2006) The study of these relationships will lead to a greater understanding of the characteristics of verbal and non-verbal behaviour in natural conversation and the specific context of learning, and will allow social scientists to explore in more detail the relationships between linguistic form and function in discourse, and how different, complex facets of meaning in discourse are constructed through the interplay of text, gesture and prosody.
>
> (Brundell *et al.*, 2008: 6)

Considering the materials which have been discussed earlier in this book, there are several potentially valuable applications for this system. The walking video could be uploaded, the transcript of the interview added and an aerial map of the area could be added from Google Earth; in addition, pre-destruction maps of Africville could be added and landmarks which are mentioned but not actually standing at the current time (Like the Seaview United Baptist church) could be added on digital photographs and arranged along the timeline to be shown as the respondent talks about them. This gives a genuinely multi-sensorial combination of stills and video images, audio and text. It would even be possible if we had organised it in advance to use some sort of satellite location device which could have given a sense of the exact route travelled on the map in real time.

Perhaps as systems like DRS (which is still at an experimental stage) become recognised tools, researchers will be able to weave together sequences giving more opportunity to examine the multi-sensorial features of research.

Acknowledgements

Digital Replay System illustration and details reproduced with permission of Nottingham University.

The development of DRS has been supported by ESRC and EPSRC grants: RES-149-25-0035 'Understanding New Forms of Digital Record for e-Social Science'; EP/C010078/1 'Semantic Media – Pervasive Annotation for e-Research'; GR/N15986/01 'Equator Interdisciplinary Research Collaboration'.

Licensing

Section II

Research practices in focus

Section II brings together essays by four visual researchers. Their detailed commentaries resonate with many of the issues and concerns discussed in the previous chapters, and go further, showing fully fledged research projects and their outcomes. These reflective essays offer insights into innovative visual practice: sources of inspiration, processes and designs, the tightrope of ethical and institutional constraints. The reflexivity of their work shows the researcher as a producer of images and visual narratives that are a means of understanding social reality within a challenging and shifting theoretical landscape.

At a recent Anthropology conference having projected up images of Sheffield and discussed the importance of looking more carefully at these everyday sights, I was asked the question 'So what?' We are saturated with images, anybody can take them, and we see them every day – what makes your images any more important? This is a good question. Visions of the city abound; there is an enormous and readily available resource (taking the Flickr repository as just one example). Perhaps the best response is that this very saturation is a reason to take them seriously, to help develop a critical respect for the image. We cannot avoid images but we do need to learn to look with discernment and be critical because of their power to convince, to hypnotise, to present a world which seems normal, while often disguising implicit political and economic motives. Further, the visual researcher must constantly strive for validity, recognising the shifting and varied cultural meanings of the image.

Images may be potentially narcoticising; Debord's everyday 'opium war' of the spectacle, without a critical appraisal which allows us to look beyond their surfaces. At the very least a critical sociology of the visual might yield insights into the everyday – the things that are *too* familiar, too close to home. This implicit dilemma of the image and image-based research is given an airing by each of the writers in this section. These authors examine facets of social life with freshness, innovation and a critical (politically attuned) eye, rather than adding to an avalanche of undifferentiated visual studies. How is this critical and political analysis achieved through imagery and what relationship do such readings have to the aesthetic sense of the visual?

These essays take the discussion of our relationship to the image (filmic or photographic) very seriously. There is often an uneasy relationship between discourses of art and the social scientist using a camera with the intention of penetrating the mundane surface of a society to analyse the social and political meanings manifest in the image; its institutional uses and its role in people's lives. However, without the aesthetic eye of the artist, the technical eye of the professional, the images we produce may lack coherency as visual evidence or the power to defamiliarise the everyday. Luc Pauwels, a key thinker and writer on visual research, speaking at a recent conference, suggested that some researchers are overlooking the 'vast expressive potential of visual representations' which can open up the way to much-needed scholarly debate and create new expressive opportunities for manifesting those things which are too elusive or subtle for language and elude measurement in any positivist fashion. In addition, Pauwels argues for a more technologically savvy research practice, but warns that this must be tempered with awareness that technology cannot resolve epistemological or ethical problems (Pauwels, 2010: 571–3).

Each of these four researchers combines a mastery of technical skills with subtle theoretical and philosophical discussion to show the expressive capacities of the visual to explore social issues. Panizza Allmark is a professional photographer who marries technical excellence with an understanding of the traditional aesthetics of urban documentary photography. In her piece 'Towards a *photographie féminine*: photography of the city', she carves out a practice between these lines; recognising the importance of her individual positionality; the significance of gender identity as an important mediating factor in the negotiated production and analysis of these urban visions. The resulting images highlight and allow contemplation of implicit contradictions in global culture: both sacred and profane, power and resistance, sights which break the boundaries of tacit social control.

Sarah Atkinson demonstrates a range of directorial skills in work which straddles several disciplinary boundaries. Her *Crossed Lines* project is an innovative enquiry into audience engagement. Nine original video pieces, each based on careful research to ensure the convincing realism of their separate contexts, were relayed through a multi-screen viewing environment. This ingenious, interactive format enabled the researcher to measure the amount of engagement viewers invested in each narrative and how they combined the stories creating their own composite narratives. This installation crosses boundaries between academic studies of audience to the exploration of an aesthetic of narrative and cinematic fiction.

At heart, Roger Brown's 'Photography as process, documentary photographing as discourse' presents a manifesto for photography. Brown seeks to integrate both technical and moral aspects of practice; combining an implicit care for the 'truth of the subject', ethical collaborative practice and concerns for quality of pictorial geometry, meaning, vision and lighting. This demanding, exploratory essay delves into hermeneutic philosophy. Brown's analysis of 'photographing' (illuminated by his diverse practice as a documentary photographer) outlines a convincing and finely grained analytical path, drawing on Ricoeur's discursive framework to bridge the hermeneutic divide between documentary photographing and nuances of language.

Finally, Roger Canals' 'Studying images through images' is concerned with the imagery associated with María Lionza, a Venezuelan folk icon whose features undergo transformation to meet the needs of different meaning systems in Venezuela's complex multiethnic society. Canals (an anthropologist and film-maker) demonstrates the importance of a reflexive study of these complex transformations as facets of global culture, but also the manner in which such an investigation might illuminate the methodology of visual research. Here is a robust defence of image-based research recognising the individual's active performative mediation in the research process; the camera as not only a means of recording but also of provoking events. Similarly the object of research guides the tools and direction of ethnographic study.

Drawing upon philosophy, visual anthropology, cultural studies and sociology, psychology, ethnography, media and communication theory, these essays provide a glimpse into the profound potential for visual research. Each author addresses the features of their chosen field of practice and explores the critical and analytical concerns which underpin and illuminate their work. There are lessons for all researchers here, not least that the passion for the subject which comes from each of these is an important prerequisite for the best research practice.

Towards a *photographie féminine*: photography of the city

Panizza Allmark

In my photography, I am interested in ways that the city can be both aestheticised and politicised. In my work I acknowledge that 'the photograph both mirrors and creates a discourse with the world, and is never, despite its often passive way with things, a neutral representation' (Clarke, 1997: 27–28). In my representations of the city I am attempting to develop a critical practice that acknowledges the cultural legacy of colonialism, capitalism, photography and the representation of gender, from a feminist position, rather than following a modernist practice concerned with the purely formal, 'visual' aesthetics that seek to promote masculine modalities of power, authority and distance. Hence, my photographs are a departure from the masculine landscape aesthetic traditions of the 'sublime' and the 'beautiful' according to Edmund Burke and Immanuel Kant, which promote the division between self and other. The allure of the site in this aesthetic tradition is that one is to stand back, be still, contemplate and 'appreciate' the scene. Rather than a place to see for the itinerant gazer my photographs of space involve the dynamic interaction of the place. My work is concerned with the commotion in public spaces in the city with particular emphasis on spaces of transition. Generally, my work focuses on places and artefacts we move past, but rarely stop to look at or engage with.

I am concerned with the gender politics of body and space, in particular drawing on the themes of the uncanny and the abject, which are aspects of society that have been repressed or excluded. Moreover, my work embraces a *photographie féminine,* drawn from the French feminist notion of *écriture féminine,* writing the feminine (body). Sellers (1996: 13), commenting on the work of French feminist theorist Helene Cixous, insists that '*écriture féminine* involves the inscription of that which is repressed within history and culture'. I am also following what Sellers (1996: 10) asserts might be 'the ultimate aim of *écriture féminine* which is to induce us to re-examine our connection to the world'.

My photographs explore notions of the 'everyday' and the 'uncanny' that may be construed as a feminist counter-aesthetic (Cixous, 1976; Giblett, 1996; Allmark, 2002, 2008a, 2008b). I read my work as presenting a feminist counter-aesthetic of the uncanny, which is an indeterminate and potentially ominous space. For example, according to Freud (1958: 153), the uncanny arouses dread and horror, 'a hidden, familiar thing that has undergone repression and then emerged'. Furthermore, the re-analysis of Freud's uncanny opens up possibilities for a feminist consideration of my photographs in exploring its resistance to submitting to the 'laws' of 'patriarchal binary thought' with its rigid boundaries, to an embracement of feminist concepts which allow for contradiction to co-exist and its attempt to uncover what is hidden and repressed.

As stated earlier, the photograph is not a 'neutral observation'. This also follows Trinh T. Minh-ha's (1993: 166) assertion that 'every spectator mediates a text to his or her own reality'. Nevertheless, as a photographer I am making overt decisions in what I choose to photograph and exhibit/publish, and most of my work that has been exhibited or published follows a feminist undercurrent, as such gender is the primary signifier. While I acknowledge that in the early twenty-first century, the term 'feminist' seems to be an 'unfashionable' label, this is due to the belief that as a result of socio-economic progress in Western society, it is a movement that is often seen as superfluous. This has certainly been my experience, as a lecturer in Photomedia over the past eight years. When I pose the question: 'Are you a feminist?' to the students at the commencement of the class, very rarely do I get more than three out of 20 students acknowledging that they hold any feminist views. The consensus seems to be that feminism is seen pejoratively and/or gender equality issues are no longer seen as relevant in our contemporary society. However, my visual work suggests otherwise.

The photographs that I produce are examples of how, as a Western, middle-class woman, I see the world. I follow the common features of feminist methodology as well as the characteristics of art/documentary photography, which includes an emphasis on the validity of personal experience as well as self-reflexivity, to attempt to convey the differing views of the world. In particular, I follow a range of (predominantly male) documentary photographers who while they have a topic of investigative research, tend to emphasise self-revelations and self-searches, along with intuitively knowing the right moment to photograph. Almost unanimously, photographers in the documentary tradition say that it is in a search for placing oneself that people find out who they are and how they are connected to each other. Style is necessary but secondary (Lacks, 1987: 35).

In foregrounding connections, my work presents binaries that co-exist, a perspective that challenges standard viewing points. My work is concerned with intertextuality. 'Intertextuality refers to the ways that the meaning of any one discursive image or text depends not only on that one text or image, but also on the meanings carried by other images and texts' (Rose, 2001: 79). The challenge lies in 'how to make the intertextual connections convincingly productive' (ibid.: 83). I endeavour to do this by evoking noise and pollution, in a political sense. My photographs attempt to cause a disturbance by bringing together disparate elements in the one visual frame. Borrowing the term 'dirt' from Mary Douglas (1966: 35), my work is littered with the concept of dirt as 'a matter out of place'. As such, it embraces the use of irony, the transgression of boundaries and the promotion of ambiguity. Furthermore, the images convey a sense of uncanny horror, a disruptive play and irony in terms of mainstream photographic conventions. For example, my visual work often focuses on what is unremarked, passed by and overlooked in the everyday street.

This documentary style, in particular, has its history in the early twentieth-century street photography of Paris by Eugene Atget. 'As a documentary project', Atget's almost 10,000 photographs were 'more comprehensive than anything previously attempted in European photography; in fact, Atget was the first photographer to undertake the description of a city in such detailed and extensive terms' (Lifson, 1980: 7). Furthermore, Atget's work was distinctive in the sense that he 'sees all his subjects in terms of metaphor' and it 'wasn't simply parks, statues, shops and so forth, but also images' (Atget cited in Lifson, 1980: 8). Benjamin (1979: 250) praises Atget's work, asserting that 'he looked for what was unremarked, forgotten, cast adrift, and thus such pictures, too, work against the exotic, romantically sonorous names of the cities'. It accomplishes what Benjamin (ibid.: 251) describes as 'the achievements of surrealist photography' which 'sets the scene for a salutary estrangement between man [*sic*] and his surroundings'.

I acknowledge that my photographs are similar on a stylistic level to Atget. I have admired his *oeuvre*. I certainly consider him a 'master' of photography and in my work I face the difficulty that Grundberg (1990: 196) identifies:

> For the documentary photographer today, there are at least two problems: to find a subject matter that has not already been exhausted by previous photographs; and to find a style that can maintain at least a medium of documentary authority without merely repeating the conventions of the documentary tradition.

Like Atget, I also try to work against the romantic and the exotic. My work, like Atget's, involves complexity, multiplicity, even contradictions. But, according to Lifson (1980: 7), 'Atget doesn't blur distinctions. He doesn't confuse the divine love of two Gothic angels with the profane love of prostitutes' – as I attempt to do similarly in my blurring of the sacred and the profane. Arguably, the streets of Paris in the early twentieth century were quite different from the dominion of acculturated images in the streets of contemporary cities, which gives me the opportunity to explore a wider diversity of subjects. But I consider my work is not about 'estrangement between "man" and his surroundings'; it is about my engagement with the scene; for example, in my street images I am a woman often facing images of 'woman' (in street advertising), and moreover, as a young woman photographer my presence on the street often attracts more attention. Hence, the notion of the *flâneur*, the male onlooker with the freedom of movement throughout the city is certainly a gendered privilege. From a feminist position it is not simply a matter of changing the term '*flâneur*' to '*flâneuse*' to acknowledge the presence of women on the street, because *flânerie* involves privileging of the gaze, which is a masculine modality and does not provide a space for a feminine mode of interaction. Massey (1994: 234) suggests that there could not be a female *flâneur* because, although a *flâneur* observed others, he was not observed. Furthermore, the *flâneur's* gaze was frequently erotic and on the look-out for sexual conquests. In this understanding the male is seen as the strategic protagonist.

Following de Certeau (1985: 127) in his discussion of practices of space, my work concerning public spaces also involves tactics that 'play upon "opportunities", catch occurrences, and the opacities of history' rather than a strategic practice which may be considered masculine and connotes a history of militarisation and organisational and institutional control. Tactics are 'a way of operating available to people displaced and excluded as "other" by the bordering actions of strategy' (Morris, 1992: 33). As such, the photographic approach involves tactics that seek to disrupt the masculine strategic hold of public space. The masculine hold of public space is related to the structured, official, linear vision of city, whereas these (feminist and subversive) tactics are characterised by a degree of uncertainty and indeterminacy. They operate on the 'fringes' of social order and seem to offer a capacity to recombine heterogeneous elements of culture.

One of my photographic tactics is to convey the uncanny through reframing found images, and hence disturb and reveal what is often repressed. In the processing of reframing, or incorporating a picture within a picture, it aims to destabilise the masculine 'realm of pleasure' of the gaze, in order to move beyond the limiting visual boundaries of the image. The longest and broadest project (over ten years) I have been engaged with is a series of images taken from various cities across the world, such as Rome, Istanbul, Perth, Singapore and London, of images of sexualised women that are found on the pavements of the city. But re-photographed in their found context, it suggests their pervasiveness as well as highlighting the female status as discarded commodities, as 'abjects of affection'. It is also an attempt to destabilise the aforementioned 'erotic' nature of the *flâneur*'s gaze at the sexualised women. Pictured within a wider perspective, the boundary edges are metaphorically blurred and the found images are photographed in a broader, sometimes contradictory cultural context. This approach of bringing together disparate elements is similar to what Steve Spencer, drawing upon Benjamin's notion of the dialectical image, asserts: 'there are dialectical images everywhere when the mind and eye is attuned to the inherent paradoxes and the multiple social realities which stir between the crumbling, over-layered facades and the sleek seamless surfaces of the city' (Spencer, Chapter 3).

An example of this form of dialectic image, which evokes the uncanny, is my photograph of the exterior of a small wedding chapel in Las Vegas (Figure 1). In the photograph the collision between the sacred and the profane can be found in the pornography stand situated outside the chapel. In the foreground, the stand contains a number of magazines with images advertising female sexual services. It represents females as a commodity. In terms of the placement of pornographic material available in the vicinity of a religious site, the photograph combines the sacred and secular.

The church is reminiscent of a Protestant country church; it is white, with a steeple and crucifix. It signifies simple Puritan family values such as community, tradition and conservatism. In the photograph, the doors of the chapel are closed; the outside lights of the building are on, which suggests that a religious service is taking place within the confines of the building. It is therefore sacred and private. This type of church is often a model for wedding cakes and therefore invested with the 'positive' values of heterosexual romance leading to marriage and monogamy. The wedding chapel is situated amongst grand scale resort hotels, elements of which can be seen near the edges of the photographic frame. Venturi

Figure 1 Las Vegas, 1999.

(1998) in his analysis of the architecture of Las Vegas considers that allusion and comment on the past or present, or on our great commonplaces or old clichés, are evident in the city of Las Vegas. This represents a postmodern pastiche; it is kitsch and is a kind of aesthetic populism.

My framing of the pornographic magazine stand juxtaposed with the white chapel suggests an 'anxious' ambiguity of traditional boundaries between the sacred and the profane. The framing disturbs the aesthetics of the chapel and is shadowed by the uncanny presence of the stand. In the pornography stand, which is a blue box, there were magazine images of commodified female sexuality on display behind glass. The stand consists of advertisements for sexual services. Young, scantily clad women in highly provocative poses gaze out longingly from the brochure covers. It is situated for full public access and visibility. The 'pure' Protestant values invested in the chapel, which are juxtaposed with the pornographic images, represent the divergence between ideas of expressions of female sexuality. Even the colours of the two constructions are in contrast: the white of the chapel represents innocence and purity, whereas the dark blue is connotative of 'blue' movies, the underworld and the forbidden. Paglia (1990: 34) claims that our pagan past is based on cultic exhibitionism. She asserts that 'pornography is pure pagan imagism' which is now commodified and reproduced mechanically. According to Paglia's interpretation of pornography, the photograph of Las Vegas represents the conflict between the Judeo-Christian religion that has sought to ban pornography, as well as paganism which Christianity has tried to suppress. Pornographic, clichéd images of female sexuality and the advertising of female sexual services less than ten metres from a chapel challenge the notion of what is considered a proper viewing act in public. It reflects a breakdown of traditional aesthetic, sexual and spatial boundaries.

Other examples of the highlighting of disparate elements are in a couple of images taken in New York.

In an image taken on Wall Street (Figure 2), the uniformed sailors are juxtaposed with the image of the free-spirited rock-and-roll image of male individuality in the fashion advert for 'True Religion'. In the image, opposing binaries are brought together. For example, there is conformity versus individuality, and the 'freedom' of the city versus the regulation of the naval service. Nevertheless, both are dependent on each other for the survival and protection of the city. Similarly, in another image (Figure 3) the notions of the armed forces and being armed with shopping bags are brought together. Military and commerce are united. The photographs play with the idea of the freedom to shop and the defence of freedom within the so-called 'land of the free'. The two images draw attention to issues of capitalism, gender and masculinity, in the city.

Gendered issues could also be associated with the use of the camera. The camera may be described as a weapon and this is particularly evident in the notion of the camera as a gun in which it is a predatory weapon in the act of aiming, focusing and shooting. For example, early twentieth-century safari photographer Carl Akeley said that he set out to design a camera 'that you can aim . . . with about the same ease that you can point a pistol' (cited in Haraway, 1989: 42).

Figure 2 New York (No. 1), 1999.

Figure 3 New York (No. 2), 1999.

Furthermore, 'he enjoyed retelling the apocryphal story of seven Germans mistakenly surrendering to one American when they found themselves faced by an Akeley' (ibid.: 43).

As a women photographer on the street, one is seen as less threatening than a male with a camera. It is more likely that passersby will approach you and want to talk to you. Often, they may be curious about your choice of framing or will simply invite you to take their photograph. Though, there are always ethical considerations when taking photographs, and I have made a point of not photographing people unless permission is granted and they want their image taken, or cannot be identified easily in the image, or alternatively are engaging in a form of public display. I therefore use a wide-angle or standard lens when working, which engages in personal space, rather than a telephoto zoom lens where there is a greater physical distance (and anonymity) of the photographer spying on the object prey, as in the analogy of the camera as a gun. In my picturing of events, such as the ones mentioned, there is always the issue of ethics. The photographs that I produced may be deemed to be 'concerned photography' because they attempt to convey features of the humanist paradigm of subjective documentary, such as a sense of empathy or complicity with the subject of representation.

I wouldn't accept that the camera is only a weapon, because this entails aggression. Therefore, in my photographic practice I consider the camera as a defensive utensil against loss of subjectivity, rather than an offensive weapon. Indeed, it is through the transitory moments of travel and the play of perspectives with the use of the camera that I present a dialectic of vision, concerning self and others. The dialectic allows 'the superimposition of fleeting images, present and past' that makes 'both suddenly come alive in terms of revolutionary meaning' (Buck-Morss, 1989: 220).

Much of my street documentary photography has also concerned the notion of protest in public spaces, hence alluding to the notion of the uncanny and its disturbing qualities. My documentary photographs in the context of public squares may be related to the feminised notion in relation to concept of the chora. Elizabeth Grosz (1995: 51) asserts, chora 'is the space in which place is made possible'. It is a place of interactions. For example, in the series of images of the man standing on a statue in Trafalgar Square (Figure 4) the physical dialogue or interaction between him, the crowd and myself is recorded. The man's relation with the 'world', and his momentary dominance and control, is expressed in his body language and positioning on the crown of the lion's head, which is also a symbol of strength. The man standing on the lion represents his supremacy over the 'king of the jungle'.

One of my first observations was as follows:

> Standing defiantly on the crown of a statue of a lion in Trafalgar Square, London, a young man with his fists clenched and arms raised together high above his head addresses the crowds beneath him. He turns towards me and we exchange looks. He gently smiles, waves, bows down and seductively

Figure 4 London, 1999.

blows me a kiss . . . he notices my camera, he repeats the gesture . . . I take another photograph.

(18 June 1999)

In terms of mastery, the man displays machismo in his stance, and his dominant position over the lion is emblematic of patriarchy. The display of his body and his bare chest resists the conformity of the clothed bodies beneath him. He subverts the western bourgeois standards of middle-class public decorum and in his dominant posture is expressing Western notions of 'primal' power of the 'primitive' or tribal male. His final gesture towards me represents a display of sexuality. It highlights my feminine presence and the significance of gender relations in social discourse.

A solitary white male facing the landscape is also a masculine, romantic notion which conveys the divide between self and other. The landscape is to be dominated. In the context of the anti-capitalist rally, his actions, both symbolically and physically, represent an act of defiance against passive bourgeois norms. This reading is particularly relevant because the image was taken as part of a series of images at the J18 anti-capitalist rally in Trafalgar Square in 1999. It is highly significant because the square as a major 'tourist attraction' of London has an historical importance as a 'strategic' place.

Street protests are a vital way of attracting public support and media attention to a cause. However, the sensationalist popular media tends to focus tendentiously on images of violence and conflict that are often there to 'shock, titillate, but never to challenge or to raise questions' (Webster, 1980: 221). Images of violence at demonstrations 'invite the public as a whole to regard all such "protest" as strategically pointless and personally dangerous' (Barnett, 2000: 52).

In contrast to the documentation of the 'strategic' practice of photojournalism, my *photographie féminine* concerned the *tactical* carnivalesque aspects. Bakhtin's (1984) notion of the carnivalesque, elaborated by literary theorists, is a form of cultural resistance. It is something that is developed when the performances twist, mutate, and invert standard themes of societal make-up. It involves focusing and picturing elements that convey some form of tension, either through performance, and/or interesting juxtapositions within the photographic frame. Isaak (1996: 20) insists that the carnivalesque 'is an instrument not only for a feminist analysis of texts, but also for feminist artistic production and cultural politics in general'.

Acts of defiance, or to reiterate the concept, a 'matter out of place' in which a space is transformed from the everyday to something extra, is a resonant theme in my work. My images of the madres of the Plaza de Mayo, in Buenos Aires, Argentina, also attempt to foreground the uncanny. These are images of the mothers and grandmothers of those victims of the military (the lost loved ones called 'Desaparecidos', or disappeared ones) have met and protested every Thursday afternoon since the mid-1970s. As Antonius Robben asserts, 'the existing patriarchal structure that valorised motherhood with the "insistence upon the woman's sacrifice for and obedience to the family and to her children" had "backfired on the military as women have demanded to know what has happened to their sons and daughters"' (Robben, 2007: 261). My photographs attempt to express their sense of empowerment and taking over of public space. The women 'are an example of sustained collective action that has little precedent in Latin America and the world in general' (Bosco, 2001: 313). In my photographs, gender and generational identities are in focus. The older matriarchal woman in the street may also be seen as reclaiming space, and challenges the notion of the mothers' relegation to the home, to the secluded domestic sphere (Allmark, 2002: 5).

There have been various outcomes of my visual work: as well as being used for teaching resources, I have published photo-essays and critical pieces, such as journal articles and book chapters drawing together a cultural studies approach to the reading of images. My images are placed within wider discourses to illustrate trends in critical inquiry. For example, in my academic article 'Flagging Australia: photographs of banal nationalism', I was interested in 'how a sense of place and national identity are continually being flagged in the aesthetics of

Figure 5 Buenos Aires (No. 1), 2008.

Figure 6 Buenos Aires (No. 2), 2008.

Australian contemporary consumer culture' (Allmark, 2007: 1). As a photographer and researcher it has been crucial to be able to articulate my practice, but an approach which presents some challenges. For example, at times my photography is instinctual. I merely take a photograph because I find the subject interesting. The challenge lies in delving deeper into what makes the subject and photograph interesting. How does it conform to what has been done before? How does it build upon, comment on, and develop wider critical inquiry? The highly constructive nature of photography to create a differing 'reality' opens up the possibility of the 'third effect'. A 'third effect' meaning can be generated from the juxtaposition of the image, with text or other images, which was not inherent in the image seen in isolation (Walker, 1997: 56).

Most of my work has been exhibited in art exhibitions. Within the art forum at times it tends to lose its textual political base, as images are open to be read in many ways, and the images may be rendered within a passive aesthetic status. However, through networking, I have been invited to exhibit work in conjunction with cultural studies conferences or events. An example of this is a solo exhibition titled 'Visual Love Categories' held in conjunction with the Australian Women's and Gender Studies Association Conference in Perth, 2008. The theme of the conference was vision, memory and spectacle and the work combined with the theme 'beautifully', and was intended to bring artistic stimulation (Baker, 2008). Another example where my images worked in collaboration with a conference is the 'Interrogating Trauma Media and Art Responses International Conference', in which the images of the Madres of the Plaza de Mayo as well as a series of images taken after the London Bombings (2005) were displayed. The opportunity to present work and artist talks in the gallery space enables my work to be seen

on a larger visual scale, thus drawing attention to the uncanny in magnified propor-
tions, and following a tenet of *photographie féminine* of the re-examination of our
connection to the world. My overall visual methodology, which requires engagement in capturing a mood, as well as framing interesting juxtapositions, conveys
dialectical images that pose questions, rather than presenting answers. It is about
contemplation of the world we live in rather than confirmation of how it is.

References

Allmark, P. (2002) 'Urban exposures. Transformations: regions, culture and society', 5.
　　Online. Available HTTP: <http://www.cqu.edu.au/transformations>, (accessed 28
　　December 2009).
Allmark, P. (2007) 'Flagging Australia: photographs of banal nationalism', *Illumina*, 2.
　　Online. Available HTTP: <http://illumina.scca.ecu.edu.au/journal_view.php?rec_id=
　　0000000041>, (accessed 28 December 2009),
Allmark, P. (2008a) 'Framing Plaza de Mayo: photographs of protest', *Continuum:
　　Journal of Media and Cultural Studies*, 22, 6 December 2008.
Allmark, P. (2008b) 'Traversing one's space: photography and the feminine', in
　　G. Backhaus and J. Murungi (eds) *Symbolic Landscapes. Geographical Sensibilities
　　in the Arts*, Dordrecht, London: Springer.
Baker, J. (2008) 'Vision, memory, spectacle', Report presented at the Australian Women's
　　and Gender Studies Association conference. *Outskirts: Feminisms Along the Edge*, 19.
　　Online. Available HTTP: <http://www.chloe.uwa.edu.au/outskirts/archive/volume
　　19/baker> (accessed 28 December 2009).
Bakhtin, M. (1984) *Rabelais and his World* (translated by H. Iswolsky), Bloomington:
　　Indiana University Press.
Barnett, B. (2000) 'Why radicals need a history lesson', *The Ecologist*, 30(5): 52–53.
Benjamin, W. (1979) 'A small history of photography', in his *One Way Street* (pp.
　　240–57), London: Verso.
Bosco, F. J. (2001) 'Place, pace, networks, and the sustainability of collective action. The
　　Madres de Plaza de Mayo', *Global Networks*, 1(4): 307–27.
Buck-Morss, S. (1989) *The Dialectics of Seeing: Walter Benjamin and the Arcades
　　Project*, Cambridge, Mass: MIT Press.
Cixous, H. (1976) 'Fiction and its phantoms: a reading of Freud's "Das unheimliche"',
　　New Literary History, 7: 525–48.
Clarke, G. (1997) *The Photograph*, Oxford: Oxford University Press, pp. 27–33. Also
　　online as 'How do we read a photograph?' Available HTTP: <http://www.aber.ac.
　　uk/media/Modules/MC10220/reading_photos.html> (accessed 28 December 2009).
de Certeau, M. (1985) 'Practices of space', in M. Blonsky (ed.) *On Signs* (pp.122–45),
　　Oxford: Blackwell.
Douglas, M. (1966). *Purity and Danger: An Analysis of the Concepts of Pollution and
　　Taboo*, London: Ark.
Freud, S. (1958) 'The uncanny', in his *On Creativity and the Unconscious: Papers on the
　　Psychology of Art, Literature, Love, Religion* (pp. 122–61), New York: Harper & Row.
Giblett, R. (1996) *Postmodern Wetlands: Culture, History, Ecology*, Edinburgh: Edinburgh
　　University Press.
Giblett, R. (2000) 'Shooting the event: the camera as a gun', paper presented at the Ethics,
　　Events, Entertainment Conference, Southern Cross University, 3–5 July.

Grosz, E. (1995) 'Women, chora, dwelling', in S. Watson and K. Gibson (eds) *Postmodern Cities & Spaces* (pp. 47–58), Oxford: Blackwell.

Grundberg, A. (1990) *Crisis of the Real: Writings on Photography*, New York: Aperture Foundation.

Haraway, D. (1989) 'Teddy bear patriarchy in the garden of Eden', in her *Primate Visions: Gender, Race, and Nature in the World of Modern Science* (pp. 26–58), New York: Routledge.

Isaak, J. (1996) *Feminism and Contemporary Art: The Revolutionary Power of Women's Laughter*, New York: Routledge.

Lacks, C. (1987) 'Documentary photography: a way of looking at ourselves', unpublished PhD thesis, Saint Louis University, Saint Louis.

Lifson, B. (1980) 'Introduction', in *Eugene Atget* (pp. 1–9), New York: Aperture.

Massey, D. (1994) *Space, Place and Gender*, Cambridge: Polity Press.

Morris, M. (1992) 'Great moments in social climbing: King Kong and the human fly', in B. Colomina (ed.) *Sexuality and Space* (pp. 1–52), New York: Princeton Architectural Press.

Paglia, C. (1990) *Sexual Personae*, London, New Haven: Yale University Press.

Robben, A.C.G.M. (2007) 'Mourning and mistrust in civil–military relations in post-Dirty War Argentina', in F. Ferrandiz and A.C.G.M. Robben (eds) *Multidisciplinary Perspectives on Peace and Conflict Research* (pp. 253–70), Bilbao: University of Deusto.

Rose, G. (1993) *Feminism and Geography: The Limits of Geographical Knowledge*, Cambridge, Mass.: Polity Press.

Rose, G. (2001) *Visual Methodologies: An Introduction to the Interpretation of Visual Materials*, London: Sage.

Sellers, S. (1996) *Hélène Cixous: Authorship, Autobiography and Love*, Cambridge: Polity Press.

Spencer, S. (2009) 'Drifting visions & dialectical images: everyday paradoxes in a northern city', *Illumina*, 3. Online. Available HTTP: http://illumina.scca.ecu.edu.au/ (accessed 28 December 2009).

Trinh T. Minh-ha. (1993) 'All-owning spectatorship', in S. Gunew and A. Yeatman (eds) *Feminism and The Politics of Difference* (pp. 157–76), St Leonards, NSW: Allen & Unwin.

Venturi, R. (1998) *Learning from Las Vegas: The Forgotten Symbolism of Architectural Form*, Cambridge, Mass.: MIT Press.

Walker, P.J. (1997) 'Documentary photography in the postmodern era', unpublished thesis, Doctor of Art, New York University.

Webster, F. (1980). *The New Photography: Responsibility in Visual Communication*, New York: Riverrun.

Multiple cameras, multiple screens, multiple possibilities: an insight into the interactive film production process

Sarah Atkinson

Summary

Crossed Lines (Dir: Sarah Atkinson) is an original fictional interactive film amalgamating multi-linear plots, a multi-screen viewing environment, an inter-active interface and an interactive story navigation form. It has been exhibited at the Electronic Literature Organisation conference at Washington State University, US; the Digital Interactive Media in Arts and Entertainment conference arts show in Athens; The Interrupt arts show in Providence, US; the EuroITV arts show in Belgium and the International Digital Interactive Storytelling conference in Portugal. This essay reflects upon the creative processes of devising, scripting, directing and authoring the interactive film installation in which the viewer is given control over the flow, pace and ordering of the video-based narratives. The entire production process from script-writing to the final installation took place over a four-year period and involved nine principal cast members, numerous crew personnel, technicians, programmers, various cameras, audio-recording equip-ment, cutting-edge computer processors, reams of cable and a precariously soldered telephone. The complexities of undertaking and delivering such a project are reflected upon and discussed within this essay from the first-person perspective of the artist herself.

Introduction

Crossed Lines constituted the practice element of my doctoral thesis, which I began in 2002 with the initial idea that I wanted to create an interactive film artwork that broke new ground and moved beyond all that had gone before it within the field. My primary method of enquiry into interactive cinema was practice-based. That is, that the research expression would be the artwork itself alongside the reflection and findings that would emanate from the direct experi-ence of the creative process and the subsequent audience responses. Practice-based research PhDs have become commonplace in art, design, creative media, performance, humanities and new media disciplines within which the researcher's own practice is foregrounded as the primary method. The bottom-line assumption of this approach is the notion that new knowledge can be generated through an artist's practice. This is not a new concept within the realm of teaching and learning. In 1934 the scholar Dewey stated:

> The sense of increase in understanding, of a deepened intelligibility on the part of objects, of nature and man resulting from aesthetic experience, has led philosophic theorists to treat art as a mode of knowledge and has induced artists, especially poets, to regard art as a mode of revelation of the inner nature of things that cannot be had in any other way.
>
> (1934: 300)

Crossed lines: influences and inspiration

Crossed Lines is a multi-plot film telling the stories of nine characters in a way that the viewer can constantly explore and switch between all nine characters and their associated narratives, and can simultaneously witness the presence of all of the characters between their nine remote locations (see Figure 1). The starting point of this unique piece was to conceive a series of compelling narratives that could be viewed as individual stories, but would also reference and link to the other stories, as is the case of the multi-plot film genre. As McKee has noted: 'multi-plot films never develop a central plot; rather they weave together a number of stories of subplot size' (1998: 227). The difference with *Crossed Lines* is that it is delivered through an interactive interface paradigm, meaning that viewers have the power to navigate and order the stories themselves, and to create a story of varying complexity depending on the number of different characters which are selected through the interface. In 1987, Joyce and Bolter imagined fictions in which:

Figure 1 The *Crossed Lines* screen presentation: all nine screens are visible throughout the film.

> Stability and certainty . . . disappear (and) there may no longer be one plot
> but several, and characters may no longer develop in a consistent fashion.
> The structure and rhythm of the text will be different for each reading (with)
> every element . . . subject to electronic fragmentation and reconfiguration.
>
> (1987: 130)

It was these imagined fictions that I wanted to attempt to realise within my research practice. Throughout the creation of the film, I drew on many influences and sources of inspiration. Some of these derived from multi-form films, which have been explored extensively in the contemporary commercial cinematic realm. For example, a groundbreaking film such as *Shortcuts* (1993, Dir: Robert Altman) traces the actions of 22 principal characters, both in parallel and at occasional points of connection. In *Magnolia* (1999, Dir: Paul Thomas Anderson), nine separate yet connected storylines are investigated. *Run Lola Run* (1999, Dir: Tom Tykwer) depicts three alternate realities triggered by the same event. Filmic examples in which the narrative has included multiple points of view of the same events include *Rashomon* (1950, Dir: Akira Kurosawa). Other influences to *Crossed Lines* have been films using complex and non-linear time structures such as *Memento* (2001, Dir: Christopher Nolan), which is a story told in two separate narratives; the first is a series of black and white scenes shown in chronological order which is intercut with the second, a series of colour scenes which are presented in reverse chronological order; the two narratives converge at the film's climax. Influences also stem from multi-screen presentations. The split screen has been used on numerous occasions throughout cinematic history in which to show two sides of a telephone conversation simultaneously. Perhaps the first example of this was in 1901 in Williamson's *Are You There?* (Salt, 1983: 57). Other notable examples of the use of split screen include *Napoleon* (1927, Dir: Abel Gance) in which three images, a triptych, were projected side by side, in a format that Gance called Polyvision, *The Boston Strangler* (1968, Dir: Richard Fleischer), *The Thomas Crown Affair* (1968, Dir: Norman Jewison), *Numero Deux* (1975, Dir: Jean Luc Godard) and *The Pillow Book* (1996, Dir: Peter Greenaway). Andy Warhol's *Chelsea Girls* (1966) continually consisted of two images side-by-side, the audio switching from left to right for the duration of the film. This aesthetic, in part due to developments in digital non-linear editing and postproduction technologies, has led us to 'an epoch of simultaneity: we are in the epoch of juxtaposition, the epoch of near and far, of the side-by-side, of the dispersed' (Foucault, 1997).

An explosion of this use of the multi-screen in fiction film occurred in the late 1990s and early 2000s including *Run Lola Run* (1998, Dir: Tom Twyker), *Requiem for a Dream* (2000, Dir: Darren Aronofsky), *My Little Eye* (2002, Dir: Marc Evans), *The Laramie Project* (2002, Dir: Moises Kaufman) and *Hulk* (2003, Dir: Ang Lee). As Talen has noted, 'the splintered aesthetic of multi-channel storytelling – once the province of the '60's avant-garde – is suddenly every-where' (2002). In addition to technological innovation, the proliferation of this aesthetic has also been attributed to 'both surveillance imaging and internet technology that has possibly been the most prominent aesthetic influence to date'

(Griffiths, 2003: 19). In the documentary *Surveillance* (1993, Dir: Chris Petit) 'Petit breaks the panoptic illusion by inserting the possibility of doubt, multiplicity, and contradiction into the experience of real time vision' (Murri, 2002).

This is evident in *Timecode* (2001, Dir: Mike Figgis), which presents the film on a screen split into quarters, and involves 20 characters whose screen space and stories overlap and shift throughout the 90-minute feature, which was shot by four cameras in real time. It is perhaps the observational and improvised style of the acting and the handheld filming in which this sense of surveillance is most defined. TV drama series, which have also adopted this aesthetic, have been the UK's *Trial and Retribution* (2002) and *24* (2002) in the US. Director Stephen Hopkins says he first got the idea for *24* because 'there were so many phone calls in the script that these people would never share any screen time together . . . I loved the idea of showing what people were saying on the phone but also what they didn't want other people to see' (Talen, 2002).

Innovative interactive film presentations have also been created through cinematic, DVD and computer interfaces. The viewer of such content 'is thus no longer merely an observer but a user of the film' (Himmelsbach, 2003: 236). Interactive interfaces have become commonplace within the DVD mode of delivery. Films such as *My Little Eye* (2002, Dir: Mark Evans) have been presented in an alternative screen interface on DVD, in this case through a web browser to effectively enhance the narrative, which is centred on a reality webcast. Interactive story navigation systems have also been delivered on DVD where the format's architecture allows 'additional content to be embedded into the experience of watching a feature film, similar to hyperlinks within a web page' (Atkinson, 2007: 22). One such example, *Tender Loving Care* (2000, Dir: David Wheeler) allows the viewer to navigate and witness alternative content dependent on questions that they answer after each chapter of the film. These types of films in both their content and story design in the former examples, and in their form in the latter, challenge the dominant conventions of traditional classical film, and are far removed from 'normative diegetic exposition' (Grieb, 2002: 157). It is precisely within this exciting context, created by the artistic and innovative deployment of new media technologies within cinema, that the conception of *Crossed Lines* was posited.

Crossed lines: the installation

Crossed Lines is presented on a large-scale monitor showing nine screens of simultaneous video (see Figure 6), which is controlled by the use of a physical telephone interface. The nine numerical buttons of the telephone keypad mirror the layout of the nine video screens, establishing a firm visual relationship between the interface and screen (see Figure 2). A familiar, simple and efficient user interface is used intentionally since it is a ubiquitous piece of hardware that can be operated intuitively, with no or very minimal instruction for the user. As McLuhan states, 'the telephone demands complete participation' (1997: 267) and is 'an irresistible intruder in time or place' (ibid.: 271).

Figure 2 The *Crossed Lines* telephone interface: the telephone keys numbered 1–9 simply map on to the nine screens.

In *Crossed Lines*, the user presses one of the keys (numbers 1–9), and the result of their action is then immediately apparent on the corresponding screen in that a dramatic action is triggered; for example, a phone rings or someone walks into frame, thus giving the operator an immediate sense of user agency. The user listens to the audio and dialogue through the telephone earpiece. In technical terms, what the user's key press actually activates is a switch in video streams. The corresponding screen (numbered 1–9 in exactly the same way the phone keys are positioned; the numbers run chronologically from left to right, top to bottom) changes to a new scene, as does one or more of the other screens depending on which characters are in conversation. This is consistent throughout the entire piece. It is therefore apparent to the user early on in the experience that they are ordering and constructing the narrative. The software works in such a way that the scenes are chronologically ordered for reasons of narrative coherence, and once a scene has been viewed, it is no longer accessible to the viewer. On the nine screens, the user is faced by nine characters, each of whom are seen or will be seen as the narrative progresses, on the telephone, and then communicating with one another solely through the use of the telephone. The approach taken to the production of the installation was to purposefully heighten and enhance the experience of the multiple narratives; and to encourage user engagement and immersion.

> With the telephone, there occurs the extension of ear and voice that is a kind of extra sensory perception. With television came the extension of the sense of touch or sense of interplay that even more intimately involves the entire sensorium.
>
> (McLuhan, 1997: 266)

The comparison to the television implied here is of note, since the aspect ratio of the screen is more akin to a television set and its 4:3 dimensions than it is to a

16:9 cinema screen. The use of DV also contributes to the installation's televisual aesthetic. The mode of viewing and interaction is also a contributing factor to this:

> the possibility of simultaneously observing a few images that co-exist within one screen can be compared with the phenomenon of zapping – the quick switching of television channels that allows the viewer to follow more than one programme.
>
> (Manovich, 2001: 97)

The nature of the technologies that were deployed within the creative process clearly influenced and affected the narrative direction and approaches to the development of the interactive film. Similarly, the approach taken to the script-writing process shaped the form and presentation of *Crossed Lines.*

Process: script-writing

This process was undertaken over the course of a year. Initial research and character preparation involved interviewing a telephone Samaritan, a telephone psychic, and various people who had worked in call-centres. I purposefully wanted to maintain realism, actuality and believability within the narratives. The writing of the screenplay was approached by first developing nine identifiable and clearly defined characters and then by mapping the various different and complex relationships between them. Contrasting character types were strategically chosen and developed. Action between the characters was broken down into scenes or 'conversations' – the motivation point of the commencement of each scene/conversation is signalled by a telephone ring (which in the interactive presentation is actually triggered by the viewer's key press), and is punctuated at the end by a character's telephone being put down. It was essential to structure the narrative segments in this way; as O'Meara has observed, 'every experience in an interactive ought to be a tiny story or scene. Even if it's short, it still needs to have a beginning, middle and end' (Garrand, 1997: 76). Given the problems that can arise within a potentially fractured viewing experience, in what has been scripted as a fully formed narrative, the challenge of ensuring that viewers received essential expositional elements was paramount.

> The same information will have to appear in a number of different scenes, but it can't be presented in exactly the same way or the player will become bored with hearing it on repeated viewings. Instead, the writer has to feed the essential information into all the possible story tracks but do it differently each time.
>
> (Garrand, 1997: 76)

The conversations are by their very nature 'dialogue-heavy', since characters are inclined to explicitly state their intentions while conversing on the telephone. The usual screen-writing rule of using 'visual before aural' indicators (Costello,

2004: 82) does not necessarily apply in this instance, especially given the fact that the conventional cinematic tools such as camera movement, shot changes, non-diegetic sound and music are also absent. Costello encourages the writer to omit unnecessary dialogue, if the same information can be given visually, but this economical approach to language was not appropriate given the nature of all the scenes and the emphasised actuality of the piece. Cinematic codes and conventions are once again not appropriate, again arguably making the piece more like television in its form, content and potential reception.

In terms of approaching the formatting of the script, Friedman claims that 'no clearly defined format has come to the fore such as those that exist for the film and television worlds' (2006: 266), and Handler Miller asserts that 'formats for interactive scripts vary widely. Sometimes they resemble the format for feature films, but incorporate instructions for interactive situations' (2004: 197). Wimberley and Samsel have conceded that there may never be a universal format since 'the power and promise of interactive multi-media are that it shifts control to the end-user' and 'unlike feature films, multi-media titles have unique and varied structures depending on its category or purpose' (1995: x). In the case of *Crossed Lines* a traditional scripting format was followed, then additional elements not present in traditional scripts were employed to identify the scene numbers. These scene numbers precede the master scene line in every instance as shown in the script excerpt below. The first digit refers to the grid number in which the scene is visible, and the second is a shooting script number, to identify the sequence of scenes to be shot during the principal photography stage.

In each we see a character.

1.1   INT. JAMES' OFFICE – DAY
James sits at a candlelit desk, next to a telephone, shuffling a deck of tarot cards.

2.2   INT. MARTIN'S OFFICE – DAY – SAME
Martin is in a darkened attic room; the light of a computer screen illuminates his face as he frantically taps into a keyboard; he stares intently at the computer screen, biting his lip and concentrating.

3.3   INT. JULIE'S CAR – DAY – SAME
Julie is driving along in a car in an inner-city setting. She taps, sings and dances in her seat to an upbeat house track playing on the radio.

4.4   INT. MANDY'S OFFICE – DAY – SAME
Mandy is sitting at a desk in a very tatty office environment next to a telephone. She is chewing gum, which she pulls in and out of her mouth with her fingers.

While a viewer is witnessing a conversation, action continues in each of the remaining 'non-conversational' frames: we see the other characters in looped action, waiting for a call or going about their business. For each scene it was therefore essential that all nine screens were scripted in the way shown above, even if there was no dialogue for a particular character. A description of the action going on within their screen was essential, since, dependent on the point in time in the story, the characters in the non-conversational frames would be waiting in a different way, which would be indicative of their current narrative stage and psychological state in their own narrative journeys. In screen seven, for example, Gary, the inhabitant of the phone box, becomes increasingly agitated as the narrative progresses as he either swigs from a bottle of neat rum or props himself against the phone. Similarly Julie, in screen three, stranded in her broken-down car, becomes visibly anxious as night falls: her camera switches to night vision as the light levels lower, increasing the sense of user surveillance. The viewer witnesses her increased anxiety as she is unknowingly, telephonically stalked by Martin, the character who inhabits his phone-hacking world within screen five.

In form and presentation, the script appears as any other, but this is only a hint at the final film, as it cannot encompass all of the narrative possibilities. The variation in order and structure of the script is set in motion by the viewer's various interactions. The script included a visual guide indicating the layout and the corresponding numbering of the scenes to enable those working on the project to have a greater understanding of the structure of the piece. As Friedman states, 'writing for interactive media will require a new layout to accommodate not only more elements of media production but also the non-linear form and the interactive possibilities of the program' (2006: 254).

Process: production

All scenes were shot in the months of June and July 2003. Each character was shot individually in separate locations (see Figures 3, 4 and 5). The actors heard the dialogue to respond to through a hidden earpiece. In later shoots, the actors heard the pre-recorded dialogue through the earpiece, which they then had to respond to in complete synchronicity. This posed a unique challenge since dialogue had to fit exactly and the overlapping of speech had to be avoided in order to eliminate any postproduction manipulation. The choice of a static locked-off camera in all nine scenes provided consistency; each of the frames needed to be similar in both composition and shot size and action needed to be relatively equal, so that no one frame was favoured, and viewers could not be influenced in their selections on this basis. This was a conceptual and thematic decision and functioned as a narrative device since the locked-off and passive camera connotes surveillance. The theme of surveillance is also prevalent in the use of the viewer's listening or eavesdropping device; the telephone handset. This is also emphasised in the fact that *Crossed Lines* does not break the 'fourth wall convention' which differentiates it from many examples of interactive narratives whereby the user is directly addressed by a character in a call-to-action scenario; examples include *I'm Your Man* (1992, Dir: Bob Bejan)

Figure 3 Crossed Lines in production: the construction of the set for the character in screen 7.

Tender Loving Care (1997: Dir: David Wheeler) and *Stab in the Dark* (2001, Dir: David Landau). The convention stipulates 'that actors treat the open stage as a fourth wall without betraying any awareness of being observed, [which] places the spectator in a voyeuristic position' (Stam, 1985).The objectified position of the viewer in *Crossed Lines* is also reminiscent of the experience of viewing cinematic narratives, and to the notion of the dominance of the cine-matic gaze articulated within psychoanalytic film theory. In Laura Mulvey's (1975) seminal 'Visual pleasure and narrative cinema', she discusses the

Figure 4
Crossed Lines
in production:
the director,
Sarah Atkinson,
on set with actor
Alan Carr who
plays the character
in screen 2.

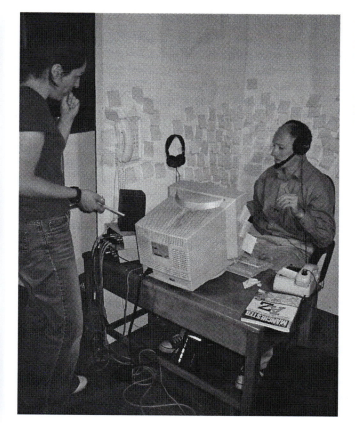

Figure 5
Crossed Lines
in production:
the director,
Sarah Atkinson,
on set with actor
Lloyd Peters who
plays the character
in screen 5.

experience of being forced to view the film from the point of view of the central male protagonist. The theme of the dominance of the gaze is evident in *Rear Window* (1954, Dir: Alfred Hitchcock), which arguably contains many parallels to the viewing experience of *Crossed Lines*. Stam (1985) refers to the windows through which the central character of the film, L.B. Jeffries, observes his neighbours as 'framed genre pantomimes' and aligns his analogy to Foucault's description of the cells of the panopticon: 'so many small cages, so many small theatres, in which each actor is alone, perfectly individualised and constantly visible' (Stam, 1985). These observations could both be applied to the aesthetic and content of *Crossed Lines*, within which the nine frames represent nine windows depicting nine separate tableaux where the characters play out their lives within the confines of the space and the genre to which they have been prescribed. In parallel with previous observations discussed with regard to the similitude of *Crossed Lines* and television, the comparison of the *Crossed Lines* viewing experience to traditional cinematic narratives is problematised, since the notion of the cinematic gaze works in opposition to television's mode of viewing, which has been referred to as the 'regime of the glance' (Ellis, 1982). That is that television viewing behaviours tend to be fractured and distracted as viewers multi-task in their home environments and the television is no longer the sole focus of their attention.

A mid-shot was selected as the most appropriate shot size since it provided a relatively close and detailed view of the character and also allowed key elements of the locale to be shown. In interactive works, says Garrand, 'special attention is paid to sets and props to provide exposition' (1997: 76). This was also enhanced through the various atmospheric audio beds that were used to provide the viewer/listener with further environmental information. The sound of keyboards tapping, and constant talking in a multiplicity of voices can be heard in screen 2 to indicate Phillip's position of working in a busy, open-plan office. In screen 4, the viewer can hear constant background dialogue, but this is rather more subdued within Maureen's environment of a Samaritan call-centre. These narrative techniques are crucial communication tools in this type of narrative and as David Riordan points out, 'if you spend time introducing the characters, the viewer is not being asked to do anything. In interactive, that is death. Instead you need to discover the back-story more as you go' (Garrand, 1997: 75).

Process: postproduction

During postproduction, all conversational scenes were matched and synchronised with one another using digital video-editing software and in the case of any overlapping dialogue, frames were trimmed to maintain audibility and fluidity. Audio beds were laid as well as additional sound effects. All phone rings were added, in addition to the voice-overs previously described. The waiting scenes also needed to be edited and looped, and scenes were reversed and edited top-to-tail with the original in order to disguise the loop point to the viewer. The separate movies were then exported at full frame resolution from the editing software using the *QuickTime* H264 codec. To emphasise the theme of voyeurism and surveillance within the piece, each individual scene was shot as one continuous take with no cuts in either sound or picture, to give the viewer the impression that they are experiencing the events in real time. This is not a usual aesthetic of the cinema, with only rare examples of a director choosing to favour long continuous takes, as opposed to cutting and reframing action; a classic example is Alfred Hitchcock's *Rope* (1948) and more recently this technique has been used in both *Timecode* (2001, Dir: Mike Figgis) and *Elephant* (2003, Dir: Gus Van Sant) to re-create a real-time sense of events. Events appear to play out in real and in correct chronological time order. If editorial cuts were to have been executed to structure scenes and if changes in shot size and camera movement were to be included, not only would the staging of real time be ruptured, the sense of 'authenticity' and 'actuality' of the piece would also be compromised.

Ongoing prototype user tests were also undertaken throughout the interactive authoring period to gauge viewer perception, particularly around the issue of interactivity and how this was communicated to the viewer when they pressed a button on the telephone keypad. Except in some scenes where a phone rang, it was initially evident through user feedback that it was not apparent to the viewer which screens were becoming active at the start of a conversational exchange. Several remedies were applied to this problem, including visual cues and audible

Figure 6 The *Crossed Lines* cinematic installation: a viewer interacts with the large-scale version of the film.

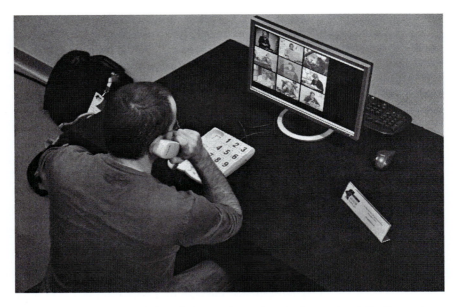

Figure 7 The *Crossed Lines* installation on the road: at the International Conference in Interactive Digital Storytelling (ICIDS), Guimarães, Portugal, December 2009.

beeps that were triggered when the viewer pressed a button. The white noise/interference effect was chosen as the optimum alert with an accompanying white noise sound effect. A user commented that 'you notice it, but you don't notice it' and this effect is also consistent with the television analogy since the simulated white noise is associated with analogue signal interference. This highlights the way in which audience responses to the piece, and my reflection upon them, drove the creative process forward and shaped my approach to the development of the project.

Process: interactivity

The interactivity of *Crossed Lines* was authored in the *Lingo* scripting environment of *Director*. The software was chosen to be the most appropriate since it is commonly considered as the industry standard package for authoring interactive media elements, particularly when using film and video.

The interface was created at the end of the process by crudely modifying a cheaply manufactured telephone to encapsulate USB computer keyboard technology. This was then connected to the computer along with an audio cable to enable the viewer to hear the sound of the film through the telephone handset.

Conclusion

I have aimed to articulate throughout this essay the fact that the resulting artwork has been influenced and shaped by three major factors: my ongoing engagement with theoretical perspectives, my reflection upon influences and sources of inspiration, and audience responses to the work. As a stand-alone art installation *Crossed Lines* has explored and has advanced past and current debates within the field of interactive cinema through the adoption of groundbreaking technologies, which allow multi-channel video to play in synchronicity and to be interrupted and reordered by the user. The practice and experience of the creation of *Crossed Lines* and my subsequent reflection and dissemination has provided many unique insights into the field, which arguably could not 'have been had in any other way' (Dewey, 1934: 300).

References

Atkinson, S. (2007) 'The versatility of visualization: delivering interactive feature film content on DVD', *Nebula*, 4(2) June: 21–39. Online. Available HTTP: <http://www.nobleworld.biz/images/Atkinson.pdf>.

Atkinson, S. (2009) 'Telling interactive stories', PhD thesis, Brunel University. Online. Available HTTP: <http://bura.brunel.ac.uk/bitstream/2438/3294/1/Telling+interactive+stories+A+practice-based+investigation+into+new+media+intrtactive+storytelling.pdf>.

Barrett, B. and Bolt, B. (eds) (2009) *Practice as Research: Approaches to Creative Arts Enquiry*, London: I.B.Tauris.

Costello, J. (2004) *Writing a Screenplay*, Harpenden: Pocket Essentials.

Dewey, J. (1934) *Art as Experience*, New York: Perigree.

Ellis, J. (1982) *Visible Fictions*, London: Routledge.

Foucault, M. (1997) *Dits et Écrits, Selections Volume 1*, New York: New Press.

Friedman, A. (2006) *Writing for Visual Media*, Oxford: Focal Press.

Garrand, T. (1997) 'Scripting narrative for interactive multimedia', *Journal of Film and Video*, 49(1–2).

Grieb, M. (2002) 'Run Lara Run', in G. King and T. Krzywinska (eds) *ScreenPlay: Cinema/Videogames/Interfaces*, London: Wallflower.

Griffiths, K. (2003) 'The manipulated image', *Convergence*, 9(4): 12–26.

Handler Miller, C. (2004) *Digital Storytelling: A Creator's Guide to Interactive Entertainment*, Oxford: Elsevier.

Himmelsbach, S. (2003) 'Toni Dove', in J. Shaw and P. Weibel (eds) *Future Cinema: The Cinematic Imaginary after Film*, Cambridge, Mass: MIT Press.

Joyce, M. and Bolter, J.D. (1987) Quoted in Joyce, M. (2002) 'Interactive planes: towards post-hypertextual new media', in B. Bushoff (ed.) *Developing Interactive Content*, Munich: High Text Verlag.

Manovich, L. (2001) *The Language of New Media*, Cambridge, Mass: MIT Press.

McKee, R. (1998) *Story: Substance, Structure, Style, and the Principles of Screenwriting*, London: Methuen.

McLuhan, M. (1997) *Understanding Media*, London: Routledge.

Mulvey, L. (1975) 'Visual pleasure and narrative cinema', *Screen*, 16(3): 6–18.

Murri, S. (2002) 'Surveillance', *Leonardo*, 35(5): 539–48.

Salt, B. (1983) *Film, Style, Technology: History and Analysis*, London: Starwood.

Stam, R. (1985) *Reflexivity in Film and Literature: From Don Quixote to Jean-Luc Godard*, Michigan: UMI Research Press.

Stam, R. (2000) *Film Theory: An Introduction*, Oxford: Blackwell.

Talen, J. (2002) '24: split screens big come back', Online. Available HTTP: <http://www.salon.com>, accessed 6 August 2008.

Wimberley, D. and Samsel, J. (1995) *Interactive Writer's Handbook*, San Francisco: The Carronade Group.

Photography as process, documentary photographing as discourse

Roger Brown

Summary

Documentary photography, as I am writing about it here, I understand as a praxis and phronesis[1] for visualising the object of the social sciences; a reflexive process of thoughtful and ethical social interaction whose value combines history, observation and aesthetics in a discourse over time.

Recent discussions about photography frequently concentrate on two primary perspectives: as a medium of illustration and source of data in a complex of sociological methods, and as a visualising text, often made by others, to be passively read, analysed and evaluated (Banks, 2007; Rose, 2001/2006). Both perspectives assume that photographs offer a description of knowledge as data and a correspondence to an empirical truth as evidence. Neither perspective offers insight into the social interaction, interpretation and reflexive process of making documentary photography. Yet there is much to be learned from doing so and, in referring to recent comments about this weakness by Becker and Banks, I am making this my starting point for discussion (Banks, ibid.; Becker, 1994).

This essay focuses on the activity of photographing, philosophical hermeneutics and ethnographic narrative; the hermeneutic activity and process of making documentary photographs of sociological value. On what Maynard refers to as the process of thinking and visualising through the medium of photography, Rorty as a hermeneutic of edification and Ricoeur as a hermeneutic of dialectical discourse, tacit knowledge, meaningful action and indirect description, comprehended in a move from explaining to understanding social worlds of inherent complexity. A redescribing of reality that is descriptive, sensory, affective and aesthetic and one not accessible to direct description alone. A visual equivalent to fixing an inscription by writing (Maynard, 2000; Morin, 2007; Ricoeur, 1991/ 2007; Rorty, 1979/2009).

While this essay is not in any sense an instruction manual for a meta-narrative of documentary photography practice I shall refer to the philosophical hermeneutics of Paul Ricoeur, the five-fold aesthetic of photography devised by the art historian John Szarkowski and to published observations from documentary photographers David Hurn and Henri Cartier-Bresson on how they think through their practices, that are offered here as thoughtful and pragmatic guides to broadening our understanding.

The essay is illustrated with examples of my past work and two case studies from current work (Appendix) as examples of a continuum of documentary practice running from an ethnography of identity to a visualisation of archaeology where empirical observation and aesthetics are indivisible to the interpretation.

Introduction: photographing

The art–science genre of documentary photography continues to offer a powerful visual means of combining phenomenological description with hermeneutic understanding of visual social science methodology. As single images but most especially when sequenced into an extended narrative, the visualisations made can act as a complement to and mediation of written, spoken or performed ethnographies; or they can stand alone as visualised ethnographic essays. By drawing attention to the process of making photographs, *photographing*, I am drawing attention to the subtle interplay of observation, tacit knowledge, new knowledge and aesthetics in their making. To not only what is being described visually but to the manner of their visualisation. As Ruskin put it many years ago and Dening more recently, that in their manner of making of observations, their rhetorical poetics and historicised performance, documentary narratives are a mutual dependency of 'Form and Mental Expression' for capturing the rhythms of daily life of a greater value than mere recording and illustration (Dening, 1995; Ruskin, 1853). Still photographs as documentary visualisations are an empirical asset and contribution to theoretical and methodological clarification in the social sciences (Hogel, 1998).

The question is how to maintain a sense of action, the activity of making, as meaningful in the process of photographing in the formation of ethnographic narratives while being able to grasp the practice critically. Ulin points to a tension between a human agency and the structural constraints imposed by the circumstances in which it is operating that connects the formal properties of a text, or visual narrative in my case, to the conditions of its generation (Ulin, 1992). The question in turn connects to mid-twentieth-century philosophical hermeneutics and a shift from the epistemological question '*How to read?*' to the ontological question of '*How do we communicate at all?*' It is a discussion that Ricoeur develops as a conflict of interpretations through a move away from a semiotic concern with structures of saying to a hermeneutic understanding of the manner of what is being said and their discourse (Ricoeur, 1974, 1991). I discuss this further.

The genre of documentary photography is alive and well. An art–science, creative process and a powerful visual means of interacting with people, the rhythms and complexities of their lives that is capable of embedding '*numerous social meanings, contexts and institutions*', to borrow from Baetens' excellent recent appraisal (Baetens, 2009: 93–96). Surprising, perhaps, that this should be so, despite the fierce criticisms of documentary photography by the proponents of critical theory in the 1970s and 1980s who, in deconstructing the practice, argued that humanist documentary photography such as that to be seen in Steichen's

(1955) *Family of Man* exhibition[2] was essentially an example of false consciousness, imperialistic and self-serving (Solomon-Godeau and Nochlin 1991); despite its more recent elevation to a supposedly higher status as an art form of subjective self-expression albeit constrained to a post-modern, post-structuralist art-historical discourse (Dexter and Weski, 2003); and despite the predicted epistemological end-game to the debates about reality, truth and falsehood of the photographic image in a digital technological environment (Ritchin, 2009). Arguably these are all closed theoretical models that 'have omitted significant aspects of our humanness . . . that fail to address the complexity of why people photograph' (Noble, 2010: 3). Langford has recently commented that the predicted closure has not occurred. Rejecting the cynical, she writes that 'Instead . . . we see signs of persistent faith in photographic evidence, however fragmented, pixellated or otherwise mediated'. Faith in an appeal to the authority of the documentary photograph as an authentic inscription of a reality and response to the brute facticity of life (Langford, 2009: 165; Savedoff, 2008).

The enduring strength of documentary photography lies in its being a genre rather than a set of prescriptive doctrines. It is a mutable and pluralist mode of discourse within which to work that links together tacit knowledge, observational and empirical content to the sensory aesthetic poetics of their performance in ways that can create levels of expectation, meaning, interpretation and understanding beyond that of mere description (Bate, 2009). As Ruskin found to his pleasure when discussing the Nature of the Gothic, there is plenty of room for innovation and creative thinking in documentary practice. Yet the results are recognisably of the genre and a Kantian idea of reason expressed in ethnographic narratives of complex thought, depth and subtlety whose articulation can achieve a horizon of insightful understanding approaching that which Ricoeur, for example, sought to achieve in his studies of the hermeneutics of language and discourses of text, time and narrative (Ricoeur, 1984–88). A mode of thought and practice about the photographing, prosody and sequencing of images to which Morin's useful metaphor of inscribing complex social meanings and behaviour can apply. Morin writes of the complexities of human life, describing them as being a construction in movement, and one that transforms in its very movement the constitutive elements that form it (Morin, 2007). To continue with Morin's musical metaphor for a moment, I often think of narrative documentary as being similar to the fugue, a marriage of precision and passion and a technique rather than a fixed form where the sequence of images can state a theme, a response, a theme, another response and so on with photographs working together as variation succeeds variation in a sequence of relational progression, to build an increasingly complex tapestry of the subject elements and an expression of reason (see e.g. Smith, 1975: *Minamata*; James Ravilious, 2007: *An English Eye)*. As Gombrich has written:

> concentration on the physiognomic properties of sights and sounds [i.e. Signs – my insertion] will never yield a theory of artistic expression unless it is coupled with a clear awareness of the structural conditions of communication

. . . the artist . . . will select from his palette . . . from among those available that to his mind is most like the emotion he wishes to represent. The more we know of his palette, the more likely we are to appreciate his choice.

(Gombrich, 1963: 62–63)

Thus, we can conceive the written, the spoken and the visual modes of representation as a complementary triad that enables us to gather empirical data, organise, structure, interpret and analyse it; that in certain areas overlap, such as combining text with images, images with sound and haptic performances, but in others remain discrete and separate in their individual modes of discourse and inscription (see, for example, Coover (2004) and the use of hypertext).[3] Howard Becker in an *Afterword* to Knowles and Sweetman's thoughtful collection of essays, *Picturing the Social Landscape,* writes of 'the need to find ways of using visual imagery that will be as natural and acceptable . . . as other forms of data' and continues that:

many people who work with visual materials have not realised that there are real skills involved and that you have to learn them, practise them and keep them in mind as you do your research and prepare it for public presentation . . . many people have failed to master the mechanics of writing clearly . . . and, similarly, most people do not know how to make a visual image that communicates clearly what's to be said . . . and certainly do not know how to deliberately control the many aspects of such images.

(Becker, 2004: 195)

Strong words – and he concludes on this theme that while there are good examples within visual social science, he none the less contends that 'we'd do well to look also at the work of photographers who never pretended to be social scientists but who we would do well to claim as our own', citing Robert Frank and Walker Evans, 'with a lot of work yet to do' (Becker, 2004: 196–197). Hogel has commented that until very recently, anthropological understanding and use of documentary photography remained to a large extent dominated by nineteenth-century ideas of realism with film or digital technologies that are 'revered' as clear, precise and undistorted methods of gathering data for subsequent reading and analysis. Simple mirrors to the world without an analytical potential or aesthetic dimension of meaning (Hogel, 1998). This is a conception in which interpretation and aesthetics often seem to be treated as synonyms for something artificial and added. An addition that corrupts the integrity of their descriptive and information value rather than being qualities that are implicit in experience and indissolubly integrated in the authoring and receiving of photographic images. The descriptive and aesthetic dimensions together form an equal music of rationality and emotion in their making, understanding and appreciation rooted in our pragmatic experience of everyday life and humanity (see Dewey, 1934).

Progress has been made in the years since Becker and Hogel published their articles. Baetens remarks that photography research has become interdisciplinary and hybrid, incorporating and then breaking the constraints of an art historical perspective, but ineluctably drawn towards issues of rhetoric, aesthetics and 'questions of the pragmatic influence exerted on a non-passive audience by considerations . . . which some may call beauty'. A move that crucially sees a shift in concern from photography as an object of picture *taking* to the appreciation of photography as a socially constructed practice of picture *making* and points to a useful distinction to be made between media theory and medium theory in understanding this (Baetens, 2009: 94–95). Pink and Edwards have, in the interim, pointed towards concerns with photography in an anthropological context: to questions of intersubjectivity, the alleged fragmenting nature of photographs, the similarity of this with fieldwork practice and to the materiality of the medium. All of which are process-related observations suggesting possible lines of development to be further worked on. Developments that allow for the recognition of affective, sensory and aesthetic subjectivities to understanding that are rooted in the experience of the aesthetic in everyday life and a category reconfiguration that makes the photographic discourse more truthful to the complex dimensions of the ethnographic object, enriching our understanding of it in meaningful ways (Dewey, 1934; Edwards, 1997; Pink, 2006; Pink *et al.*, 2004; Saito, 2007). Yet for all this, in talking about the business of making photographs in the field, Banks comments that while there are useful guides such as Wright's *The Photography Handbook* (Wright, 2007) there is nothing published 'quite equivalent for still photography' as Barbash and Taylor's *Cross-Cultural Filmmaking* (Banks, 2007: 124; Barbash and Taylor, 1997).

Photography or photographing?

To talk in terms of photography is too abstract a category for so hybrid a medium, and conceptually not helpful to us. The category is too broad to be meaningful and passive in its spectator orientation, as Elkins has recently discussed (Elkins, 2007). I am talking in terms of *photographing* and the specific and limited photographic genre of documentary photography. This may be characterised as a social activity and a reflexive process of making, interpretation and discourse of thinking about effective visualisations of social life, and also as their reception by varieties of other people and circumstances; a means and not an end whose instrumentality expands the domain of our understanding. This is an intentional sociological action that I understand as an ethical Aristotelian praxis and phronesis directed towards interpreting cultural circumstances in ways that are meaningful and inscribing human beings actively living their lives in relation to each other and their cultural worlds, natural environments and their history in webs of semantic understandings.

In speaking of *photographing* I am also drawing attention to the distinction between merely seeing and incisive looking; and to the nature, the prosody of the visual frameworks of understanding being used in their inscription. Frameworks that mediate, shape and constrain our capacity to experience, interpret, understand and communicate intelligibly to others and that reciprocally mediate their reception. We tend to think of seeing and looking as synonymous, but they are not. Seeing is to be aware in a disinterested way. Looking is to scrutinise, to be fully engaged with the detail and minutiae of the object. A distinction akin perhaps to Barthes' *studium* and *punctum* dichotomy. Both seeing and looking are not immediately obvious and both are about perception and questioning the nature of our perceptions (Elkins, 1997). Documentary photographing is very much about looking. Scrutinising the object of the enquiry with all senses alert to its visual possibilities, moods and qualities. In this it has a great deal in common with anthropological fieldwork and participating observation. Both have the quality of immediacy and presence yet both can only come to full realisation over an extended period of time and deepening understandings of the object of enquiry.

Photographing as a hermeneutic discourse

Gombrich writes: 'No artist is worth his salt who cannot keep the various dimensions of his language apart and use them for different articulations' (Gombrich, 1963: 65). The significant question to be answered in documentary photographing is 'How?' It is not only the choice of subject matter but *how* am I going to make photographs of it? Music is so much more than merely playing the notes so photographing is more than pointing the camera with all the settings on automatic.

Hermeneutic philosophy has been largely overlooked as an idea of reason that adds unity and coherence to our experience and as a guide to our thinking in discussions of photography. Ricoeur in his analysis of the text makes a crucial distinction between the speech act of *saying*, which is a dialogue, with what is *said*, which is the enunciation of the speaking transposed to writing. What we write, he says, is the noema of speaking, the meaning of the speech event, not the event as event (Ricoeur, 1991: 146–47).[4] Writing captures the fleeting event that appears and disappears in speech. In a similar way, photographing seeks to fix visually the fleeting and transient in the swirl of events. But it also seeks to capture and describe the event as event, exhibiting connections and distinctions which have hitherto lain hidden or cannot be as well expressed in writing.

The answers to the question 'How' to make the photographs that fulfil their intention is by no means obvious, although we have the habit of thinking photography is so easy as to be self-evident. Simply put the camera on automatic and take a picture. What could be easier? Ulin and Gombrich each in their distinctive ways point to a tension between human agency and the contingency of the circumstances under which work is necessarily performed. In using hermeneutic thinking to help conceptualise and evaluate this I am drawing most particularly on the work in hermeneutics of Paul Ricoeur who writes on the task of hermeneutics as being to resolve an aporia and perceived opposition between explanation and understanding, that is, between an epistemological mode of knowing and an ontological understanding as a way of being and meaningful social behaviour (Ricoeur, 1991: 53–74).[5] Hermeneutics in relation to documentary photographing should be viewed as a regulative idea, rather than constitutive, adding meaning, unity and coherence to our experience. A help and guide to our thinking and understanding, I argue.

Ricoeur defines hermeneutics as being the rules required for the interpretation of written documents. In his development of hermeneutics to the humanities and social sciences he distinguishes between a Weberian *verstehen* as a generalised comprehension and understanding and the concept of *auslegang* as stated by Dilthey. *Auslegang* being an interpretation and exegesis that implies something more specific, a limited category of signs fixed by writing in documents and in monuments that entail a fixation 'similar to writing'. Ricoeur's stated hypothesis is that the human sciences (in which are included anthropology and sociology) may also be said to be hermeneutical, because they raise similar problems in their interpretation as are raised in the interpretation of written and spoken texts. He argues that the object of the human sciences displays some of the features of a text as a text, and the methodology of their interpretation develops similar procedures as those of *auslegang* or text interpretation (Ricoeur, 1991: 144–45).

I am suggesting that documentary photography, when used as a medium of inscription and method of analysis (i.e. *photographing*) in the social sciences displays features that are similar to those in writing – especially so in the construction of linked sequences of photographs. Further that photographing as the action of inscription is a visualising discourse of a regulative equivalence, enabling us the adoption of Ricoeur's assertion that it is in discourse that language is either written or spoken. Ricoeur tells us that discourse, as he defines the category, is 'language-event or linguistic usage' and the counterpart of what linguists call language systems or linguistic codes (ibid.: 145). Because language is capable of multiple semiosis that the word alone cannot encompass, he shifts the unit of analysis from the semiotic word (sign) to the sentence as the base unit of discourse because it is better able to capture a plurality of multiple meanings. Therefore, he says, 'it is the linguistics of the sentence which supports the theory of speech as an event' (ibid.). Without getting ahead of myself, I shall say here that for my purposes of analysis I regard the single photograph as the visual equivalent to the sentence in language.

Ricoeur proposes that discourse has four distinctive traits. First, discourse is always realised temporally and in the present (language is a-temporal and virtual). Second, discourse refers back to a speaker. It has a complex set of indicators that amount to an instance of discourse (unlike language which lacks a subject in the sense of 'who is speaking?'). Third, discourse is always about something, it refers to a world that it claims to describe, to express or to represent (language signs refer only to other signs within the same system). Only in discourse is the symbolic function of language actualised. Fourth, in discourse, all messages are exchanged. Discourse alone has a world that includes another, an interlocutor that is being addressed (language is only the condition for communication, for which it provides codes); thus we arrive at the category of speech as an event (ibid.: 145–46).

He continues with a problem, the distinction between spoken and written language. Examining how these four traits are present in spoken and written language he realises there is a fundamental difference between the two modes of language. Speech is a transient fleeting event, which is why there is a problem in fixing it, of inscribing it. What we want to fix, he says, is what disappears. Referring to Plato's *Phraedrus*, it is writing, the *grammata* of external marks, that solves the problem. Writing 'is discourse's destination', Ricoeur says. Writing fixes the fleeting event of speech that would otherwise disappear. That same fleeting reality when all the faculties converge into 'that moment that mastering an image becomes a great physical and intellectual joy' for Cartier-Bresson in photography (Cartier-Bresson, 1999: 16). Ricoeur continues by asking 'what in effect does writing fix?' In answer he proposes that writing does not inscribe the event of speaking but the 'said' of speaking. Here is our bridge between a hermeneutics of writing and a hermeneutics of photographing and visualisation in documentary photography. The 'said' of speaking is, Ricoeur contends, the intentional exteriorisation of discourse thanks to which the saying, *sage*, wants to become the enunciation, *aus-sage*. For writing this means the written text. For documentary photographing this means the visualised narrative. In short, he says, what we write is the meaning of the speech event. Speech itself insofar as it is said (ibid.: 146).

Drawing on the theories of the speech act to be found in the work of Austin and Searle, Ricoeur deepens his analysis. A speech act, or the act of speaking, has, according to Austin and Searle, three levels:

1   The propositional or locutionary: the act of saying (Inscription).
2   The illocutionary act: that which we do in saying (Inspiration).
3   The perlocutionary act: what we do by saying (Aspiration).

Unwrapping these categories, Ricoeur reveals their implications, which are that:

(a) The locutionary act is fixed in the sentence. The sentence thus becomes a propositional utterance with descriptive content that because of its sign structure can be identified and re-identified.
(b) The illocutionary is less completely inscribed in grammar, it dwells on the expressive aspects of the speech act that calls on prosody to articulate and inspire what could not otherwise be known.
(c) The perlocutionary is the least inscribable aspect. The perlocutionary is the level of discourse as stimulus and aspiration; it acts upon the emotions, imagination and affective dispositions of people, typically through metaphor.

Thus to fully understand the meaning of a speech act it is necessary to understand all three rational and aesthetic aspects of language where they are codified and gathered into paradigms that can be identified and re-identified as having the same meaning.

When transposed to writing the sentence is a diverse indicator of subjective factors such as the personality of the speaker, Ricoeur states. This too is an assertion also frequently made about photography. But there is a further problem because the subjective author and the written text are dissociated. The author's intention and the meaning of the text no longer necessarily coincide. Thus, 'the dissociation of verbal meaning of the text and the mental intention is what is really at stake in the inscription of discourse' says Ricoeur, and interpretation is the only recourse we have to recover the meaning (ibid.: 147–48). Finally, discourse is what refers to a world, it cannot fail to be about something. 'Only man has world' he says, a text has only a situation. The text has an ostensive reference but people have an ensemble of references, tacit knowledge, that are opened up by the text. People encountering a text are an audience that constitutes itself and one that utilises their prior knowledge. Thus, he concludes, to understand a written text is at the same time to understand something of ourselves and a new dimension to Self being-in-the-world. A Heideggerian *project* of discourse as projecting-a-world which is, he argues, its justification as a social action: to establish the relation of man to the world. Discourse is addressed to someone. This is the foundation of communication, Ricoeur writes, universal in its address as meaningfully-oriented behaviour (ibid.: 148–50).

I am suggesting that documentary photographing in a social science context can be found to share significant similarities and characteristics in its discourse with Ricoeur's three-fold delineation of the written text. The photographs have locutionary description, illocutionary affects and perlocutionary aesthetics that arouse and fire the imagination. Both are evidence of a somebody saying something about something to a somebody. Ricoeur's analysis of the hermeneutics of discourse gives us a fresh understanding of the way in which documentary photographing can be critically understood to operate and how it does so. The reflexive participation of the observer is recognisable in the locutionary manner by which the observation is described and visualised in photographs, what Wright has called the primary message (Wright, 2007). Ricoeur calls this the reference, a literal description and in his nomenclature, *mimesis$_1$*. The illocutionary he calls the intentional sense of the inscription. A message and discourse that reveals aspects, qualities and values of a reality that he categorises *mimesis$_2$*. The perlocutionary he calls the indirect reference, redescribing a reality inaccessible to direct description and categorises *mimesis$_3$*. These different aspects become apparent through the skill (*phronesis*) with which we photograph and the manner in which the primary and lateral messages that are descriptive, explanatory, affective, sensory, revealing values that stimulate the imagination are communicated that in their total, 'make the world one that can be inhabited' (Ricoeur, ibid.).

Documentary photographing is a skill and no less a skill to be learned than the skill of writing. It is a practical way of thinking about the complexity of life that refuses the photography to be reduced and polarised as either science or art but in form and mental expression is dependent on both (Morin, 2007; Ruskin, 1853).

Photographing as practice

> [I]f I make a judgement it can only be on a psychological or sociological level
> . . . in order to give meaning to the world one has to feel oneself involved in
> what one frames through the viewfinder. This attitude requires concentration,
> a discipline of mind, sensitivity, and a sense of geometry . . . by an economy
> of means . . . one arrives at simplicity of expression. One must always take
> photographs with the greatest respect for the subject and for oneself.
>
> (Cartier-Bresson, 1999)

Photographing is about looking and imaginatively evoking worlds visually. For
myself, I reject the collapsing of documentary photography into Art and a mere
art form as the only worthwhile form. It is entirely capable of standing on its own
feet in a sociological context as method and analysis and to categorise it
wholesale as Art and therefore 'worthy' is singularly unhelpful. As Paul Newman
did not quite say, why eat hamburger when you are already eating fillet steak?

As with the written word we can do it well or we can do it half-heartedly or
even misleadingly. This places considerable responsibility on the photographer
and demands from them other skills in terms of prior knowledge and understanding; perception and sensitivity to current and unfolding events; an ability to
build rapport and good working relations with other people; integrity and humility
in recognition of the ethical responsibilities to the people, their lives and
circumstances that they are allowing to be photographed, often intimately. To this
we can then add the skills needed in a confident marshalling and selection of the
visualising technologies and picture-making techniques available; sensitivity to
the structural and rhetorical tropes possible in the making of the photographs and
integrity in the building of the sequence of images into a satisfactory and
authentic narrative. None of this is specific to photography alone but would apply
to a greater or lesser degree to film and video makers as it would to fieldworkers
more concerned with writing their fieldwork and data than rendering it visually.
As Becker has pointed out, writing doesn't come easily!

There are some additional factors peculiar to both photography and film/video
visualisation to be aware of, as Flusser reminds us. Flusser suggests there is a
potential conflict of intentions between the users of camera-based technologies
and the intentions of the manufacturer of the equipment such that the camera may
dictate to an uncomfortable extent what is possible and what is not possible to
record on the film or sensor (Flusser, 2000/2007). To my mind it simply means
recognising the limitations of the medium and working within them.

In 1964 The Museum of Modern Art, New York, staged an exhibition of
photographs called *The Photographer's Eye*. The exhibition was curated by the
then Director of Photography, John Szarkowski, against a background that sought
to establish photography as a sovereign fine art medium. Szarkowski published a
book of the same name in 1966 based on the exhibition. The thesis of the book is
to investigate why photographs look the way they do, to move our appreciation of them from a picture-making process of synthesis to one of selection.

Szarkowski argued that a study of the photographic form 'must consider the medium's "fine art" tradition and its "functional" tradition as intimately inter-dependent aspects of a single history'(Szarkowski, 1966/2007). Szarkowski proposed five key considerations a photographer must decide upon in the 'How to' process of making photographs. In summary these are:

1) *The Thing* itself, the subject of the photograph.
2) *The Detail*, the small but significant and meaningful elements of the picture.
3) *The Frame*, the boundaries of the picture that determine what is included, what is excluded and what is hinted at lying on the edges and beyond the frame. It also is a significant element of the internal geometry of the picture and creating the illusion of space, of a foreground and background *gestalt*.
4) *Time*, when to press the shutter and what shutter speed to select for the inscription of movement or freezing motion.
5) *Vantage*, where to stand in relation to the subject, how close, how far, how low and how high, to one side or another.

By such means, suggested Szarkowski, pictures made with a mindless mechanical process could 'be made to produce pictures meaningful in human terms' (ibid.). Szarkowski is writing as a museum curator and photographic art historian. In seeking to identify what made photography distinctive as a collectable art form he devised what amounts to an aesthetics of the medium that remains a thought-provoking and influential text today.

David Hurn, the long-time member of the Magnum photo agency and former head of documentary photography at Newport, Gwent, and Bill Jay, the writer and critic of photography have written an excellent book together that attempts to unravel the processes of 'how to think and act like a photographer'. (Jay and Hurn, 2007). It is a distillation of common denominators and basic principles they have found in a lifetime of their own and many other photographers' experience. Among the hundreds of books available that give advice on how to make better pictures, Jay and Hurn's is unique. The book is arranged as a Socratic dialogue of questions and answers so, for example, when Jay asks what is it that transforms a simple record photograph of the appearance of something into something of lasting merit, Hurn replies that it comes down to the choice of subject. The photographer must have an intense curiosity and not just a passing visual interest in the subject, he says. A curiosity that leads to intense examination, reading, talking, researching, and not least to many failed attempts at finding a satisfactory visualisation over a long period of time (ibid.: 48).

This sits well with fieldwork of course. It may sound trite to say it but photographing has to be worked at and a common mistake is to treat it as an add-on, an afterthought. So put time aside to concentrate on making photographs, immerse yourself in photographing. It takes time, persistence and patience. Unlike working with formal or informal interview techniques, with listening and participating in conversations and the ebb and flow of the dialogue, or with observations and research that are going to be transcribed into spoken, and above all written language in monographs and journal articles, photographing means looking for the visual. You are using a different part of the brain and a quite different mind-set. You are making yourself alive to line, shape, form, colour, texture, patterning and configurations of elements, and above all light and the tone or mood of the photographs. James Ravilious frequently chose to shoot into the light, for example. The subject matter becomes backlit, shadows are cast forward towards the viewer and the overall tone of the photographs of rural Devon farming communities is lyrical (Ravilious: ibid.).

When photographing, you are in control, deciding where to stand and when to press the shutter release; how to draw the image on the film or sensor according to the ways in which different lens focal lengths render light at the camera focal plane – so long focal length telephotos compress perspective, limit depth of field and allow differential focus to be used to isolate a subject from its surroundings, whereas short focal length/wide-angle lenses expand and even distort perspective, and increase depth of field, rendering foreground and background distinct. Different shutter speeds will impact on how movement is made apparent in the image (slow speed) or stopped in its tracks (fast speed). What ISO rating of film or sensor will be used? In making the crucial decisions about how to photograph something, a person or an event, the photographer can choose which technology, which lens, the level of exposure, the shutter speed, the handling of contrast ratios and qualities of light, mood and atmosphere, the lens aperture, the depth of field and point of focus, whether to work in colour or black and white, the extent of post-production enhancement and manipulation of the image, all grounded in a web of empirical references and significations. Not for nothing did Edward Steichen say that 'Photography is a medium of formidable contradictions. It is both ridiculously easy and almost impossibly difficult.' So it comes as a relief that he also felt able to say with great conviction that photography, 'I believe . . . is potentially the best medium for explaining man to himself and his fellow man'. All that is required is, as Hogel says, 'that we work seriously with the media' (Hogel, 1998: 33).

Some examples

Oil rigs are noisy, fascinating, and at times tedious places. In the early 1980s I was on the North Sea oil rig Piper Alpha. Soon after dawn I wandered the rig looking for interesting subject matter when I noticed a roustabout standing by the nozzle of the gas flare. When they burn, the gas flare booms with noise. That morning it was quiet and there were no flames because he had been cleaning the burner of carbon deposits. The rig, however, was noisy and flexing with vibrations from the well-drilling deck.

I watched in amazement as he reached into his pocket, and taking out an ordinary cigarette lighter, stretched an arm to the nozzle and lit the gas jet. It ignited and billowed and roared into flame. My camera was loaded with colour film, the lens focal length, settings and exposure already chosen because I had beforehand measured and evaluated the light and picture-making possibilities of

Figure 1
Igniting the flare
stack, Piper Alpha,
North Sea
(Occidental
Petroleum).

the early morning activities. But not this, I had no idea this is what happened. I managed to frame and shoot one exposure. Serendipity.

When not on the rigs I was undertaking research and fieldwork for an ethnography of the North East of Scotland inshore fisheries for a postgraduate degree. Then, as now, my ethics were humanist. I was steeped in the realist tradition, discourse and expectations of documentary photography being 35mm, available light, black and white, shot on Kodak Tri-X at 400 ISO or more. The rhetoric of this photograph was formed by these expectations and by the light of a single fluorescent strip light in the ceiling of the railway arch housing a small family business. It was very cold and steam drifted from the buckets of hot water that the working women and one man used to warm their hands frozen from filleting the cold, wet fish. I tried hard to catch that sense of a Dickensian

Figure 2
Fish filleting and
processing shed,
Aberdeen.

atmosphere and relentless hard work processing the morning catch and sending it to market as fresh as possible. The aesthetic of grainy black and white photographs fitted that. Colour would not. The photographs were always intended to be sequenced into a photo-essay and visual narrative with text and resulted from many months of work building personal relationships, gaining acceptance and developing an understanding of the complex social structure through which the fisheries were organised and operated. I had seen the same events in this and other similar fish houses for a number of weeks before photographing them, during which time I worked out my story line and my visual rhetorics through which to make the photographs.

In 2004 to 2005 I spent six months photographing the workforce, plant and manufacturing processes of the Royal Doulton ceramics company in their last British factory at Nile Street, Burslem, Stoke-on-Trent. After years of decline and loss making, the factory was to close, production shipped overseas and the brand name sold to the Wedgwood Group. I chose to work on 6cm x 7cm medium format cameras with colour negative film. I was intending as complete a record as possible for exhibition, publication and as a doctoral research case study, with high-quality negatives and archival durability. I was very conscious that I was photographing history. For this reason I wanted great detail and clarity in the photographs. Lighting governed the aesthetics and mood of the photographs with a complex mixture of ambient daylight and fluorescent strip lighting which I controlled and softened by using on camera fill-in flash.

My current work is with documentary visualisations of archaeological skeleton remains for an HEA/JISC funded research project producing photographs for a Forensic Archaeology and Forensic Science teaching and learning DVD (Cassella *et al.*, 2008). The skeletons have been excavated from Hulton Abbey, Stoke-on-Trent, Staffordshire over a period of time (Klemperer and Boothroyd, 2004). One unique skeleton has recently been identified as probably that of Hugh le Despenser the Younger, favourite of Edward II, executed for high treason by being hanged, drawn and quartered in November 1326 at Hereford. The bones of

Figure 3
Royal Doulton Plc:
Anne, aerobrush
figurine decorator.

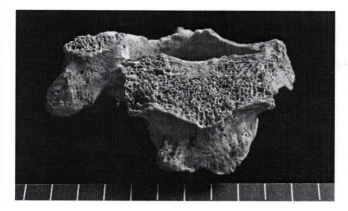

Figure 4
Hugh le Despenser the Younger, 1326, executed for high treason. Cervical vertebra C3 showing the inter-vertebral surface of the living bone where it has been sliced through by beheading.

the skeleton are scarred with axe and swords cut and chopping marks where the body was butchered into pieces and the head struck off. The intention was to produce clear and detailed images that can be used for teaching diagnostics of the pathology of peri-mortem trauma without the need to handle the fragile bones. Lighting and the aesthetic quality of the light is the key to this. Here I have used contre-jour lighting that produces glowing highlights, clearly defined shadow regions and three-dimensional drawing of the bone surfaces and butchering cuts and fractures. So successful has this been that the research project is continuing with further photography of these and other archaeological specimens.

Documentary photography can readily span a range of intended methodologies in the social sciences as I have sought to show in these few examples. Common to all the different applications is an appreciation of the aesthetic qualities of the photographing that far from corrupting the empirical content, add immeasurably to our appreciation, understanding and interpretation of them.

Appendix: Case studies

HASDiP: The Hulton Abbey Skeleton Digitisation Project

HASDiP is an HEA/JISC funded research project to digitally photograph skeleton remains excavated from Hulton Abbey, Stoke-on-Trent, in the recent past (Klemperer and Boothroyd, 2004). The purpose was to document the remains with as much aesthetic clarity and detail as possible to show their pathology. The photographs are to be used as a diagnostic teaching and learning aid in forensic science, forensic archaeology, forensic anthropology and other related fields. The final outcome has been published as a DVD for in-class use, the intention being to remove the need to handle the very fragile remains (Cassella *et al.*, 2008).

Hulton Abbey is a minor medieval Cistercian monastery (AD1219–1538). One skeleton stood out labelled as HA16. The decapitated remains are heavily scarred with what were, on initial diagnosis, suggested to be the cut marks of battle injuries. A recent re-analysis by Dr Mary Lewis suggests the skeleton is of a male and well-known political figure who had been executed by being hanged, drawn and quartered. Lewis contends the remains are those of Hugh le Despenser the Younger, executed for high treason in November 1326 at Hereford on the orders of Queen Isabella, wife of Edward II. Lewis's analysis and the new photographs that I made are the first osteological description and visualisation of the lesions associated with this form of execution (Lewis, 2008: 315).

Hugh le Despenser was the Chamberlain and favourite courtier of Edward II and widely hated by his Queen, Isabella, the Barons, Bishops and population for exploiting his position of power and authority to enrich himself at their expense (Fryde, 1979). When Queen Isabella and the Marcher Baron Sir Roger Mortimer invaded England in September 1326 to depose him from the throne, Despenser

Figure 5 Froissart: The execution of Hugh le Despenser, Hereford, 1326.

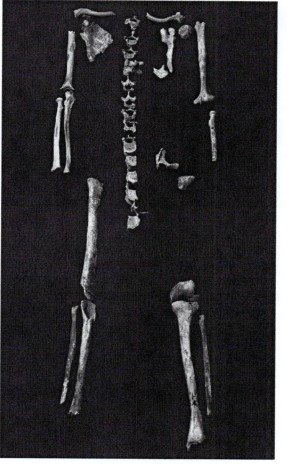

Figure 6 HA16 (the surviving skeleton remains).

was chased, captured and taken to Hereford for trial and execution for high treason. He was sentenced to death by being publicly drawn, hanged, emasculated, eviscerated and beheaded while still conscious and his body then quartered. The manner of execution being reserved only for high-status individuals, carbon-dating of the bones and the absence of several parts of the body including the head all point to Despenser and if so then 'this is the first time such an execution victim has been identified' says Lewis (ibid.).

The head was displayed on London Bridge and his quartered body parts sent to the four corners of the kingdom and displayed there to confirm his death. Significantly, the body was not only quartered but cut into smaller sections by being halved below the rib cage and the spine cut vertically. The chop marks on the bones show that the butchering was crudely done. Despenser's widow,

Figure 7 Cervical vertebra C3. This shows the moment of beheading. The spongy appearance of the inter-vertebral surface shows the living bone where the axe sliced through the flesh and fractured the neck vertebra.

Eleanor, later petitioned Edward III for the return of his bones to be buried in his family mausoleum in Gloucester Cathedral, but only the head, a thigh bone and a few vertebrae were returned to her. These are the bones missing from the Hulton Abbey skeleton. Hulton Abbey formed part of the estate of Hugh Audley, Despenser's brother-in-law and a Knight in Edward II's household. It is possible the family may have chosen to bury what remained of him there to save him from eternal purgatory.

As well as producing photographs of record, the aesthetics of the lighting is crucial to the photographing.

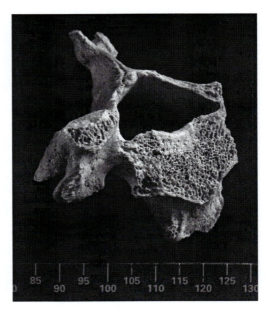

Figure 8 Cervical vertebra C3. Another view of the same site of beheading.

I used a lighting technique known as contre-jour and macro levels of magnification of each specimen. The lighting places the source high and behind the subject. The effect is to create glowing highlights as the light reflects from surfaces and builds shadows that create texture and three-dimensional form.

Cuts, slices, chopping marks and stress fractures are all brought out in great detail and clarity as can be seen on the right clavicle where the arm was cut away at the shoulder (Figure 10). Multiple cut marks are visible, suggesting that the butchering was crude, hasty and difficult.

The photographic techniques used have been so successful that further evidence of the peri-mortem trauma has been revealed by the photography that visual examinations had missed. The research programme is continuing with quantitative laser 3-D scanning of the bones.

Together the qualitative photography and the quantitative laser scans will establish new national visualisation protocols for this type of documentation, new

Figure 9 Lumbar vertebrae showing living bone surfaces. The body was quartered and cut vertically down the lower spine from below the rib cage to the pelvis.

Figure 10 The right clavicle where the right arm was cut away at the shoulder. The bone shows as many as 12 cut lines, evidence of repeated slashing and the difficulty of cutting through the flesh and sinews.

Figure 11
The thoracic
section of the spine
was also cut
through vertically
as the body was
butchered.

knowledge to science and open new understandings of medieval life and the highly theatrical performance of public execution by drawing, quartering and beheading.

Place, space and identity: Waterside South, Hanley, Stoke-on-Trent

In 2007 I was awarded an Arts Council West Midlands/RENEW Regeneration North Staffordshire community arts commission to document an area of Stoke-on-Trent undergoing Pathfinder 1 regeneration. The area I chose is called Wellington traditionally, and Waterside South in the regeneration scheme. It is an area of nineteenth-century terraced housing, built for the people working in the paper mills and potbanks that lined the district to the south along the Caldon canal.

Up to four generations of people living in the district give it a vivid sense of self and community identity, with many having lived there all their lives, marrying their neighbours, working in the same factories, sending their sons and daughters to war. Typical of these is Mrs Lottie Hughes who has lived all her life in the house she was born in and her parents and grandparents before her. Mrs Hughes' home was recently demolished and she has been rehoused in a small bungalow development for the elderly.

I had three winter months in which to produce a series of documentary photographs and hold a public exhibition of them. The question was: how to photograph something so insubstantial and transient as 'Identity'?

Figure 12
New housing along
the Caldon canal
where potbanks
previously stood.

Figure 13
Mrs Lottie Hughes,
fourth-generation
resident.

It seemed to me only possible through a visual narrative of portraits, events and localities in the district and to combine the photographs with captions. The captions were extracted from interviews with the residents and professionals involved in the regeneration of the district.

I worked through the Residents' Association by giving a presentation of my past work and asking people to come forward and help me by giving their permission to photograph them and their homes.

Tensions were high because demolition was taking place, new housing being built, many older properties condemned, and a lot of uncertainty about what was going to happen and when. People living in the district did not like the changes being forced on them and the manner in which they were being carried out without, it was felt, sufficient and proper consultation.

Many, like Mr and Mrs Jeffries, were happy to welcome me into their homes, others were not.

Figure 14
Residents'
Association
meeting with the
Regeneration
Agency.

Figure 15
Former paper mill
and Victorian
housing and new-
build housing,
Cresswell Street.

Figure 16
Mr and Mrs
Jeffries.

The older community was fracturing and with it a sense of self and identity that none the less people worked hard to maintain through the church, school and community centre organising luncheons, social activities and events such as the traditional children's Christmas lantern parade through the streets of the district (Figure 17).

North Staffordshire is famous for a local delicacy, the oatcake. This is a pancake of fermented wheat and oat flour. 'The Hole in the Wall' is the last traditional shop selling from what used to be the front room of the house. The shop was to be demolished, and it caused an outcry and became the focus for people's frustrations (Figures 18 and 19).

The photographs were exhibited in the district Community Centre and the church hall of the parish church, St Mary's. My work continues with documenting the changes and regeneration of Wellington, old identities and loyalties broken up and new forms emerging, and a book is planned for publication in late 2010.

Figure 17
The Christmas children's lantern parade through the district.

Figure 18
The Hole in the Wall oatcake shop.

Figure 19
Glenn Fowler and
the Oatcake Girls.

Figure 20
Exhibition at the
Community
Centre.

Bibliography

Adams, R. (1996) *Beauty in Photography*, New York: Aperture.

Baetens, J. (2009) 'Theorising photography as a social and artistic practice', *Visual Studies*, 24(2): 93–96..

Banks, M. (2007) *Using Visual Data in Qualitative Research*, London: Sage.

Barbash, I. and Taylor, L. (1997) *Cross-Cultural Filmmaking: A Handbook for Making Documentary and Ethnographic Films and Video*, London: University of California Press.

Bate, D. (2009) *Photography: The Key Concepts*, Oxford: Berg.

Becker, H. (1994) 'Afterword: Photography as Evidence, Photographs as Exposition', in Knowles and Sweetman (eds) *Picturing the Social Landscape: Visual Methods and the Sociological Imagination*. London: Routledge.

Cartier-Bresson, H. (1999) *The Mind's Eye: Writings on Photography and Photographers*, New York: Aperture/Magnum.

Cassella, J., Brown, R., Lewis, M. and Lucking, P. (2008) *HASDiP, The Hulton Abbey Skeleton Digitisation Project.* Online. Available HTTP: <http://www.heacademy.ac. uk/assets/documents/digitisation-project-report-pdf>.

Coover, R. (2004) 'Working with images, images of work: using digital interface, photography and hypertext in ethnography', in S. Pink (ed.) *Working Images, Visual Research and Representation in Ethnography,* London: Routledge.

Coppock, C. and Seawright, P. (eds) (2009) *So Now Then, With Essays by David Campany, Martha Langford and Jan-Erik Lundstrom,* Cardiff: Ffotogallery, in association with the Hereford Photography Festival, 2006.

Dening, G. (1995) *The Death of William Gooch, a History's Anthropology,* Melbourne: Melbourne University Press.

Dewey, J. (1934/2007) *Art as Experience,* New York: Perigee.

Dexter, E. and Weski, T. (eds) (2003) *Cruel and Tender: Photography and the Real,* London: Tate Publishing.

Edwards, E. (1997) 'Beyond the boundary', in M. Banks and H.Morphy (eds) *Rethinking Visual Anthropology,* New Haven, CT, and London: Yale University Press.

Elkins, J. (1997) *The Object Stares Back: On the Nature of Seeing,* New York: Harvester Harcourt.

Elkins, J. (2007) *Photography Theory, The Art Seminar Volume 2,* London: Routledge.

Flusser, V. (2000/2007) *Towards a Philosophy of Photography,* London: Reaktion Books.

Fryde, N. (1979) *The Tyranny and Fall of Edward II 1321–1326,* Cambridge: Cambridge University Press.

Gombrich, E. (1963) *Meditations on a Hobby Horse,* London: Phaidon.

Hogel, J. (1998) 'In anthropology, the image can never have the last say', Group for Debates in Anthropological Theory (GDAT) 1997: 9, P. Wade (ed.) University of Manchester: Department of Social Anthropology.

Jay, B. and Hurn, D. (2007) *On Being a Photographer: A Practical Guide,* Anacortes,WA: LensWork Publishing.

Klemperer,W. and Boothroyd, N. (2004) 'Excavations at Hulton Abbey, Staffordshire 1987–1994', *Society for Medieval Archaeology Monograph 21,* London.

Knowles, C. and Sweetman, P. (eds) (1994) *Picturing the Social Landscape: Visual Methods and the Sociological Imagination,* London: Routledge.

Langford, M. (2009) 'What use is photography?', in Coppock and Seawright (eds) *So Now Then,* Cardiff: Ffotogallery.

Lewis, M.E. (2008) 'A traitor's death? The identity of a drawn, hanged and quartered man from Hulton Abbey, Staffordshire', *Antiquity,* 82(315): 113–24.

Maynard, P. (2000) *The Engine of Visualisation: Thinking Through Photography,* Ithaca, NY: Cornell University Press.

Morin, E. (2007) *On Complexity,* Cresskill, NJ: Hampton Press.

Noble, D. (2010) 'The distance between theory and practice', Staffordshire University Department of Photography/Stockholm 2010 conference paper: 'Photography Next'.

Pink, S. (2006) *The Future of Visual Anthropology, Engaging the Senses,* London: Routledge.

Pink, S., Kurti, L. and Afonso, A.L. (eds) (2004) *Working Images: Visual Research and Representation in Ethnography,* London: Routledge.

Ravilious, J. (1998/2007) in P. Hamilton (ed.) *An English Eye,* Oxford: The Bardwell Press.

Ricoeur, P. (1974) *The Conflict of Interpretations,* Evanston: Northwestern University.

Ricoeur, P. (1984–88) *Time and Narrative* (3 vols), trans. Kathleen Blamey and David Pellauer, Chicago and London: Chicago University Press.

Ricoeur, P. (1991/2007) *From Text to Action: Essays in Hermeneutics II*, Evanston: North Western University Press.

Ritchin, F. (2009) *After Photography*, New York: W.W. Norton.

Rorty, R. (1979/2009) *Philosophy and the Mirror of Nature* (30th Anniversary edition), Princeton, NJ: Princeton University Press.

Rose, G. (2001/2006) *Visual Methodologies: An Introduction to the Interpretation of Visual Methods*, London: Sage.

Ruskin, J. (1853) 'The nature of the gothic'. Essay first published in *The Stones of Venice*, vol. 2, 1853.

Saito, Y. (2007) *Everyday Aesthetics*, Oxford: Oxford University Press.

Savedoff, B. (2008) 'Documentary photography and the art of photography', in S. Walden (ed.) *Philosophy and Photography: Essays on the Pencil of Nature*, Oxford: Blackwell.

Smith, W.E. and Smith, A.M. (1975) *Minamata*, London: Chatto & Windus.

Solomon-Godeau, A. and Nochlin, L. (1991) *Photography at the Dock: Essays on Photographic History, Institutions and Practices*, Minneapolis: University of Minnesota Press.

Steichen, E. (ed.) (1955) *The Family of Man*, New York: The Museum of Modern Art.

Szarkowski, J. (1966/2007) *The Photographer's Eye*, New York: The Museum of Modern Art.

Ulin, R.C. (1992) 'Beyond explanation and understanding: anthropology and hermeneutics', *Dialectical Anthropology*, 17(3): 253–69.

Ulin, R.C. (2001) *Understanding Cultures: Perspectives in Anthropology and Social Theory*, Oxford: Blackwell.

Walden, S. (ed.) (2008) *Philosophy and Photography: Essays on the Pencil of Nature*, Oxford: Blackwell.

Wright, T. (2007) *The Photography Handbook*, 2nd edn, London: Routledge.

Studying images through images: a visual ethnography of the cult of María Lionza in Venezuela

Roger Canals

In 2003, I began a research project on the images of María Lionza, one of the most popular divinities in Venezuela.[1] I was sure that studying this still unexplored subject could shed a little more light on this important Venezuelan belief, as well as articulate, using the analysis of a specific case, a more general, and decidedly anthropologic, reflection on the meanings and functions of images in contemporary society.

María Lionza represents a unique case in the Venezuelan religious universe: a main figure in an important cult of possession, she is described and represented in many different and apparently contradictory ways (as Indian, white, mixed race or black, good or evil, seductress or virgin). Moreover, the image of María Lionza is present in diverse contexts in contemporary Venezuelan society, where she takes on heterogeneous roles and meanings. We can find her, for example, on the altars of the cult of possession which honour her, in the artistic world and world of handicrafts (galleries, museums, workshops), in publicity, in films or on the internet, among other contexts.

Having selected my subject, and before embarking on my first trip to Venezuela, I asked myself the following question: which strategies (theoretical and methodological) are the most appropriate for addressing such a vast and complex subject from a specifically anthropological perspective? My first fieldwork experience, which lasted approximately a month and a half, was enlightening in this regard. It was then that I realised that my study of the image of María Lionza could only proceed if it were framed within a project which included and critically connected the three essential branches of visual anthropology: the study of the image as *object*, the use of the image as *method* and the incorporation of the image in anthropological *discourse* – in other words, the consideration of the image *as language*.

The main aim of this essay is to show, through my own ethnographic study of the representations of María Lionza, the possible relationships between these three areas of visual anthropology. Of these three areas, we will focus here on the use of *visual methods* during fieldwork. Before discussing the uses I made of the image throughout my research, however, it is important to offer more detailed information on the goddess María Lionza and the cult which worships her.

María Lionza and her cult

María Lionza is a widely known divinity in Venezuela. So much so, that often she is regarded, by believers and non-believers alike, as the autochthonous goddess of the nation, symbol of Venezuelan history and identity (Barreto, 1998). The versions of the myth of María Lionza – as present both in oral tradition and written literature – are as innumerable as the images representing her (see Garmendia, 1980; Antolínez, 1995; Manara, 1995; Barreto, 2005). On the other hand, the term 'cult of María Lionza' designates a group of healing, divination and initiation rituals in honour of María Lionza and her pantheon of divinities, where possession rituals play a crucial role (see Clarac de Briceño, 1970, 1983, 1996; Pollack-Eltz, 1972; Ferrándiz, 2004). These rituals mainly take place in large Venezuelan cities (Caracas, Valencia or Maracaibo), as well as on the *Montaña de Sorte* (Sorte Mountain), a centre of pilgrimage for believers. Despite its close connection with Venezuela, the belief in and worship of María Lionza has spread in recent decades to other South American and Caribbean countries (Colombia, the Dominican Republic and Brazil, among others), as well as to the United States and Europe. From a historical perspective, the origin of the figure of María Lionza and her cult is still diffuse. Everything seems to indicate, however, that this belief stems from ceremonies which the inhabitants of present-day Venezuela held in honour of female deities – deities related with the water, animals and the forces of Nature – before the arrival of the Spanish (Barreto, 1990). Later, these beliefs combined with Catholicism and with the rituals brought over by West African slaves. The cult would have also been influenced, at the start of the twentieth century, by Allan Kardec's Spiritism, Cuban *Santería* and Haitian voodoo, among other belief systems.

The pantheon of the cult of María Lionza includes hundreds of divinities, also known as 'spirits' (*espíritus*) or 'brothers' (*hermanos*). Among these are mythic figures (such as *Santa Barbara* or *La India Yara*), spirits of historical figures (such as past Venezuelan presidents or Indian despots who died during the Spanish conquest), as well as characters from comics or television (such as the Vikings or Tarzan). It should also be mentioned that the cult of María Lionza continuously incorporates new divinities stemming from other religions or belief systems. As such, it is common to see figures of the Buddha or the image of Shango, one of the main figures from the Yoruba pantheon, on altars of worship. In fact, the cult of María Lionza maintains a close relationship with other neighboring cults – especially with the Cuban *Santería* and the *Umbanda* of Brazil – to such a degree that at times these religious expressions appear to be inextricably tied. The influence between the different cults is reciprocal, as demonstrated by the presence of statues of María Lionza in Afro-American religious ceremonies, such the Dominican *Misterios*.

A comparative analysis of the myths and representations of María Lionza shows how this divinity is characterised by three essential ambiguities. Firstly, by an ethnic ambiguity (she is represented as an indigenous, white, mixed race or black woman); secondly, by a moral ambiguity (at times she appears as an evil deity and at others as a benevolent one); and, thirdly, by an ambiguity regarding her femininity (at times she is represented as a figure of great beauty with an explicitly sexual component and at times she is depicted as a mature woman without any particular physical attractiveness). An especially complex aspect of this goddess is that she frequently appears as associated with other deities. It is not uncommon to meet believers who claim that María Lionza is the Virgin Mary or who identify her with figures like *Santa Barbara* or *Yemayá*. Despite the plurality of the representations of the goddess, there are two which are decidedly popular: one in which she is represented as a white woman with a crown – and which is commonly named *La Reina* (The Queen) (see Figure 1) – and one in which she is depicted as an indigenous woman riding naked on a tapir (Figure 2).

That said, we will now consider the three aspects I used to analyse the image of María Lionza in my doctoral research on the representations of this goddess.

Figure 1 (Above) María Lionza as *La Reina* (The Queen).

Figure 2 (Right) María Lionza as an indigenous woman riding naked on a tapir.

The image as object

The anthropological research tradition devoted to the study of the image as *object* is a long one. These studies – a cross between material anthropology, symbolic anthropology and the anthropology of art – range from research on religious images by Tylor (1871) or Lévy-Bruhl (1927) to contemporary studies on graffiti or digital images. From this perspective, image is defined as a singular object whose main property is to make visible anything which is situated in a transcendental plane – whether this referent be, from our point of view, 'real' or 'imaginary', 'concrete' or 'abstract'. Certainly, anthropology – and more specifically, visual anthropology – is not the only discipline which has expressed interest in this type of object. Aesthetics and the history of art, to name only a few, are branches of knowledge which are explicitly dedicated to this end.

That said, in contrast to other disciplines, visual anthropology places the importance of *relationships*, or more specifically, the importance of *social relationships*, at the heart of its analysis of images. Without forgetting the iconographic relationships which images have with each other, anthropology is especially interested in two aspects: the interactions which individuals have *with* images and the interactions which individuals form with one another *through* images. Image is understood, as such, as an agent which weaves social fabric, and as an active element which contributes to the maintenance and reconfiguration of the ties existing in a particular community. This perspective does not forgo, however, the symbolic importance of the image – that is the analysis of its aesthetic characteristics – but rather the contrary. In fact, what visual anthropology aims to do is to demonstrate the interrelationship between symbol and function, showing how the function of images developed in a specific cultural context is intimately related with the meaning of these images, and viceversa (Banks and Morphy, 1999). Expressed another way, it is based on the idea that it is only possible to fully understand what an image symbolises by analysing the use which is made of it and, inversely, that the functions of these images are partially determined by the aesthetic characteristics of the work, characteristics which the anthropologist can only interpret if he or she knows the 'cultural' particularities of the human collective which he or she is studying.

Interpreted from a relational perspective, the image of María Lionza appears as a *hybrid*, *dynamic* and *global* image. Hybrid because of its presence in distinct forms and in highly varied contexts in Venezuelan society, where it takes on heterogeneous meanings and functions. For example, in the context of worship, the image of the goddess takes on an explicitly religious role. Placed on altars in the form of a statue or seal, the representations of the goddess act as mediator between this world and the afterlife, thus acquiring a partially transcendent dimension. During the rituals, these altar images contribute, on the one hand, to *establishing a connection* between men and gods and, on the other hand, to forming a bond between the believers themselves, who are gathered around the religious images. The representation of María Lionza most often found on altars – at least, public ones – is that of the queen, that is, of a white woman. This fact is not at all strange considering the influence of Catholicism, which traditionally has rejected representations of black or indigenous divinities in its regard for these as 'pagan', on the cult. Due to this influence, the image of the queen has acquired a level of prestige for the believers of the cult superior to that of the image of the Indian, which is not to say that the latter has disappeared, but rather that it has taken on other meanings and functions.

The image of María Lionza also appears as an artistic one. We find it in galleries and museums in the form of sculpture, paintings or performance. In contrast to the religious context, María Lionza is frequently represented in the artistic world as an indigenous woman or as a highly sensual white woman[2] (see Figure 3), something which is probably due to the idealised representation of the Indian woman presented by a series of Venezuelan painters and poets in the 1940s. At first glance, everything seems to indicate that the artistic image is deprived of all religious function. The immanence of the artistic image should thus contrast with the transcendence of the religious image. The difference between the religious image and the artistic image in the cult of María Lionza is, however, much more diffuse than this divide would suggest. The ethnographic

Figure 3 María Lionza as a highly sensual white woman.

examples demonstrating this continuity are numerous. During my fieldwork, for example, I was able to observe how artists regard their creative task related with María Lionza as a religious activity which they use to pay homage to the divinity and enter into a relationship with her. Another clear example of this interdependence is an occurrence which I observed during the inauguration of an extensive exhibition dedicated to María Lionza in the most important museum of the city of San Felipe (in the Yaracuy region). Over the course of the event, some visitors prayed before the 'artistic' paintings and sculptures and one of them even fell into a state of trance provoked by the supposed presence of María Lionza in the building. This ontological ambiguity of the image of the goddess which is observable in the artistic and religious images is also evident in the images which are used commercially, politically or for publicity purposes.

On the other hand, I have referred to the image of María Lionza as dynamic because the same representation can take on different meanings in function of the context and the uses made of it. I recall, for example, an event which took place in Maracaibo, the second most important city in the country. In a shop selling religious items, a believer bought an image of María Lionza. She paid the amount due and they wrapped it up and put it in a bag, just like any other piece of merchandise. Not long after, this very image presided over a magnificent altar where healing rituals were held. The image-merchandise had become a religious image. This dynamic character of the image of María Lionza refers to the uses made of specific representative models. For example, the image of María Lionza as an Indian woman riding a tapir was, early on, an artistic and monumental image. Shortly afterwards, however, the cult worshippers reproduced this image in the form of a statue and used it for rituals, thus converting the artistic image to a religious one.

Finally, the representation of María Lionza can be regarded as a global image, since it is found in different parts of the world (South America, Europe, China, the United States), thus participating actively in the interrelationship process at a planetary scale, which we call globalisation. The aesthetic recreations of this figure are, for example, widely present on the internet (more than 16,000 entries on the most popular search engines). The types of representations which we find on the web and the tone and character of the websites where these appear are even more varied. In fact, the internet is becoming the most important space for the reinvention and diffusion of the image of the goddess. At the same time, the web has become a unique medium for *establishing a connection* between believers around the world.

The above reflections on the image of María Lionza as object do not come from nowhere; they are based on extensive fieldwork in Venezuela and other countries where the cult of María Lionza is present. The key issue which the ethnographer must address during fieldwork is that of method. In order to understand the *relational* characteristics of the image of María Lionza, I chose to design an ethnographic research method where the image played a specific role. Before outlining the methodological characteristics of the fieldwork, however, it is important to reflect on the notion of method.

The use of the image as an ethnographic research method

In the objectivist and positivist conception of scientific knowledge, method is defined as a group of more or less fixed and predetermined rules which lead to the gathering and interpretation of data on the outside world, to which a truth may be assigned regardless of the subject's perspective. This paradigm, which I have simplified here, has been surmounted. We know that the world – and, more specifically, what we may call the 'social world' – does not constitute a coherent and unique whole, but rather a complex and constantly transforming context. We also know that there is not one objective and neutral truth which is independent from the viewpoint of the subject, a subject which is understood not as an immutable unit, but rather as a multifarious and changing being which is historically and culturally defined. This is not to say, however, that the world is an unintelligible chaos in which there are no rules of social organisation which the anthropologist can decipher through critical and rigorous research.

In this epistemological revolution, the notion of 'method' has changed meaning, but only partially. The final objective of the scientific method in anthropology is still to deepen one's knowledge of man's life in society. That said, the scientific method no longer consists of a group of predetermined rules aimed at revealing an assumed truth inherent in the world, but rather in revealing a range of strategies for interacting in it, for relating with it, for questioning it. And since the method is no longer established ahead of time, *but rather forms part of the problem which the anthropologist must address*, it acquires a, shall we call it, 'creative' dimension which implies, in turn, a reflexive stance on the part of the researcher – that is, which obliges him to specify, in the presentation of the research's conclusions, the conditions of origin of the ethnographic data. It is necessary, therefore, to question the methods we use, to subject these to analysis, to 'deconstruct' these and, at the same time, to accept that if the method (or 'methods') is a creation, we, too, can legitimately invent new ones or dare to mix and combine *already existing* methods which, for one reason or another, have been regarded as antagonistic. That said, what criteria should be used when 'creating' new social research methods or selecting from among already existing ones?

I propose that the characteristics of the object of study can orient us in designing our methodological strategies. Moreover, I propose that there should be a certain *affinity* between the nature of the object of analysis and the method by which we intend to understand it. Here, however, we run into an apparent contradiction: I said that it is precisely the nature of the object of study which should inspire our choice of method; however, to get close to this reality, we already need a strategy, that is, a method. The key for overcoming this vicious cycle is to understand that before we initiate an ethnographic study, it is first necessary to go through a previous phase of designing a method, a type of 'pre-fieldwork' in which the anthropologist informs him/herself of what is written on or filmed about the subject. And, if he or she does travel to the place of study, it is necessary to carefully and attentively observe the social reality in-depth, leaving aside, to the extent that this is possible, any ideological biases about the subject in question. It is from this first phase that the design of the 'method' (which may be the sum of various methods and, more importantly still, which may change over the course of the investigation) should emerge.

My fieldwork was established on the basis of this necessary affinity between the method and the object of study. Early on, I observed that the image of María Lionza was a multifarious and changing object of strong social significance. It was thus necessary to devise a research method which enabled me to capture the creative and relational dimension of this representation. To achieve this aim, I designed a method based on two different, yet complementary, uses of this image.

Firstly, during my fieldwork excursions, I always carried reproductions of maybe 20 images of María Lionza in which she appears represented in different ways: as white, black, mixed race (*mestiza*), Indian, good, evil, etc. I often organised meetings with diverse groups of people who did not know each other so that they could comment on this plurality of representations. The comments which emerged in these *mise-en-situation* ('putting into situation') were extremely valuable for my research. Secondly, since I began my doctorate, I have had the intention of incorporating the camera as a fieldwork tool. My objective was not only to use the camera to record events but also to provoke these. And that is exactly what happened: thanks to the presence of the camera, I was able to establish a series of social ties and provoke a series of research situations which hardly would have emerged otherwise and which enabled me to obtain highly valuable ethnographic data. These *performative* strategies associated with the use of the camera in fieldwork, while legitimate, must satisfy certain scientific and ethical standards. More specifically, they oblige the anthropologist to be *reflexive*, that is, to make explicit in the study's conclusions – visual or textual – the process by which the ethnographic knowledge was produced. Of particular interest were the experiences where these two visual methods blended together – one using pre-existing images and the other producing new images – and where I filmed the discussions which emerged around the different images of the goddess María Lionza.

An ethnographic study does not end when the fieldwork is over, but rather when the ethnographic data obtained over the course of the study have been analysed and interpreted within a determined theoretical framework and articulated through discourse. It is with a brief commentary on this process of writing and presenting the results obtained during my fieldwork that I will end this essay.

The image as discourse

I have always felt there was a certain contradiction in studies of images which only employ text or, at most, in which the image is given a secondary role, subordinate to the pre-eminence of the verbal discourse. The same goes for anthropologists who use visual methods to obtain ethnographic data in their fieldwork but who then, at the time of presenting the research conclusions, merely use this material as an instrument of support, and who avoid making this available to the readers in the final publication of their research. These two attitudes stem from a theoretical principle – of which perhaps the researcher is not always fully aware – in which all that is said *about* an image (or which has been learned from the use of images as a research *method*) can be directly and fully expressed through conceptual language.

I consider this principle to be erroneous and based on a devaluation of the image with relation to the text as a medium for transmitting ethnographic knowledge. Image and text are *ontologically* different mediums which are irreducible. From my point of view, the question which the anthropologist should pose is not whether or not to make films or write articles, but rather how textual and visual records complement each other so that the best of each is extracted while maintaining their *significative autonomy*.

In presenting the conclusions of my research on the image of María Lionza, I aimed to critically complement verbal and visual records. With regard to the image, this was used in three distinct ways. Firstly, from the visual material harvested during my fieldwork, I made one full-length film and two short films on the representations of María Lionza. Due to its mimetic character – that is, due to the opportunity it offers for capturing and reproducing a moving reality – film is a medium which is especially indicated for showing *actions*, *bodies*, as well as the *material* elements of social reality. It is for this reason that in the film *The Many Faces of a Venezuelan Goddess*[3] I focused on showing the relationship which different individuals in Venezuelan society (artists, believers, mediums, actresses) establish *with* and *through* the image of María Lionza. On the other hand, thanks to editing, film becomes a medium especially suitable for expressing the symbolic relationships established *between the images themselves*. In fact, through 'intellectual' editing inspired by the principles of the dialect, we can evoke the symbolic continuities and discontinuities between the representations as found in diverse contexts. At the time of editing, I used this resource to demonstrate the bond which unifies the representations of María Lionza as presented in different forms and found in highly varied geographic and cultural contexts. In doing so, I aimed to demonstrate the ties between the material, corporal and mental image or between the artistic, religious or publicity image (see Belting, 1994, 2004).

It must also be said that film is a privileged medium for transmitting not only anthropological information (as could be done in this essay) but also an ethno-graphic *experience*. *The Blood and the Hen*,[4] for example, is a short film about a healing ritual – sacrifice included – performed by a group of the cult of María Lionza in Maracaibo (Venezuela) in 2007 (see Figure 4). From the spectator's point of view, no written commentary, no matter how brilliantly written, can compare to the experience of seeing this ceremony represented in the moving image. Thanks to film, we can understand essential aspects of this ritual – the nonverbal language used by the mediums, the rhythm of the prayers and enchant-ments, the expressions of the patient or the physical or social characteristics of the context where the ritual is carried out – *through the senses*. Of course, upon seeing this short film (in which there is no voice-over narration), a spectator who is not a specialist in Afro-American rituals will not fully understand the *meaning* of the ritual (why kill a hen to cure a woman of her headache, he will ask). But despite this, and thanks to film, the spectator will have learned new aspects of man's life in society and, more importantly, he/she will have had the *experience* of coming face-to-face with an event from another cultural universe, all the codes of which she cannot possibly understand. When all is said and done, this is the most truly ethnographic experience. Film enables us, then, to place the spectator in a position analogous to that of the anthropologist during the fieldwork (or at least during its early phases, when he/she does not yet dominate the cultural patterns of the community being studied).

The other two uses made of images in the presentation of the study's conclusions do not involve film, but rather photography. On the one hand, I used photographs in my fieldwork to illustrate the written reflections on the images of María Lionza. This use of image as a complement to the text (which is the case in this essay up until now) is familiar to us, but this does not mean that it is any less problematic. In books on ethnography, the image is often present as a mere illustration of the text when, in fact, and if we try to reconstruct the intellectual evolution of the author, we realise that it is the text which has been constructed *based on the image*.

On the other hand, for the publication of my doctoral thesis, I elaborated a series of fixed image sequences through which I aimed to demonstrate the relational character of the image of María Lionza. The process of elaborating these visual schemes was useful for the interpretation of the images themselves and, in this sense, also became a *method* of reflection. See an example of these

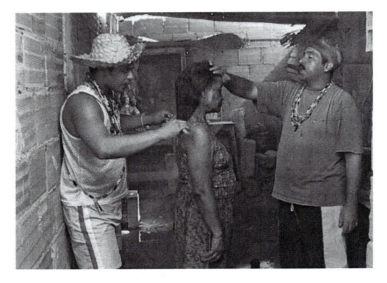

Figure 4 The Blood and the Hen.

schemes in Figure 5. At the top we see an unpainted bust of María Lionza represented as a queen. If the bust is painted according to traditional songs (a) it becomes a *religious image*. However, when it is painted in a unique way, provocatively and deliberately personal[5] (b), it becomes, in principle, an *artistic image*. We can see how the iconographic or aesthetic characteristics of the image *partially* condition the use and, as a consequence, the range of possible interactions which can be established. Nevertheless, and as I have explained earlier, this differentiation between the religious image and the artistic image is not as clear as it may seem, due to the fact that it is a difference which does not depend so much on the intrinsic characteristics of the image as on the context in which it is found and the intention with which it is used.

Towards a normalisation of the image in social sciences

Visual anthropology has been constituted as a partially autonomous discipline within the field of social and cultural anthropology. For a good number of years, it has had its departments, its conferences, its journals and its film festivals. This

a   b

Figure 5 Visual schemes to demonstrate the relational character of the image of María Lionza.

relative autonomy does not imply, however, that it has been widely recognised as a fully fledged member of the academy – especially in some countries, such as Spain. In fact, there still exists a lack of appreciation for and an undervaluation of visual anthropology as a discipline. A specific example will help demonstrate this oversight. A kinship anthropologist, specialist in the notion of family and matrimonial alliances, is not at all expected to know the theoretical and practical problems of visual anthropology. Moreover, it is possible to spend one's entire professional career ignoring this discipline and be no less respected. The opposite case, however, would be unthinkable: any visual anthropologist who wants to have an academic career and be respected as an anthropologist must demonstrate competence in the main branches of anthropology – which undoubtedly includes that of kinship.

One of the causes of this disparity is that visual anthropology has been judged by many anthropologists solely by its method or, better said, by one of its possible methods: the use of the camera in fieldwork. In fact, the visual anthropologist is still regarded by many as someone who captures images during ethnographic research and who makes films or photographic sequences. This simplification of the field of visual anthropology isolates the discipline and establishes a clearly *asymmetric* relationship between visual anthropology and its peers, which save for some exceptions, do not use visual methods in their research. I call this relationship *asymmetrical* because there is no institutional equivalent to visual anthropology called 'textual anthropology' which groups together all anthropologists who express themselves only through text. As such, the visual anthropologist stands alone against the rest, and with everything to lose. This characterisation of the visual anthropologist, based on one of the possible methods, is, moreover, clearly reductionist. There does not, nor has there ever, existed any anthropologist – from Mead to Rouch to MacDougall – who is interested only in the visual; and there is no anthropologist who has not written articles and books, that is, who has not addressed the problems inherent in *ethnographic writing*.

I am increasingly convinced that the authentic consolidation of visual anthropology would consist not only in the establishment of more specific university courses, but rather in the *normalisation* of the use of audiovisual techniques in the social sciences. If image as a method and discourse were to be accepted once and for all as just another option, visual anthropology would cease to be viewed as a strange and marginal body of work, interloper in a world where only the written word is deemed legitimate, and the anthropologists who receive (and adopt) the label of 'visual' would come to be anthropologists who *also* make use of image in their research. As such, it would be normal for a kinship anthropologist to conduct research using visual and textual resources in a complementary way and to present his research conclusions, for example, on CD-ROM with both images and text. With this normalisation, a professor of political anthropology could make use of an ethnographic documentary to show how clan societies live or to analyse the forms of commerce taking place in North African markets without the need to justify himself. All anthropologists should address the problems inherent in the use of image in the social sciences in an analogue way, just as visual anthropologists writing an article today must address the intrinsic characteristics of written language.

This normalisation of the use of image is not only desirable, but also necessary. Contemporary society poses unprecedented problems for anthropologists. The study of images and, above all, the use of images in research and in the presentation of research results can provide new elements for addressing classic anthropological issues (identity, cultural otherness, gender), as well as for understanding more current phenomena, such as globalisation, advances in reproductive techniques or the emergence of new religions. Image, in all of its aspects, must play a central role in the social sciences and, more specifically, anthropology. The intellectual and political challenges we face are too complex to cast aside one of the greatest resources available to us and which, to a more or less silenced degree, has accompanied anthropology since its inception.

Bibliography

Antolínez, G. (1995) *Los ciclos de los dioses*, San Felipe: Ediciones La Oruga Luminosa.

Augé, M.(1997) *La guerre des rêves*, Paris: Seuil.

Banks, M. and Morphy, H. (1999). *Rethinking Visual Anthropology*, London: Yale University Press.

Barbash, I. and Taylor, L. (1997) *Cross-Cultural Filmmaking*, Berkeley: University of California Press.

Barreto, D. (1990) 'Perspectiva histórica del mito y culto a María Lionza', *Boletín Americanista*, 39–40: 9–26.

Barreto, D. (1995) 'El mito y culto de María Lionza: identidad y resistencia popular', *Historias de Identidad Urbana*, Caracas: UCV, pp. 61–73.

Barreto, D. (1998) 'Genealogía de un mito', Tesis de doctorado en Antropología, Universidad Central de Venezuela.

Barreto, O. (ed.) (2005) *La diosa de la danta*, San Felipe: UNEY.

Belting, H. (1994) *Likeness and Presence*, Chicago: The University of Chicago Press.

Belting, H. (2004) *Pour une anthropologie des images*, Paris: Gallimard.

Clarac de Briceño, J. (1970) 'El culto de María Lionza', *América Indígena*, XXX (2): 359–74.

Clarac de Briceño, J. (1983) 'Una religión en formación en una sociedad petrolera', *Boletín Antropológico*, 4: 29–33.

Clarac de Briceño, J. (1996) *La enfermedad como lenguaje en Venezuela*, Mérida: Universidad de Los Andes.

Colina, C. (ed.) (2002) *Alejandro Colina: El escultor radical*, Caracas: Publicaciones Universidad Católica Andrés Bello.

Colleyn, J.-P. (1993) *Le regard documentaire*, Paris: Éditions du Centre Pompidou.

Fernández, A. and Barreto, D. (2001–2002) 'El culto de María Lionza: Del pluralismo espiritista a la contestación', *Antropológica*, 96: 13–30.

Ferrándiz, F. (2004) *Escenarios del Cuerpo*, Bilbao: Universidad de Deusto.

Garmendia, H. (1980) *María Lionza. Angel y Demonio*, Caracas: Seleven.

Gell, A. (1998) *Art and Agency*, Oxford: Clarendon Press.

Grimshaw, A. (2001) *The Ethnographer's Eye: Ways of Seeing in Modern Anthropology*, Cambridge: Cambridge University Press.

Gruzinski, S. (1990) *La guerre des images*, Paris: Fayard.

Gruzinski, S. (1999) *La pensée métisse*, Paris: Fayard.

Henare, A., Holbraad, M. and Wastell, S. (eds) (2007) *Thinking Through Things*, New York: Routledge.

Herrera Salas, J. M. (2003). *El negro Miguel y la primera revolución venezolana*, Caracas: Vadell Hermanos Editores.

Hockings, P. (ed.) (1975) *Principles of Visual Anthropology*, La Haye: Mouton.

Jiménez Sierra, E. (1971) *La Venus Venezolana*, Caracas: Chicuramay.

Latour, B. and Weibel, P. (eds) (2002) *Iconoclash*, Karlsruhe: Center for Art and Media.

Lévy-Bruhl, L. (1927) *L'âme primitive*, Paris: Bibliothèque de Philosophie Contemporaine.

MacDougall, D. (1998) *Transcultural Cinema*, Princeton, NJ: Princeton University Press.

Manara, B. (1995) *María Lionza: Su identidad, su culto y la cosmovisión anexa*, Caracas: Universidad Central de Venezuela.

Piault, M.H. (2000) *Anthropologie et Cinéma*, Paris: Nathan.

Pink, S. (2006) *The Future of Visual Anthropology*, London: Sage.

Pollack-Eltz, A. (1972) *María Lionza, mito y culto venezolano*, Caracas: Universidad católica Andrés Bello.

Taussig, M. (1993) *Mimesis and Alterity*, London: Routledge.

Tylor, E.B. (1994)[1871] *Primitive Culture*, London: Routledge.

Conclusions

A democratic civilization will save itself only if it makes the language of the image into a stimulus for critical reflection – not an invitation for hypnosis.
(Umberto Eco (1979) 'Can television teach?' *Screen Education* 31: 12)

Thirty years on Eco's point is perhaps even more significant today in a society where we are ever more dependent on electronic visual media for so much of our knowledge of events in the outside world through vicarious consumption of images, especially television and the new electronic media. The types of visual study being advocated in this book have emphasised that active critical approaches to the image are essential if we are to understand the power and potential latent in images.

Visual studies highlight features of social reality in special ways. Although the image is not reducible to language, we nevertheless depend on language to anchor the meanings of images, to harness them to our arguments and demonstrate processes and illustrate theoretical effects with them. The relationship between language and images is complex, as Roger Brown (p. 202) notes: 'we can conceive of the written, the spoken and the visual modes of representation as a complementary triad that enable us to gather empirical data, organise, structure, interpret and analyse it; that in certain areas overlap, such as combining text with images, images with sound and haptic[1] performances, but in others remain discrete and separate in their individual modes of discourse and inscription.'

The discussion about these complex relationships and the manner in which sensory information is presented and framed through discursive structures has been a key contribution of this text. Images have enormous productive potential due to their ambiguity. It has become apparent that the image is at once 'real' and explicit and capable of seductive deception. As John Hartley points out: 'Just as it is very hard for photographers to get their subjects to remain still for long enough to be photographed, so pictures themselves are never still, either in signification or social circulation' (1992: 34). This book contains dozens of 'readings' of different images showing the restless semiotic fluidity of their interpretation over time, between different media, and through the different institutional settings which might produce or use them.

Visual research is special because it throws issues of subjectivity, reflexivity and interpretation into sharper focus. Subjective understandings are central to some forms of visual research. The fact that visual data are already perceived and interpreted by others – part of a 'double hermeneutic' – indicates that people will evaluate visual messages differently based on complex differences and commonalities between their experience of the world, their political, social and cultural values. Researchers are no different in this – they also have cultural baggage which they must declare when they frame an analysis. Where studies present visual records of people and communities, the researcher strives for a collaborative *intersubjective* approach which avoids 'outsider arrogance' and hopefully leads to a more negotiated understanding of other people rather than one that merely *imposes* a set of cultural and theoretical values.

The relationship between images in a case may be seen to provide a form of 'thick description' whereby the unfolding dynamics of the case are interwoven to show the interplay of discourses. Images as well as words are central to the circulation of cultural meaning: producing and reproducing and regulating social meanings and affirming individual and group identities. Chapters 1 and 2 discussed the complex social and political uses of the image and suggested some applications to research methods. In particular, the discussion centred on a range of phenomenological approaches which utilise visual materials, allowing a vivid and deeper examination of evidence. The suggestion that the experience of generating, looking, analysing and using images aids the development of a more critical 'eye', more attuned to the visual dimension of social life, has been further borne out in Section II where four visual researchers explained their developing visual practices revealing the insights such studies can yield.

The chapters are not intended as a definitive guide to the practice of visual methods; such research, is of necessity, always 'in progress', developing creative and versatile approaches. This is the enduring strength of visual research practice; it maintains the critical fluidity needed in sociology, eschewing the 'god's-eye view' in favour of the everyday vision which informs the researcher's ignorance. We need to look and listen more carefully and be less hasty to dismiss the most 'mundane' sights. It is clear from the first five chapters that research is less linear than some might pretend and, where the image is concerned, positivist procedural doctrines must be revised to include our own compromised subjectivities. The visual may highlight this more than conventional research methods because it focuses on images whose meanings are not easily or objectively measured. By their very nature images are polysemic and depend on the cultural capital and intertextual knowledge of their beholders and producers.

Therefore visual sociology challenges and disrupts the mindset which seeks to reduce all research to numerical analyses, supporting instead those forms of research which recognise the importance of human reflexivity as an essential component of fallible and open research. In his recent article, Denzin (2009) emphasises the severity of the attack which presents plural forms of qualitative research as dangerously subjective, attacking the reflexivity of the researcher as an underlying malaise which needs to be rooted out: 'Global efforts to impose a new orthodoxy on critical social science inquiry must be resisted, a hegemonic politics of evidence cannot be allowed. Too much is at stake' (Denzin, 2009: 155). Such efforts are to be resisted, but given the inescapable importance of subjectivity in qualitative research, it is difficult to see how the whirlwind of social reality can ever be restored to some positivist Pandora's box.

The examples in this book indicate the power of accepting subjectivity as central to the research project, rather than something to be excised from the process. The use of visual evidence and the focus on the manifestations of social phenomena proves to be not only an enriching and indispensable part of social research, but one which exposes the weaknesses of more traditional objectivist paradigms.

Glossary

Aberrant decoding

A term coined by Umberto Eco (1965) to highlight the problems of interpreting (decoding) a text by means of a different code from that used to encode it (e.g. what are the conventions for understanding rhythm and blues music or the Mona Lisa? One may be ethnocentric and time bound to US black culture of the post-war period, the other dependent on complex codes of expression employed in society and art of the time of Da Vinci) (see, for example, Eco's *Misreadings*, 1994). In another example, Eco, entertainingly, imagines a (post-holocaust) world 2,000 years in the future. Archaeologists picking through the layers of our lost civilisation, fragments fused together and misinterpreted; popular lyrics from musicals (*Oklahoma*) interpreted as rites of fertility and evidence of human sacrifice, fused in turn with fragments of mythology (Fraser's *Golden Bough* or *Golden Bowl*).

Bricolage/Bricoleur

Lévi-Strauss derived the meaning of bricolage from the 'bricoleur' – someone who does odd jobs, making and mending things from bits and pieces which have been left over from previous jobs. It provides a 'science of the concrete' by which the world is ordered in minute ways.

Discourse

The term encompasses a spectrum of uses from the directly linguistic analyses of spoken or written language, especially important in our analyses of research data (interview transcripts, media texts, advertising, institutional documents) but also textual analysis in the broadest way is seen as mediated by discursive practices which stem from much more complex socio-historical sources. Issues of gender and sexuality as well as race ethnicity, age and class have all been presented as shaped and affirmed (or challenges and trangressions) of discursive structures.

This relationship of power/knowledge and institutional and textual processes has led to a range of strategies for researchers examining not just language but a whole range of constitutive codes and practices. We could ask ourselves what are the discourses of educational practice within HE which have recently shaped our relationships with one another? How are discursive relationships between disciplines maintained and policed to create a sense of distinct identity? Communications and cultural studies, sociology, psychology, criminology, politics. Similarly we could ask what are the shifts in pedagogical thinking and their effects in shaping and constraining our practice – student-centred learning, autonomous learning, e-learning, learning hubs, student engagement, research, informed teaching, employability, internationalisation – have I missed any? And aren't discourses in this sense highly political discursive practices which are characterised by the delimitation of a field of objects, the definition of a legitimate perspective for the agent of knowledge, and the fixing of norms for the elaboration of concepts and theories? Thus each discursive practice implies a play of prescriptions that designate exclusions and choices (Foucault, 1977: 199).

Epistemology

'The philosophical theory of knowledge, which seeks to define it, distinguish its principal varieties, identify its sources and establish its limits' (*Fontana Dictionary of Modern Thought*).

'The philosophical theory of knowledge – of how we know what we know' (*The Oxford Dictionary of Sociology*, Oxford University Press, p. 197).

Habitus

> The habitus, a product of history, produces individual and collective practices – more history – in accordance with the themes generated by history. It ensures the active presence of past experiences, which, deposited in each organism in the form of schemes of perception, thought and action, tend to guarantee the 'correctness' of practices and their constancy over time more reliably than all formal rules and explicit norms.
>
> (Bourdieu, 1990: 54)

Bourdieu is suggesting that the objective conditions of existence – material events in social history – generate the habitus which, like a grammar of behaviours, in turn generates certain dispositions, attitudes and behaviours; a lexicon from which each individual may choose. This might allow a view of ethnic identity and boundaries which does not treat focus on social class or socio-cultural aspects as either/or. All such influences are part of the habitus and have been ultimately derived from the history of an individual, a group, or indeed a population. The habitus is most definitely not an idealist or abstract concept:

> the habitus only exists in, and through and because of the practices of actors and their interaction with each other and with their environment: ways of talking, ways of moving, ways of making things, or whatever.
>
> (Jenkins, 1992: 27)

The habitus clearly has features in common with a Marxist notion that the material conditions giving rise to a social class will be reproduced in the material practices of those experiencing such conditions. At the same time, the habitus can avoid the pitfalls of Marxian and plural society theories which presuppose some inevitable cycle of ethnic conflict or class struggle. The following section will more thoroughly assess the value of Bourdieu's theory of practice to the study of ethnic relations in Guyana.

Bourdieu's concept of habitus appears to be a valuable theoretical tool. The following points summarise the advantages as well as possible shortcomings of using the Theory of Practice.

(1) The habitus enables a view of identity and boundaries which allows focus on social class and socio-cultural interactions rather than appraising these sets of factors as competing explanatory variables or assigning primacy to one or the other. All acts of cultural expressions can be explained in terms of lived experiences, habitual practices which produce the codes, and inscribe meanings onto the body and psyche of the individual.

(2) A corollary of the above point is that the theory of practice allows for analysis of both individual and group. There are differences in each individual's habitus – unique individuals construct their own. However, the individual has also been steeped in the specific traditions of a group, embodying all its social codes. Therefore, while the habitus has a potentially infinite capacity to produce practices, the actual behaviours brought into active practice are 'constrained': 'without violence, art or argument'. The group habitus tends to exclude all 'extravagances' ('not for the likes of us'), that is, all the behaviours that would be negatively sanctioned because they are incompatible with the objective conditions (Bourdieu, 1990: 56).

Haptic

This term refers to the perception through the sense of touch in which contours, textures, shapes, edges, etc. of objects and surfaces are sensed through the skin in a directly somatosensory manner. It also includes the internal proprioception of body in which we have a sense of the physical relation between parts of the body (e.g. in the dark, knowing where our hands are in relation to our heads). Gibson (1983) defined the haptic system as 'The sensibility of the individual to the world adjacent to his body by use of his body'.

So haptic visuality might include active exploration of movement, shape and textures, physical sensations, wetness, dryness, temperature, etc. and the perceptions of images which convey these sensory data.

Some prime examples can be seen on Flickr: http://www.flickr.com/groups/haptic/.

'In haptic seeing, all our self rushes up to the surface to interact with another surface' (Marks, 2004).

Identity politics

While the origins of the term are obscure it is likely to have emerged from within specific ethnic women's groups in the late 1960s – especially with Black Feminism.

Identity politics is often used to indicate the fragmentation of social movements towards particular facets of identity: ethnicity, nation, sexuality, etc. Similarly, multiculturalism is seen to be a certain stage in the movement of identity politics which has arguably divided once united resistance movements of the left (e.g. the Anti-Nazi League, which as an umbrella group included a sort of rainbow coalition of ethnicities and left-leaning political groups). The argument that there was a need for 'strategic essentialism' in consciousness raising and political resistance sometimes united groups (e.g. of feminists or 'black' activists) and at other times divided their ranks as a specific strand (e.g. lesbian feminists or black feminists) became the platform for the struggle and being subsumed under the general banner of feminism ignored these important identities which differentiated these groups and reflected different challenges and patterns of disadvantage.

Institutional ethnography

A highly influential approach to combine both method and practice in empirical social research pioneered by prominent Canadian sociologist Dorothy Smith: 'Institutional ethnography recognises the authority of the experiencer to inform the ethnographer's ignorance' (Smith, 2005). Using a broadly Foucaultian vision of power and ethnomethodological approach, i.e. enables the analysis of internal systems of institutions – placing the individual perception within the bounds of institutional rules and discourses. It has been applied in a wide variety of analyses.

Intersubjectivity

The term implies the individual's subjectivity is dependent on networks of relationships. In a very real sense our identity is constantly negotiated and re-negotiated through communicative encounters with others. Marcia Langton writes: '"Aboriginality" . . . is a field of intersubjectivity in that it is remade over and over again in a process of dialogue, of imagination, of representation and interpretation. Both Aboriginal and non-Aboriginal people create "Aboriginalities"'(1993: 33).

Richard Jenkins introduced the term internal/external dialectic as a central argument in the formation of both individual and collective identities (see Jenkins, 2004: 18–26).

Intertextuality

The interrelationship between texts: usually one text's reference to another. This location of a cultural reference point (most often a historically prior one) usually takes the form of diffuse memories, echoes and reworkings of other texts. Intertextuality is particularly prevalent in 'postmodern' texts, which often play on the notion that everything is a reworking of something else to produce a 'pastiche aesthetic' (the hotchpotch of historical styles visible in postmodern architecture).

Mediasphere

When identities and complex cultural meanings are the object of study, understanding is always positioned and subjective. Knowledge produced by research, through the visual researcher's collection and interpretation of data, is socially constructed. Hence only by pursuing a reflexive approach, in which a rigorous analysis of motives behind the interpretative path chosen takes place might a tentative sense of validity be achieved. Central to this view is the process by which social and cultural meanings (including interpretative paradigms) are mediated between the wider cultural sphere (semiosphere), the mediasphere and the public sphere. It is important to examine and reveal the disciplinary discourses – their language, texts, and institutional practices which shape our interpretations if validity is to be strengthened (see Hartley, 2002: 142).

Meaning and Communication

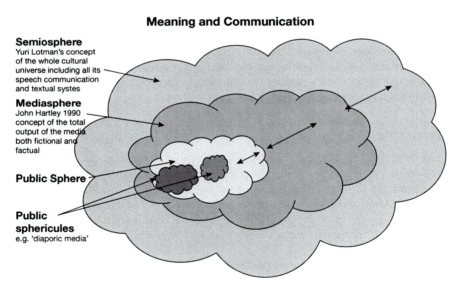

Semiosphere
Yuri Lotman's concept of the whole cultural universe including all its speech communication and textual systes

Mediasphere
John Hartley 1990 concept of the total output of the media both fictional and factual

Public Sphere

Public sphericules
e.g. 'diaporic media'

Figure 46 Different spheres of cultural meaning

Myth

Based on the work of structuralist anthropologist Claude Lévi-Strauss, two fundamental principles of myth can be suggested: first, that the meaning of myth does not lie in isolated elements, but in the combination of these, and meaning is a dynamic produced by transformation of meaning between surface and deep structures.

Second, myth has a language which exhibits properties over and above the ordinary linguistic level. Like ordinary language, myth is composed of constituent units. In linguistics, these are morphemes and phonemes – but in the language of myth these units differ from natural language because they belong to a higher and more complex language. Lévi-Strauss (1958) suggested the existence of 'mythemes', arguing that each version of a myth could be broken down into a series of sentences consisting of a relation between a function and a subject. Sentences with the same function were given the same number and bundled together – and these were mythemes, the smallest constituent of myth. We might regard myth, he said, as an orchestral score; working along two axes simultaneously, the diachronic and the synchronic. The score for the orchestra must be read diachronically; page by page, yet must also be understood synchronically – we hear resonances – bundles of meaning. His work affirms that there is no direct relationship between a work of art and the reality it is supposed to portray. Myth works as a moulding or mediating force rather than as a reflective agency.

Barthes' approach to myth focuses considerable time and energy on the elaboration of systems as these are designed to 'make the world heavy with meaning' to convert objects to signs (see Culler, 2002: 46). Yet the nature of myth for Barthes is one in which its socially constructed nature is hidden, and instead it is presented as natural or commonsense. Some of the examples in this book demonstrate this vividly; images used in media, advertising, photojournalism and ethnography often illustrate different degrees of naturalism. Figure 47 is adapted from Barthes' *Mythologies* (1957: 115) and shows myth as operating at a meta-level as a second order level of signification. This suggests that a transformation takes place of 'the materials of mythical speech (language itself, photography, painting, posters, rituals, objects, etc.)' (p. 114). Once they are caught up in the web of myth, these are 'reduced to pure signifying function' (ibid). Barthes is suggesting that myth constructs these different codes as mere means to an end:

> Whether it deals with alphabetical or pictorial writing, myth wants to see in them only a sum of signs, a global sign, the final terms of a first semiological chain. And it is precisely this final term which will become the first term of the greater system which it builds and of which it is only a part.
>
> (pp. 114–15)

The importance of the techniques discussed in this book is to demystify those texts which are often presented as presenting an unchallenged, inevitable view of social reality.

MYTH

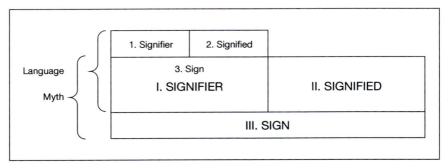

Figure 47 The structure of myth

Phronesis

Gr. Wisdom, good sense, good judgement, prudence n. one of the four cardinal virtues.

(*Penguin Dictionary of Philosophy*, edited by Thomas Mautner, 2000)

> Aristotle is the classic philosopher of phronesis. In Aristotle's words, phronesis is an intellectual virtue that is 'reasoned, and capable of action with regard to things that are good or bad for man'. Phronesis concerns values and interests and goes beyond analytical, scientific knowledge (episteme) and technical knowledge or know-how (techne) and it involves what has been called 'the art of judgment', that is to say decisions made in the manner of a virtuoso social actor. Aristotle was explicit in his regard of phronesis as the most important of the three intellectual virtues: episteme, techne, and phronesis. Phronesis is most important because it is that activity by which the analytical and instrumental rationality of episteme and techne is balanced by value-rationality.
>
> (Flyvbjerg Bent (2009) *What is Phronetic Planning Research? What is Phronetic Social Science?* http://flyvbjerg.plan.aau.dk/whatisphronetic.php)

Positionality

The complex and elusive term used to recognise individual subject position in relation to the research practice or indeed to any interactive context. Paulo Friere's radical pedagogy suggests that teachers ought to embrace their own and their students' narratives of experience and hence a consciousness of our relative positionality is significant in the classroom where our own subjectivity is part of the dynamic of the teaching context. For example, a white middle-class male may be responded to very differently to a white working-class female where his or her identities are visibly different to the pupils. In visual terms the complex intersubjective relationships between the viewer and the image also accentuate the value of this concept.

Preferred reading

This is a concept coined by Stuart Hall ([1973] 1980) used in media and cultural studies to suggest that there are implicitly favoured interpretations of media stories embedded into the text. By the language used and the social context of the source, the meaning is socially positioned.

A problematic concept which suggests that texts often contain cues which favour a certain reading and constrain the openness of the text. This may not be a consciously manipulated meaning but the implication is that a dominant ethos of ideology is able to hold sway in the manner the text is structured. John Fiske has demonstrated this in several places. If there is an 'ideal audience' for a newspaper article then surely a preferred reading of the story is equally possible. The way this is achieved may not be through overt propagandist techniques (although in tabloid journalism it may certainly seem so!) but the language and imagery may be part of complicit codes of certain social groups (e.g. white, middle-class male, over 25, etc.).

Ritual condensation

From this perspective, image is defined as a singular object whose main property is to make visible anything which is situated in a transcendental plane – whether this referent be, from our point of view, 'real' or 'imaginary', 'concrete' or 'abstract'.

Scopophilia

A term used by Laura Mulvey to describe voyeurism and 'the look' in cinema. Derived originally from Freud's theoretical canon, Mulvey has convincingly shown that the look defines and possesses the other. Furthermore, by viewing films or other texts, we are positioned as the voyeur. Some feminist theorists have employed the term as a way of discussing the 'male gaze' and the patriarchal and colonial view of the colonial female body.

Simulation

The notion that the image has arrived at a stage where it is indistinguishable from that which it represents. Baudrillard suggests there has been a historical transition through successive phases of the image:

- it is the reflection of a basic reality
- it masks and perverts a basic reality

- it masks the *absence* of a basic reality
- it bears no relation to any reality whatever: it is its own pure simulacrum.

(Baudrillard, 1983: 11)

This appears to be an extreme contention questioning the foundations of realism. Baudrillard's nihilism, however, has garnered support from critiques of the mass media and its global corporate management which at times appears to present a restricted, centralised model of world events like wars and global disasters. Hand in hand with these globalising processes, technological advances have allowed increasingly accurate visual models (e.g. computer animations) while surveillance and media intrusions into everyday life as entertainment (reality TV) add grist to the nihilistic mill that we are living in a world of constructed appearances, of artifice.

Thick description

This is a concept which Geertz developed from the philosopher Gilbert Ryle. Ryle cites the example of the wink in a cultural context where it could be interpreted as an involuntary physiological movement – 'blinking' or a symbolic cultural sign – 'winking'. Geertz argues that understanding the role and meaning of such symbols in the patterning of culture is a major task of ethnography. Such behaviours are intrinsically cultural and hence the proper object of study in social anthropology.

> The concept of culture I espouse is essentially a semiotic one. Believing, with Max Weber, that man is an animal suspended in webs of significance he himself has spun, I take culture to be those webs, and the analysis of it to be therefore not an experimental science in search of law but an interpretive one in search of meaning
>
> (Geertz, 1973: 5)

Geertz gives a vivid description of this sort of ethnography in the following quote:

> The point for now is only that ethnography is thick description. What the ethnographer is in fact faced with – except when (as, of course, he must do) he is pursuing the more automatised routines of data collection – is a multiplicity of complex conceptual structures, many of them superimposed upon or knotted into one another, which are at once strange, irregular, and inexplicit, and which he must contrive somehow first to grasp and then to render. And this is true at the most down-to-earth, jungle field work levels of his activity: interviewing informants, observing rituals, eliciting kin terms, tracing property lines, censusing households . . . writing his journal. Doing ethnography is like trying to read (in the sense of 'construct a reading of') a manuscript – foreign, faded, full of ellipses, incoherencies, suspicious

emendations, and tendentious commentaries, but written not in conventionalised graphs of sound but in transient examples of shaped behavior.

(Geertz, 1973)

However, if thick description is employed to interpret the signs and symbols of
a culture which may be alien to the researcher, this therefore begs the question of
how the outsider can be better equipped to provide an accurate analysis of the
'native's' cultural experience than the natives themselves.

The third effect

The 'third effect' is what happens when any two photographs are juxtaposed –
without captions, titles or any other textual clues. We read meaning into each
photograph individually. But we also read a third meaning into the fact that they
have been juxtaposed. This third meaning is highly subjective, shifting and
enigmatic. It is an extension of what Barthes termed the 'obtuse' meaning in all
photographs.

The bigger the 'gap' between the photographs [subject matter, source, genre,
time etc] the greater the third effect. http://www.3rdeffect.net/.

See the striking examples in the following site:

http://www.viewbookphotostory.com/2009/08/the-third-effect/.

Notes

Introduction

1 Term used by Eric Margolis to address the collected ranks of visual researchers at the International Visual Sociological Association conference in 2006 in Urbino.

Chapter 1

1 Term used by Eric Margolis to address the collected ranks of visual researchers at the International Visual Sociological Association conference in 2006 in Urbino.
2 Includes all the output of the mass media, both fictional and factual. The mediasphere, in turn, encloses the public sphere, and the 'public sphericules' that seem to have proliferated within it. The idea is that the public sphere is not separate from but enclosed within a wider sphere of cultural meaning, which is itself mediated as it is communicated back and forth from the cultural to the public domain. See Figure 46 in Glossary.
3 See Glossary.
4 See Glossary.
5 See Glossary.
6 See Glossary.
7 See Adam Curtis – *Century of Self* (BBC4 – Part 2).
8 See Glossary.
9 See Glossary.

Chapter 2

1 See Glossary.
2 See Heidegger (2001) where he cites the derivation of the term from the Greek 'phainomenon' – 'that which manifests itself'.
3 African-Guyanese President.
4 African-Guyanese President, the dictatorial and charismatic founder of the People's National Congress.
5 There was even a David Cameron anecdote generator, (http://www.fridgemagnet. org.uk/toys/dave-met.php) which randomly generated other possible stories Cameron might regale the electorate with.
6 The legal fiction of *Terra Nulius* – the notion that Australia was effectively unoccupied before British colonisation – justified land theft by settlers. Indigenous concepts of stewardship of the land were alien to European traditions of private ownership.
7 The Subject Network for Sociology, Anthropology and Politics, part of the Higher Education Academy based at Birmingham University.
8 Video may capture these less-rehearsed pre-reflective aspects of social interaction, but ethically such material must be carefully considered and its uses discussed carefully

with those involved. For example, during the brief video recording of members of an indigenous community several interviews were not used because they featured individuals who were intoxicated with alcohol. Some have argued that such material should be retained, since it presents a more truthful record of the vulnerable and marginal conditions of Australian indigenous peoples. However, there is an important duty of care which must be asserted here. Even if permission is granted to film – or in some cases involvement is eagerly sought – how responsible are the subjects, and further what are the consequences of using this material in a video text? Of course it is a fine line between sanitising and distorting the final document or producing something which reaffirms dominant prejudices or could be seen as dwelling on the victimist discourse of so many well-meaning ethnographies.

9 The campaign to regenerate a derelict area of Broomhall had begun in 2000, when the failed Genesis Centre was put up for sale. Local residents responded by establishing the Broomhall Cosmopolitan to develop this area, which comprised the triangle of land bordered by Broomhall Street, Upper Hanover Street and the Inner Ring Road, as the commercial heart of Broomhall's community. The scheme was intended to be capable of being funded commercially, with the role of support from the South Sheffield Partnership, as well as significant levels of expertise in community-led regeneration, through the Manor and Castle Development Trust. The proposed scheme links the local communities with the two Universities and other key players in the voluntary sector, including Sheffield YMCA and the Black and Ethnic Minorities Initiative within the South Sheffield Partnership. The scheme aimed to build on the strength in the cultural diversity in Broomhall.

10 For example, David Goodhart's 2004 article 'Too Diverse' in *Prospect* magazine, Trevor Phillips, the head of the Commission for Racial Equality, and many tabloid journalists inveighed against multiculturalism around this time.

11 In addition, a formal set of ethical guidelines governing the practice of visual sociology have been set up by the Visual Sociology Group (2006) of the British Sociological Association: http://www.visualsociology.org.uk/about/ethical_statement.php.

12 Hurn, D. (1997) *On Being a Photographer: A Practical Guide/David Hurn in Conversation with Bill Jay,* Lenswork Publishing.

Chapter 3

1 *Globalization: Social Theory and Global Culture* (London: Sage, 1992).

2 Dreamings are said to be the lived experience of the Dreamtime – continuing to be manifest in the physical world through totemic beliefs and complex spiritual connections:'We don't have boundaries like fences, as farmers do. We have spiritual connections' (quote on Aboriginal Art and Culture website: http://aboriginalart.com. au/culture/dreamtime2.html).

3 This map of Australia's indigenous languages was created by David Horton (based on language data gathered by Aboriginal Studies Press, AIATSIS and Auslig/Sinclair, Knight, Merz, 1996). The map can be seen to represent all of the language, tribal or nation groups of indigenous people of Australia. This is only one possible representation of a complex indigenous network showing only the general location of larger groups of people which may include smaller enclaves of clan or dialect groupings. View the map at: http://www.abc.net.au/indigenous/map/.

4 In 1993, historian Geoffrey Blainey used the term in a magazine called *Quadrant,* arguing that the telling of Australian history had moved from an unduly positive rendition (the 'Three Cheers View') to an unduly negative view (The 'black armband'). John Howard used the term when he strongly rejected the 'black armband view of history' in a speech made in 1996 and refused to make an official apology to Indigenous people.

5 Respectively two of the wealthiest and poorest suburbs of Sheffield.

6   Picturesque beauty spot in Nova Scotia.
7   This is a link to complex map produced by Africville Genealogical Society, Nova Scotia (http://www.cca-acc.org/cca-nrc009.asp).
8   The display in the National Gallery of Canada captures this sense of dispossession of community in its title – Positive Presence of Absence: A History of the African Canadian Community through Works in the Permanent Collection of the National Gallery of Canada.
9   A short animation directed by Micro Chen and Mike Rizkalla (http://watch.muchmusic.com/artists-a-z/b/bucket-truck/#clip78984).
10 The area was flooded in 1999; the people lived from fishing in the Euphrates and farming along the riverbank. After the dam was built and the water flooded the town a 'new' Halfeti was built. Some buildings, including the jail, were pulled down and rebuilt in the new town. However, the old town of Halfeti is only partially submerged and attracts visitors who come to see the ruins.

Chapter 4

1   See Glossary.
2   See Glossary.
3   Australian version of mods and rockers.
4   Term used to denote the delinquent youth (usually male) identified by the hooded garment worn.
5   See Glossary.
6   However, there is evidence that viewers become inured to shock tactics in advertising and that such messages gradually diminish in potency. This is what has been termed 'advertising wearout' (see e.g. Scott and Solomon, 1998).
7   Vance Packard coined this term in 1957 in the book of the same name.

Chapter 5

1   An association of people at One Mile Dam to incorporate their claim on the small site (Kumbutjil means black wattle – tree species found around this area).
2   Up to 35 per cent of indigenous men do not drink alcohol compared with 12 per cent of non-indigenous men; 29 to 80 per cent of Indigenous women do not drink alcohol compared with 19 to 25 per cent of non-indigenous women. In the Northern Territory, 75 per cent of Aboriginal people do not drink alcohol at all.
3   In this instance, however, the images were made with the collaborative assent of the community and sent back to the community for their approval along with the finished video material. Links to the text and images are still available on a website about the community (www.pariahnt.org/onemiledam/).
4   See Glossary.
5   On the face of it this appears to present a useful model, but such an interpretation of discourse practice could be criticised as a 'catch-all' concept, a mediating agent for enormously complex social processes of self, identity, gender, family, class, ethnicity, cultural location and time, etc. ultimately reducing the importance of agency.
6   While Foucault would have challenged the concept of 'ideology' as problematic because it always appears to be opposed to something like 'truth'.

Brown

1   See Glossary.
2   Edward Steichen (ed.) (1955) *The Family of Man*, New York: The Museum of Modern Art.
3   Sadly, perhaps, the visual has a dynamic range of expression of about an octave because of its inherent and limiting semantic uncertainties and lack of syntax, unlike

the written text. Limitations that perhaps suggest a smaller scale of competition such as the essay in its natural form.

4 *Noema* is Husserl's term for 'the meaning of an object that is formed in the domain of consciousness'. Husserl endeavours to give a detailed analysis of those features of consciousness that make it as if of an object. The collection of all these features Husserl calls the act's 'noema'. The noema unifies the consciousness we have at a certain time into an act that is seemingly directed towards an object. The noema is hence not the object that the act is directed towards, but is the structure that makes our consciousness be as if of such an object (*Routledge Encyclopedia*, 2000: 369).

5 *Aporia* – From the Greek 'obstacle', 'blocked passage', 'unpassable path'. In philosophy (mostly used by classic logicians and rhetoricians) it denotes a philosophical puzzle, paradox or insoluble problem (*Fonatana Dictionary of Modern Thought*, 1999: 42).

Canals

1 This project relates to my doctoral thesis *Images du culte à María Lionza: un essai d'anthropologie visuelle*, which was carried out under the joint tutelage of the *École des Hautes Etudes en Sciences Sociales* in Paris and the University of Barcelona, and which was defended In September 2008. I would like to express my gratitude to my two thesis advisers, Jean-Paul Colleyn (EHESS) and Joan Bestard (UB), for their guidance and involvement in this research.

2 Felipe Guevara, *Sin título*. Mixed media on canvas. 200 × 100 cm. 2002. Artist's collection.

3 Roger Canals, *The many faces of a Venezuelan goddess*, CNRS-Images, Cellule Audiovisuelle du IIAC, 2007.

4 Roger Canals, *The blood and the hen*, CNRS-Images, 2009.

5 Patricia Proaño, *Transmutación de la imagen*. 46 × 70 × 62 cm. 2006. Artist's collection.

Conclusion

1 See Glossary.

Bibliography

Abercrombie, M. (1960) *The Anatomy of Judgement,* London: Hutchinson.

Adelman, C., Kemmis, S. and Jenkins, D. (1980) 'Rethinking case study: notes from the second Cambridge conference', in H. Simon (ed.) *Towards a Science of the Singular: Essays About Case Study in Educational Research and Evaluation*, Norwich: Centre for Applied Research in Education, University of East Anglia.

Adorno, T. (1992) *Notes on Literature.* 2 vols, trans. Shierry Weber Nicholson, New York: Columbia University Press.

Ali, T. (2006) 'The spectacle is all', *Guardian*, 9 September.

Allan, S. and Zelizer, B. (2004) *Reporting War: Journalism in Wartime*, London: Routledge.

Allmark, P. (2007) 'Flagging Australia: photographs of banal nationalism', *Illumina*, 2. Online. Available HTTP: <http://illumina.scca.ecu.edu.au/journal_view.php?rec_id= 0000000041>.

Allmark, P. (2009) 'City symbolism: discourses of space and place', presentation at a colloquium on discourse, Sheffield Hallam University.

Appadurai, A. (1986) *The Social Life of Things: Commodities in Cultural Perspective*, Minneapolis: University of Minnesota Press.

Asch, S.E. (1951) 'Effects of group pressure upon the modification and distortion of judgment', in H. Guetzkow (ed.) *Groups, Leadership and Men*, Pittsburgh, PA: Carnegie Press.

Asch, S.E. (1955) 'Opinions and social pressure', *Scientific American,* 193: 31–35.

Atkinson, M. (2004) 'Tattooing and civilizing processes: body modification as self-control', *The Canadian Review of Sociology and Anthropology*, 41: 41–53.

Atkinson, P. (1990) *The Ethnographic Imagination: Textual Constructions of Reality,* London: Routledge.

Atkinson, P. and Silverman, D. (1997) 'Kundera's *Immortality*: The interview society and the invention of the self', *Qualitative Inquiry*, 3(3): 304–25.

Auerbach, A. (2007) 'Imagine no metaphors: the dialectical image of Walter Benjamin', *Image & Narrative*, 18 (September).

Bachelard, G. (1964) *Poetics of Space*, Boston: Beacon Press.

Ball, M. and Smith, G. (1992) *Analyzing Visual Data*, London: Sage.

Banks, M. (1995) 'Visual research methods', *Social Research Update*, Department of Sociology, University of Surrey, Winter 1995. Online. Available HTTP: <http://www.soc.surrey.ac.uk/sru/SRU11/SRU11.html> (accessed 20 December 2005).

Banks, M. (2001) *Visual Methods in Social Research*, London: Sage.

Banks, M. (2007) *Using Visual Data in Qualitative Research*, London: Sage.

Banks, M. (2009) 'Slow research, or letting the image breathe', plenary keynote, First International Visual Methods Conference, University of Leeds, 15–17 September.

Barbiani, E. (2005) 'Kalighat,the home of goddess Kali', *Sociological Research Online*. Online. Available HTTP: <http://www.socresonline.org.uk/10/1/barbiani.html> (accessed 21 June 2010).

Barbour, R. (2007) *Introducing Qualitative Research: A Student's Guide to the Craft of Doing Qualitative Research*, London: Sage.

Barth, F. (1969) *Ethnic Groups and Boundaries: The Social Organization of Culuture Difference*, London: George Allen & Unwin.

Barthes, R. ([1957] 1974) *Mythologies*, Paladin.

Barthes, R. ([1970] 1991) *S/Z*, cited from J. Lewis, *The Ideological Octopus: An Exploration of Television and its Audience*, London: Routledge.

Barthes, R. (1973; 1984) *Image, Music, Text*, London: Flamingo.

Barthes, R. (1982) *Camera Lucida: Reflections on Photography*, London: Jonathan Cape.

Baudrillard, J. (1983) *Simulations*, New York: Semiotexte.

BBC News (2009) 'UN condemns Aboriginal treatment', Online. Available HTTP: <http://news.bbc.co.uk/1/hi/world/asia-pacific/8223881.stm> (accessed 16 April 2010).

BBC News (2010) 'Britain is surveillance society', Online. Available HTTP: <http://news.bbc.co.uk/1/hi/uk/6108496.stm> (accessed 21 June 2010).

Becker, H. (2002) 'Visual sociology, documentary photography, and journalism: it's (almost) all a matter of context', *Visual Sociology*, 10: 5–14.

Benjamin, W. (1999) *The Arcades Project*, (ed. R. Tiedemann, trans. H. Eiland and K. McLaughlin), Cambridge, Mass.: Belknap/Harvard University Press.

Bennett, S. (2009) *Culture, Class, Distinction*, London: Routledge.

Berger, J. (1971) *Ways of Seeing*, London: Penguin.

Berger, J. (1972) 'Ways of seeing, episode four: the language of advertising', BBC.

Berger, P.L. and Luckmann, T. (1966) *The Social Construction of Reality: A Treatise in the Sociology of Knowledge*, New York: Garden City.

Best, S. (2005) *Understanding Social Divisions*, London: Sage.

Billig, M. (1995) *Banal Nationalism*, London: Sage.

Blain, J. and Wallis, R.J. (2007) *Sacred Sites, Contested Rites/Rights: Contemporary Pagan Engagements with Archaeological Monuments*, Brighton: Sussex Academic Press.

Blake, W.P. (1959) *The Gap: A Book to Bridge the Dangerous Years*, Adelaide: Applied Journalism.

Bobier, R. (1995) 'Africville: the test of urban renewal and race in Halifax, Nova Scotia', *Past Imperfect*, 4: 163–80.

Boellstorff, T. (2008) *Coming of Age in Second Life: An Anthropologist Explores the Virtually Human*, Princeton, NJ: Princeton University Press.

Bone, V. (2009) 'Is it a crime to take pictures?' BBC News, 16 February. Online. Available HTTP: <http://news.bbc.co.uk/1/hi/uk/7888301.stm> (accessed 22 January 2010).

Borges, J.L. ([1935] 1998) 'On exactitude in science', in *Collected Fictions*, part of *A Universal History of Infamy*, New York: Viking Penguin, p. 325.

Bourdieu, P. (1986) *Distinction, A Social Critique of the Judgement of Taste*, London: Routledge.

Bourdieu, P. (1990) *In Other Words, Essays Toward a Reflective Sociology*, Oxford: Policy Press.

Boyd-Barrett, O. and Braham, P. (1987) *Media, Knowledge and Power*, London: Croom Helm and Open University.

Brown, R. (2009) 'Photography, ongoing moments and strawberry fields, the active presence of absent things'. Conference paper at the International Visual Sociology Associaiton, Annual Conference, University of Cumbria, Carlisle.

Brundell, P., Knight, D., Tennent, P. *et al.* (2008) 'The experience of using the Digital Replay System for social science research', Proceedings of the Fourth International e-Social Science Conference, 18–20 June, University of Manchester: ESRC NCeSS.

Buck-Morss, S. ([1989]1991) *The Dialectics of Seeing. Walter Benjamin and the Arcades Project*, Cambridge, Mass., and London: MIT Press.

Bunt, B. (2001) 'Halfeti: only the fishes shall visit'. Online. Available HTTP: <http://www.broganbunt.net/work/halfeti/halfeti_main.html>.

Burr, V. (1999) *An Introduction to Social Construction*, London: Routledge.

Cai, Y. and Terrill, J.D. (2006) 'Visual analysis of human dynamics: an introduction to the special issue', *Information Visualisation*, 5: 235–36.

Castells, M. (1978) *City, Class and Power*, London and New York: Macmillan and St Martin's Press.

Castree, N. and Braun, B. (2005) *Social Nature, Theory, Practice And Politics*, London: Wiley-Blackwell.

Catona, K. and Santosa C.A. (2007) 'Closing the hermeneutic circle: photographic encounters with the other', *Science Direct*, 2 March.

Chandler, D. (1994) *Semiotics for Beginners*. Online. Available HTTP: <http://www.aber.ac.uk/media/Documents/S4B/semiotic.html> (accessed 23 January 2010).

Chandler, D. (2010) 'Notes on "The Gaze"'. Online. Available HTTP: <http://www.aber.ac.uk/media/Documents/gaze/gaze09.html>.

Chandler, D. (2010) 'Notes on the construction of reality in TV News Programmes', Online. Available HTTP: <http://www.aber.ac.uk/media/Modules/TF33120/news.html>.

Clark-Ibáñez, M. (2004) 'Framing the social world with photo-elicitation', *American Behavioral Scientist* 47: 1507–27.

Clifford, J. and Marcus, G.E. (1986) *Writing Culture: The Poetics and Politics of Ethnography*, Ewing, NJ: University of California Press.

Cohen, A. (1985) *The Symbolic Construction of Community*, London: Routledge.

Cohen, A. (2003) 'Ethnography and case study: a comparative analysis', *Academic Exchange Quarterly*, September.

Cohen, S. (1972) *Folk Devils and Moral Panics*, London: MacGibbon and Kee.

Collier, J. Jr. and Collier, M. (1986) *Visual Anthropology. Photography as a Research Method*, Albuquerque: University of New Mexico Press.

Coover, R. (2009) 'On verite to virtual: conversations on the frontier of film and anthropology', *Visual Studies*, 24(3), December.

Corey, F.C. (2006) 'On possibility', *Text and Performance Quarterly*, 26(4): 330–32.

Cottle, S. (2000) *Ethnic Minorities and the Media*, London: Allen & Unwin.

Coughlin, P. (2003) 'Postmodern parody and the subversion of conservative frameworks', *Literature/Film Quarterly*, January.

Cresswell, J.W. (2007) *Qualitative Inquiry and Research Design: Choosing Among Five Approaches*, London: Sage.

Critcher, C. (2003) *Moral Panics and the Media,* London: Open University Press.

Csordas, T. (1999) 'Embodiment and experience: the existential ground of culture and self', in G. Weiss and H. Haber (eds) *Perspectives on Embodiment*, London: Routledge, p. 143.

Culler, J. (1981) *The Pursuit of Signs: Semiotics, Literature, Deconstruction*, London: Routledge & Kegan Paul.

Culler, J. (2002) *Structuralist Poetics: Structuralism, Linguistics and the Study of Literature*, London: Routledge.

Curtis, A. (2002) 'The Century of the Self – Two: The Engineering of Consent', 30 April, BBC4.

Curzon, L. (2003) 'Introduction: visual culture and national identity', *Invisible Culture: An Electronic Journal for Visual Culture*, 5.

Da Silva, M. (2009) 'Valuing subjectivity in documentary photography and the media', ANZCA09*Communication, Creativity and Global Citizenship*. Online. Available HTTP: <http://www.cpe.qut.edu.au/conferences/2009/anzca/proceedings/DaSilva_ANZCA09.pdf>.

Davies, C.A. (1999) *Reflexive Ethnography: A Guide to Researching Selves and Others*, London: Routledge.

Davies, C.A. (2003) *Reflexive Ethnography*, London: Routledge.

Davis, M. (1990) *City of Quartz: Excavating the Future in Los Angeles*, New York: Verso, pp. 240–44.

Day, W.B. (2001) 'Aboriginal fringe dwellers in Darwin: cultural persistence or culture of resistance?' PhD Thesis, The University of Western Australia Department of Anthropology. Online. Available HTTP: <http://www.country-liberal-party.com/pages/Bill_Day_Thesis.c.htm>.

Debord, G.-E. (1958) 'Theory of the dérive', *Internationale Situationniste*, 2. Translation: Ken Knabb. Online. Available HTTP: <http://library.nothingness.org/articles/SI/en/display/314> (accessed 21 June 2010).

Debord, G. (1967) *The Society of the Spectacle*, Paris: Editions Buchet-Chastel.

De Certeau, M. ([1984] 1993) 'Walking in the city', in S. During (ed.) *The Cultural Studies Reader*, London: Routledge, pp 151–60.

De Certeau, M. (1985) 'Practices of space', in M. Blonsky (ed.) *On Signs*, Oxford: Blackwell, pp. 122–45.

Delamont, S. (2007) 'Arguments against auto-ethnography', *Qualitative Researcher*, 4 (February). Online. Available HTTP: <http://www.cardiff.ac.uk/socsi/qualiti/QualitativeResearcher/QR_Issue4_Feb07.pdf> (accessed 21 June 2010).

Delgado, R. (1998) 'Storytelling for oppositionists and others', in R. Delgado and J. Stefancic (eds) *The Latino/a Condition: A Critical Reader*, New York: New York University Press, pp. 259–70.

Denzin, N. (2001) 'The reflexive interview and a performative social science', *Qualitative Research*, 1(1): 23–46. Online. Available HTTP: <http://grj.sagepub.com/cgi/content/abstract/1/1/23> (accessed 19 October 2007).

Denzin, N.K. (2009) 'The elephant in the living room: or extending the conversation about the politics of evidence', *Qualitative Research*, 9: 139.

Denzin, N.K. and Lincoln, Y.S. (2008) *Collecting and Interpreting Qualitative Materials*, 3rd edn, London: Sage.

Dickens, D. and Fontana, A. (eds) (2004) *Postmodernism and Social Inquiry*, London: Routledge.

Dreher, J. (2003) 'The symbol and the theory of the life-world: "the transcendences of the life-world and their overcoming by signs and symbols"', *Journal of Human Studies*, 26(2):141–63.

du Gay, P., Hall, S., Janes, L., Mackay, H. and Negus, K. (1997) *Doing Cultural Studies*, London: Sage.

Dyer, G. (1982) *Advertising as Communication*, London: Methuen.

Dyer, R. (2003) *Heavenly Bodies: Film Stars and Society*, 2nd edn, London: Routledge.

Eade, J. and Mele, C. (eds) (2002) *Understanding the City: Contemporary and Future Perspectives*, Oxford: Blackwell.

Eco, U. ([1965] 1980) 'Towards a semiotic enquiry into the television message', in Corner and Hawthorn (eds) *Communication Studies: An Introductory Reader*, London: Edward Arnold, pp. 131–50.

Edensor, T. (2002) *British Industrial Ruins*, Manchester: Manchester Metropolitan University. Online. Available HTTP:<http://www.scieng.mmu.ac.uk/british_industrial_ruins/default.asp>.

Edensor, T. (2005) *Industrial Ruins: Space, Aesthetics and Materiality*, Oxford: Berg.

Elder, B. (1998) *Blood on the Wattle: Massacres and Maltreatment of Aboriginal Australians Since 1788*, Revised edn, New South Wales: New Holland.

Elleston, P. (2004) 'Community Harmony strategy' – ATNS Agreements, Treaties, Negotiated Settlements, Northern territories policy (2003) Indigenous Studies Program, The University of Melbourne 2007. Online. Available HTTP: <http://www.atns.net.au/agreement.asp?EntityID=1956>.

Emmison, M. and Smith, P. (2000) *Researching the Visual*, London: Sage.

Engels, F. (1845; 1958) *The Condition of the Working-Class in England in 1844*, translated and edited by W.O. Henderson and W.H. Chaloner, Stanford, CA: Stanford University Press and Blackwell, pp. 54–73.

Entrekin, N. (1991) *The Betweenness of Place: Towards a Geography of Modernity*, Basingstoke: Macmillan Education.

Essed, P. (2002) 'Everyday racism', in. D.T. Goldberg, and J. Solomos (eds) *A Companion to Racial and Ethnic Studies*, Oxford: Blackwell, pp. 202–16.

Fahlman, B. (2006) 'Current research on the art of industry artists at work: imaging place, work, and process', *I.A., The Journal of Industrial Archaeology*, 32(2).

Fairclough, N. (1995) *Media Discourse*, London: Edward Arnold.

Faris, J.C. (1992) 'Anthropological transparency: film, representation and politics', in P.I. Crawford and D. Turton (eds) *Film as Ethnography*, Manchester: Manchester University Press.

Farrar, M. (2005) 'Photography: making and breaking racialised boundaries: an essay in reflexive, radical, visual sociology', *Sociological Research Online*, 10(1). Online. Available HTTP: <http://www.socresonline.org.uk/10/1/farrar.html> (accessed 21 April 2008).

Ferreira, V.S. (2009) 'Youth scenes, body marks and bio-sociabilities', *Young*, 17(3): 285–306. Online. Available HTTP:<http://you.sagepub.com/cgi/content/abstract/17/3/285>.

Ferris, D.S. (2004) *The Cambridge Companion to Walter Benjamin*, Cambridge: Cambridge University Press.

Finlay, L. (2008) 'Introducing phenomenological research'. Online. Available HTTP: < http://www.lindafinlay.co.uk/phenomenology.htm>.

Fiske, J. (1987) *Television Culture*, London: Routledge.

Fiske, J. (1989a) *Reading the Popular*, London: Unwin, Hyman.

Fiske, J. (1989b) *Introduction to Communication Studies*, London: Routledge.

Fiske, J. and Hartley, J. (2003) *Reading Television*, London: Routledge.

Flick, U. (2002) *An Introduction to Qualitative Research*, Thousand Oaks, CA: Sage.

Floch, J.-M. (2000) *Visual Identities* (trans. P. V. Osselaer and A. McHoul), London: Continuum.

Foley, G. (1997) 'Muddy waters: Archie Mudrooroo and Aboriginality', *The Koori History Website*. Online. Available HTTP: <http://www.kooriweb.org/foley/essays/essay_10.html>.

Foucault, M. ([1967] 1984) 'Of other spaces heterotopias', *Architecture/Mouvement/ Continuité*.

Foucault, M. ([1976] 1999) 'Of other spaces heterotopias', Lecture, in N. Mirzoeff (ed.) *The Visual Culture Reader*, London: Routledge.

Foucault, M. (1977) *Discipline and Punish: The Birth of the Prison*, Harmondsworth: Peregrine.

Foucault, M. (1980) *Power/Knowledge: Selected Interviews and Other Writings 1972–1977*, New York: Pantheon.

Garson, G.D. (2008) 'Accepted practices and processes – case study management'. Online. Available HTTP: <http://www.adizesgraduateschool.org/AGSPDF/casestudymgmt.doc>.

Gauntlett, D. (2007) *Creative Explorations: New Approaches to Identities and Audiences*, London: Routledge.

Gauntlett, D. and Howzarth, P. (2006) 'Creative and visual methods for exploring identities', *Visual Studies*, 21(1): 82–91.

Geertz, C. (1973) 'Thick description: toward an interpretative theory of culture,' in *The Interpretation of Cultures*, New York: Basic Books.

Gibson, J.J. (1983) *The Senses Considered as Perceptual Systems*, New York: Greenwood Press.

Giddens, A. (1976) *New Rules of Sociological Method*, New York: Basic Books.

Gilroy, P. (2006) *Postcolonial Melancholia*, New York: Columbia University Press.

Gombrich, E.H. (1996) *The Essential Gombrich: Selected Writings on Art and Culture*, London: Phaidon.

Goodchild, S. (2007) 'Britain becoming a Big Brother society, says data watchdog', *Independent*, 29 April. Online. Available HTTP: <http://www.independent.co.uk/news/uk/this-britain/britain-becoming-a-big-brother-society-says-data-watchdog-446700.html>(accessed 21 June 2010).

Gos, S. (2003) 'Hole in the road (including an ode)' [Archive] – *Sheffield Forum* 27April. Online. Available HTTP: <http://www.sheffieldforum.co.uk/archive/index.php/t-2524.html>.

Grady, J. (2001) 'Becoming a visual sociologist', *Sociological Imagination*, 38(1/2): 83–119.

Grady, J. (2008) 'Visual research at the crossroads', *Forum: Qualitative Social Research*, 9(3): 38. Online. Available HTTP: <http://www.qualitativeresearch.net/index.php/fqs/article/view/1173>.

Grayson, K. (1998) 'The icons of consumer research: using signs to represent consumers' reality', B.B. Stern (ed.) *Representing Consumers: Voices, Views and Visions*, London: Routledge, pp. 27–43.

Guba, E.G. and Lincoln, Y.S. (1994) 'Competing paradigms in qualitative research', in N.K. Denzin and Y.S. Lincoln (eds) *Handbook of Qualitative Research*, Thousand Oakes, CA: Sage, pp. 105–17.

Hall, E.T. (1959) *The Silent Language*, New York: Doubleday.

Hall, S. ([1973] 1980) 'Encoding/decoding', in Centre for Contemporary Cultural Studies (ed.) *Culture, Media, Language: Working Papers in Cultural Studies, 1972–79*, London: Hutchinson, pp. 128–38.

Hall, S. (1990) 'Cultural identity and diaspora', in J. Rutherford (ed.) *Identity*, London: Lawrence & Wishart.

Hall, S. (1996) *Race, the Floating Signifier*, a film directed by Sut Jhally (videotape lecture), Northampton, Mass.: Media Education Foundation.

Hall, S. (ed.) (1997) *Representation: Cultural Representations and Signifying Practices*, London: Sage.

Hammersley, M. and Atkinson, P. (1997) *Ethnography: Principles in Practice*, 2nd edn, London: Routledge.

Hammerton, Sir J. (1933) *Peoples of All Nations*, London: Amalgamated Press.

Haraway, D.J. (1992) 'The promises of monsters: a regenerative politics for inappropriate/d others', in L. Grossberg, C. Nelson and P. Treicher (eds) *Cultural Studies*, New York: Routledge, pp. 295–337.

Hardy, C., Phillips, N. and Clegg, S. (2001) 'Reflexivity in organization and management theory: a study of the production of the research "subject"', *Human Relations*, 54: 531–60.

Harper, D. (1988) 'Visual sociology: expanding sociological vision', *The American Sociologist*, Spring: 54–70.

Harper, D. (2005) 'What's new visually?', in N. Denzin and Y. Lincoln (eds) *Handbook of Qualitative Research,* 3rd edn, Beverly Hills and London: Sage, pp. 747–62.

Harper, D. (2006) 'Cultural studies and the photograph', in P. Hamilton (ed.) *Visual Research Methods*, London: Sage, pp. 211–48.

Hartley, J. (1992) *The Politics Of Pictures: The Creation of The Public in the Age of Popular Media*, London: Routledge.

Hartley, J. (1998) *The Politics of Pictures*, New York: Polity Press.

Hartley, J. (2002) *Communication, Cultural and Media Studies*, London: Routledge.

Harvey, D. (1985) *The Urbanization of Capital: Studies in the History and Theory of Capitalist Urbanization*, Baltimore, MD: Johns Hopkins University Press.

Hayles, N.K. (2002) 'Virtual bodies and flickering signifiers', in N. Mirzoeff (ed.) *The Visual Culture Reader*, 2nd edn, London: Routledge, pp. 152–60.

Hayward, S. (1996) *Key Concepts in Cinema Studies*. London: Routledge.

Heidegger, M. (2001) *Phenomenological Interpretations of Aristotle: Initiation into Phenomenological Research*, Bloomington: Indiana University Press.

Helmling, S. (2003) 'Constellation and critique: Adorno's constellation, Benjamin's dialectical image', Online. Available HTTP: <http://pmc.iath.virginia.edu/textonly/issue.903/14.1helmling.txt>.

Hensher, P. (2008) *The Northern Clemency*, London: Fourth Estate.

Hermes, J. (1995) *Reading Women's Magazines: An Analysis of Everyday Media Use*, London: Polity Press.

Hiles, D. (1999) 'Paradigms lost – paradigms regained', summary of the paper presented to the 18th International Human Science Conference, Sheffield, 26–29 July.

Hine, C. (2000) *Virtual Ethnography*, London: Sage.

Hockings, P. (ed.) (1995) *Principles of Visual Anthroplogy*, 3rd edn, Berlin: Mouton de Gruyere.

Hogan, S. (ed.) (1997) *Feminist Approaches to Art Therapy,* London: Routledge.

Hogan, S. (2001) *Healing Arts: The History of Art Therapy*, London: Jessica Kingsley.

Hollinshead, K. (1991) '"White" gaze, "red" people – shadow visions: the disidentification of "Indians" in cultural tourism', *Journal of Leisure Studies,* 11(1), London: Routledge.

hooks, bell (1997) *Cultural Criticism & Transformation*, video produced and directed by Sut Jhally, Media Education Foundation.

Hughes, E.C. (1971) *The Sociological Eye – Selected Papers,* New Brunswick: Transaction Books.

Hughes, I. (1995) 'Dependent autonomy: a new phase of internal colonialism', *Australian Journal of Social Issues*, 30(4): 369–88.

Hurn, D. and Jay, B. (2003) *On Being a Photographer: A Practical Guide*, 3rd edn, Anacortes, US: Lenswork Publishing.

Husserl, E. ([1913] 1931) *Ideas: General Introduction to Pure Phenomenology*, London: George Allen & Unwin.

Iannucci, A. (2003) 'Shoot now, think later', *Guardian*, 28 April. Online. Available HTTP: <http://www.guardian.co.uk/Iraq/Story/0,2763,944902,00.html>.

Ingold, T. and Vergust, J. (2006) 'Fieldwork on foot: perceiving, routing, socialising', in S. Coleman and J. Collins (eds) *Locating the Field: Space, Place and Context in Anthroplogy*, Oxford: Berg.

Ingold, T. and Lee Vergust, J. (eds) (2007) *Ways of Walking: Ethnography and Practice on Foot, Anthropological Studies of Creativity and Perception*, London: Ashgate.

Jacka, T. and Petkovic, J. (2000) 'Ethnography and video: researching women in China's floating population', *Intersections*, back issues, Parts 1 and 2. Online.Available HTTP: <http://wwwsshe.murdoch.edu.au/intersections/back_issues/tampt1.html> (accessed 2 January 2005).

Jay, B. and Hurn, D. (2007) *On Being a Photographer: A Practical Guide*, Anacortes, WA: LensWork Publishing.

Jay, M. (1994) *Downcast Eyes: The Denigration of Vision in Twentieth-Century French Thought*, Ewing, NJ: University of California Press.

Jayne, M. (2006) *Cities and Consumption*, London: Routledge.

Jenkins, R. (1992) *Pierre Bourdieu*, London: Routledge.

Jenkins, R. (2004) *Social Identity*, 2nd edn, London: Routledge.

Jenkins, R. (2007) 'Inarticulate speech of the heart: nation, flag and emotion in Denmark', in T.H. Eriksen and R. Jenkins (eds) *Flag, Nation and Symbolism in Europe and America*, London: Routledge, pp. 115–35.

Jenkins, R. (2008) *Social Identity*, 3rd edn, London: Routledge.

Jenks, C. (ed.) (1995) *Visual Culture*, London: Routledge.

Johnson, P. and Duberley, J. (2003) 'Reflexivity in management research', *Journal of Management Studies*, 40: 1279–303.

Judelman, G.B. (2004) 'Knowledge visualization problems and principles for mapping the knowledge space', MSc Thesis Dissertation, International School of New Media, University of Lubbock, Germany, June.

Kampfner, J. (2003) 'How truth was edited in saving Private Lynch', *The Age*, 18 May.

Karp, D.A., Stone, G.P. and Yoels, W.C. (1991) *Being Urban: A Sociology of City Life*, New York: Praeger.

Kaufman, K.J. in E. Kaufman and K.J. Heller (eds) (1998) *Deleuze & Guttari: New Mappings in Politics, Philosophy and Culture*, Minneapolis: University of Minnesota Press.

King, A. (ed.) (1996) *Re-presenting the City: Ethnicity Capital and Culture in the 21st Century Metropolis*, New York: New York University Press.

Knowles, C. (2006) 'Seeing race through the lens', *Ethnic and Racial Studies*, 29(3).

Kress, G. (1988) *Culture and Communication*, New South Wales University Press.

Kress, G. and Hodge, R. (1979) *Language as Ideology*, London: Routledge & Kegan Paul.

Kress, G. and Hodge, R. (1988) *Social Semiotics*, New York: Polity Press.

Kristeva, J. (1980) *Desire in Language: A Semiotic Approach to Literature and Art*, New York: Columbia University Press.

Kuhn, A. (2007) *Photography and Cultural Memory: A Methodological Exploration*, Visual Studies, Vol. 22, No. 3, Abingdon: Routledge.

Kuper, A. (ed.) (1992) *Conceptualizing Society*, London: Routledge.

Kvale, S. (1995) 'The social construction of validity', *Qualitative Inquiry*, 1(1): 19–40.

Ladson-Billings, G. and Tate, IV, W.F. (1985) 'Toward a critical race theory of education', *Teachers College Press*, 97(1): 47-68.

Lahire, B. (2001) *Le Travail Sociologique de Pierre Bourdieu: Dettes et Critiques*, Paris: La Decouverte/Poche.

Lakoff, G. and Johnson, M. (1980) *Metaphors We Live By*, Chicago: University of Chicago Press.

Lally, E. (2002) *At Home with Computers*, Oxford: Berg.

Lang, S.B. (2004) 'The impact of video systems on architecture', Dissertation, Swiss Federal Institute of Technology.

Langton, M. (1993) *Well I Heard It on the Radio and Saw it on the Television . . .*, Sydney: Australian Film Commission.

Lawler, S. (2007) 'Stories and the social world', in M. Pickering (ed.) *Research Methods for Cultural Studies*, EUP.

Lee, A. and Ingold, T. (2006) 'Fieldwork on foot: perceiving, routing, socializing', in S. Coleman (ed.) *Locating the Field: Space, Place and Context in Anthropology*, Oxford: Berg.

Lee, A. and Poynton, C. (eds) (2000) *Culture and Text: Discourse and Methodology in Social Research and Cultural Studies*, St Leonards, NSW: Allen & Unwin.

Lemert, C. (2006) 'Racism and atlantic violence', *Keynote Address Centre for Sociology, Anthropology and Politics, of the British Higher Education Academy*, 27–28 June, London.

Lester, S. (1999) *An Introduction to Phenomenological Research Developments*, Taunton: Stan Lester.

Lévi-Strauss, C. (1958) 'La structure des mythes' (in French), in *Anthropologie Structurale*, Paris: Plon.

Lewis (2007) 'Contemporary culture, cultural studies and the global mediasphere', in Lewis (ed.) *Cultural Studies*, London: Sage, pp. 1–33.

Lotman, Y. (2005) 'On the semiosphere', *Sign Systems Studies*, 33(1).

Lury, C. (1999) *Consumer Culture*, Cambridge, Mass.: Polity Press.

Macnaghten, P. and Urry, J. (1999) *Contested Natures*, London: Sage.

McCannell, D. (1999) *The Tourist: A New Theory of the Leisure Class*, Ewing, NJ: University of California Press.

Madriaga, M. (2007) 'The Star-Spangled Banner and whiteness in American national identity', in T.H. Eriksen and R. Jenkins (eds) *Flag, Nation and Symbolism in Europe and America*, London: Routledge, pp. 53–68.

Malinowski, B. (1961) *Argonauts of the Western Pacific: An Account of Native Enterprise and Adventure in the Archipelagoes of Melanisian New Guinea*, New York: E. P. Dutton.

Marcus, A. and Neumann, D. (2007) *Visualising the City*, London: Routledge.

Marcuse, H. (1965; 1969) 'Repressive tolerance', in R.P. Wolff, B. Moore Jr. and H. Marcuse (eds) *A Critique of Pure Tolerance*, Boston: Beacon Press, pp. 95–137.

Margolis, E. (2004) 'Blind spots: thoughts for visual sociology upon reading Martin Jay's "Downcast eyes: the denigration of vision in twentieth century French thought"', Website of the International Visual Sociology Association. Online. Available HTTP: <http://courses.ed.asu.edu/margolis/review.html> (accessed 20 April 2008).

Marks, L. V. (2004) 'Haptic visuality: touching with the eyes', Frameworks, 2. Online. Available HTTP:http://www.framework.fi/2-2004/visitor/artikkelit/marks.html.

Martin, R. (2001) 'Phototherapy and re-enactment: the performative body', *Afterimage*, Fall.

McCannell, D. (1999) *The Tourist: A New Theory of the Leisure Class*, Ewing, NJ: University of California Press.

McDonald, H. (2003) 'Exploring possibilities through critical race theory: exemplary pedagogical practices for indigenous students', paper for *NZARE/AARE Joint Conference*, James Cook University, Australia.

Mead, M. (1995) 'Visual anthropology in a discipline of words', in P. Hockings (ed.) *Principles of Visual Anthroplogy*, 3rd edn, Berlin: Mouton de Gruyere.

Mejstrik, M. (1999) 'Czech Republic: the revolution's fading velvet', *Transitions – Changes in Post-Communist Societies,* 6(1): 38–41.

Metz, C. (1982) *The Imaginary Signifier* (trans. C. Britton, A. Williams, B. Brewster and A. Guzzetti), Bloomington: Indiana University Press.

Mill, C.W. (1959) *The Sociological Imagination*, Oxford: Oxford University Press.

Miller, D. (2009) *The Comfort of Things*, New York: Polity Press.

Mills, C.W. ([1959] 1976) *The Sociological Imagination*, New York: Oxford University Press.

Mirzeoff, N. (ed.) (1999) *Visual Culture Reader*, London: Routledge.

Mitchell, W.J.T. (1994) *Picture Theory: Essays on Verbal and Visual Representation*, Chicago: University of Chicago Press.

Moores, S. (2005) *Media/Theory: Thinking About Media and Communications*, London: Routledge.

Morley, D. (1981a) 'The nationwide audience: a critical postscript', *Screen Education*, 39: 3–14.

Morley, D. (1981b) *Interpreting Television. In Popular Culture and Everyday Life* (Block 3 of U203 Popular Culture), Milton Keynes: Open University Press, pp. 40–68.

Morley, D. (1992) *Television, Audiences and Cultural Studies*, London: Routledge.

Muecke, S. (1982) 'Available discourses on Aborigines', in P. Botsman (ed.) *Theoretical Strategies*, Sydney: Local Consumption Press.

Muecke, S. (1994) 'Narrative and intervention in Aboriginal filmmaking and policy', *Continuum: The Australian Journal of Media and Culture*, 8(2):1–7.

Mulvey, L. ([1992] 2001)'Visual pleasure and narrative cinema', in M.G. Durham and D. Kellner (eds) *Media and Cultural Studies: Keywords*, Malden, MA, and Oxford: Blackwell; pp. 342–52.

Mulvey, L. (1999) 'Visual pleasure and narrative cinema', in L. Braudy and M. Cohen (eds) *Film Theory and Criticism: Introductory Readings*, New York: Oxford University Press, pp. 833–44.

Murdock, G. and Pink, S. (2005) 'Ethnography bytes back: digitalising visual anthropology', *Media International Australia, Incorporating Culture & Policy*, 116 (August): 10–23. Online. Available HTTP:http://search.informit.com.au/document Summary;dn=012416226662116;res=IELHSS, ISSN: 1329-878X. (accessed 30 July 2010).

Nájera-Ramírez, O. (1994) *Engendering Nationalism: Identity, Discourse, and the Mexican Charro*, The George Washington University Institute for Ethnographic Research.

Nisbet, R.A. (1967) *The Sociological Tradition*, London:, Heinemann Educational Books.

PARIAH (2007) *People Against Racism In Aboriginal Homelands*, Online. Available HTTP: <http://pariahnt.org/>.

Patton, M.Q. (2002) *Qualitative Research and Evaluation Methods*, 3rd edn, London: Sage, pp. 411–41.

Pauwels, L. (2010) 'Visual sociology reframed: an analytical synthesis and discussion of visual methods in social and cultural research', *Sociological Methods Research*, 38: 545.

Petkovic, J. (dir.) (1983) *Frame on Dreaming*, Western Australia: Edith Cowan University.

Philo, G., Hewitt, J., Beharrell, P. and Davis, H. (Glasgow University Media Group) (1982) *Really Bad News*, London: Writers and Readers Publishing Cooperative Society.

Pickering, M. (ed.) (2008) *Research Methods for Cultural Studies*, Edinburgh: Edinburgh University Press.

Pink, S. (2003) 'Interdisciplinary agendas in visual research; re-situating visual anthropology', *Visual Studies*, 18(2): 179–92.

Pink, S. (2004) *Home Truths: Gender, Domestic Objects and Everyday Life*, Oxford: Berg.

Pink, S. (2007) *Doing Visual Ethnography*, London: Sage.

Pink, S. (2008a) 'Sense and sustainability: the case of the Slow City movement', *Local Environment*, 13(2): 95–106.

Pink, S. (2008b) 'Mobilising visual ethnography: making routes, making place and making images', *Forum Qualitative Research*, 9(3): art. 36.

Pole, C. (ed.) (2004) *Seeing is Believing? Approaches to Visual Research*, London: Elsevier Science & Technology.

Polkinghorne, D. (1983) *Methodology for the Human Sciences*, Albany: State University of New York Press.

Pool, R. (1991) 'Postmodern ethnography?', *Critique of Anthropology*, 11: 309.

Potter, J. and Wetherell, M. (1987) *Discourse and Social Psychology*, London: Sage.

Propp, V. ([1927] 1968) *Morphology of the Folktale*, 2nd edn, trans. L. Scott, Austin: University of Texas Press.

Prosser, J.D. (1998) *Image-based Research: A Sourcebook for Qualitative Researchers*, London: Falmer Press.

Prosser, J. (2000) 'The moral maze of image ethics', in H. Simons and R. Usher (eds) *Situated Ethics in Educational Research*, London: RoutledgeFalmer, pp. 116–32.

Prosser, J. (2006) 'Working paper: researching with visual images: some guidance notes and a glossary for beginners', Real Life Methods, University of Manchester and University of Leeds.

Prosser, J. and Schwartz, D. (1998) 'Photographs within the sociological research process', in J. Prosser (ed.) *Image Based Research: A Sourcebook for Qualitative Researchers*, London: Falmer Press, pp. 115–29.

Prosser, J. (2008) 'Introducing visual methods', ESRC National Centre for Research Methods Review Paper, October.

Ratcliff, D. (1995) 'Validity and reliability in qualitative research'. Online. Available HTTP:<http://www.vanguard.edu/uploadedFiles/faculty/dratcliff/qualresources/Validity.pdf> (accessed 25 April 2008).

Relph, E. (1976) *Place and Placelessness*, London: Pion.

Richardson, J.T.E. (1996) *Handbook of Qualitative Research Methods for Psychology and the Social Sciences,* Oxford: Blackwell.

Ritzer, G. and Goodman, D. (2003) *Sociological Theory*, 6th edn, London: McGraw Hill.

Rose, G. (2007) *Visual Methodologies,* 2nd edn, London: Sage.
Rose, G. (2008) 'Using photographs as illustrations in human geography', *Journal of Geography in Higher Education,* 1466–1845, 32(1): 151–60.
Rouch, J. (1954) *Les Maitres Fous* (The Mad Masters), Ghana/France, documentary film.
Rouch, J. (1959) *The Human Pyramid,* documentary film.
Sapir, E. (1966) *Culture, Language and Personality: Selected Essays,* 8th edn, Berkeley: University of California Press.
Saunders, K. (1984) *Indentured Labour in the British Empire, 1834–1920,* London: Croom Helm.
Schutz, A. (1962) *Collected Papers 1: The Problem of Social Reality,* The Hague: Martinus Nijhoff.
Schwartz, T. (ed.) (1980) *Socialization as Cultural Communication: Development of a Theme in the Work of Margaret Mead,* Berkeley: University of California Press. Online. Available HTTP: <http://ark.cdlib.org/ark:/13030/ft1p300479/>.
Seamon, D. (2002) *Sources: Phenomenology, Place, Environment, and Architecture: A Review of the Literature.* Online. Available HTTP: <http://www.phenomenology online.com/articles/seamon1.html>.
Seamon, D. and Sowers, J. (2008) 'Place and placelessness', in P. Hubbard, R. Kitchen and G. Vallentine (eds) *Key Texts in Human Geography,* London: Sage, pp. 43–51.
Seattle Post-Intelligencer (2003) 'Tech Briefs: Sony says it's sorry for "shock and awe" idea', 18 April. Online. Available HTTP: <http://seattlepi.nwsource.com/business/118102_tbrf18.html>.
Scott, D.R. and Solomon, D. (1998) 'What is wearout anyway? (advertising)', *Journal of Advertising Research,* 38(5): 19–28.
Sharrow/Nether Edge/Broomhill Area Panel (2003) Meeting held 4 September at the Salvation Army Citadel, Sheffield Council.
Sheffield City Council and Arcus (2007) *Brightside Weir and Steelworks,* Public Information Panel.
Sheffield City Council Website (2009) Available HTTP: <http://www.sheffield.gov.uk/out—about/tourist-information/visitor-attractions/heritage/town-hall/exterior-of-the-building> (accessed 10 December, 2009).
Shields, R. (1996) 'A guide to urban representation and what to do about it: alternative traditions of urban theory', in A. King (ed.) *Re-Presenting the City: Ethnicity, Capital and Culture in the 21st Century Metropolis,* New York: New York University Press.
Shilling, C. (1993) *The Body and Social Theory,* London: Sage.
Short, J.R. (2006) *Urban Theory: A Critical Assessment,* London: Palgrave.
Silverman, D. (2005) *Doing Qualitative Research,* 2nd edn, London: Sage.
Silverman, D. and Torode, B. (1980) *The Material Word: Some Theories of Language and its Limits,* London: Routledge.
Sjöberg, J. (2006) 'The ethnofiction in theory and practice', in *NAFA Network* 13.3a (August), Newsletter of the Nordic Anthropological Film Association.
Smith, D.E. (2005) *Institutional Ethnography: A Sociology for People,* Toronto: AltaMira Press.
Smith, L.T. (1999) *Decolonizing Methodologies: Research and Indigenous Peoples,* NewYork: Zed Books.
Sontag, S. (1978) *On Photography,* New York: Farrar, Strauss & Giroux.
Spencer, S. (2003) Unpublished interview with Prof. Bob Franklin, University of Sheffield.
Spencer, S. (2004) *Framing the Fringe Dwellers,* Academic Video, C-SAP Website. Available HTTP: <http://www.teachingrace.bham.ac.uk/video_resources/>.

Spencer, S. (2005) 'Contested homelands: Darwin's "itinerant problem"', *Pacific Journalism Review*, University of Auckland, The indigenous public sphere, 11(1): 174–97.

Spencer, S. (2006a) *Race & Ethnicity: Culture, Identity and Representation*, London: Routledge.

Spencer, S (2006b) 'Framing the fringe dwellers: visual methods for research and teaching race and ethnicity: a sample case study', in M. Farrar and M. Todd (eds) *Teaching Race in Social Sciences – New Contexts, New Approaches*, Birmingham: C-SAP Monograph, pp 144–83.

Spencer, S. (2007) 'Visualising the multicultural city', in P. Facioli and J.A. Gibbons (eds) *Framing Globalisation: Visual Perspectives*, Cambridge: Scholars Press.

Spencer, S. (2009) 'Drifting visions and dialectical images: everyday paradoxes in a Northern city', *Illumina*, 3 (December), e-journal, Edith Cowan University. Editor: Dr Mardie O'Sullivan, [ISSN 18347274]. Online. Available HTTP: <http://illumina.scca.ecu.edu.au>.

Spencer, S. and Radley, K. (2006) *Under the Skin of Multiculturalism*, Academic Video, Available on C-SAP website (film is divided into separate video clips). Available HTTP: <http://www.teachingrace.bham.ac.uk/video_resources/>.

Spencer, S. and Samuels, L. (2008) Video Interview with Denise Allen, 2007, in *Identities in Transition: Five African Canadian Women Discuss Identity*, video published in EliSS Journal, CSAP, Online Publication, 1(2) 184–205. ISSN:1756848X, Available HTTP:<http://www.eliss.bham.ac.uk/PreviousEditions/Volume1Issue2/Video Gallery/IdentitiesinTransition/tabid/139/Default.aspx>.

Stake, R. (1988) 'Case study research', in R. Jaeger (ed.) *Complementary Methods for Research in Education*, American Educational Research Association.

Stake, R. (1995) *The Art of Case Research*, Newbury Park, CA: Sage.

Stallybrass, P. and White, A. (1986; 1993) 'Bourgeois hysteria and the carnivalesque', in S. During, (ed.) *The Cultural Studies Reader*, London: Routledge.

Stanczak, G.C. (ed.) (2007) *Visual Research Methods: Image, Society, and Representation*, London: Sage.

Stoller, P. (1992) *Cinematic Griot*, Chicago: The University of Chicago Press

Stratton, J. (1998) *Race Daze: Australia in Identity Crisis*, Sydney: Pluto Press.

Strinati, D. (1996) *Theories of Popular Culture*, London: Routledge.

Susser, I. (2002) *The Castells Reader on Cities and Social Theory*, Oxford: Blackwell.

Sweetman, P. (ed.) (2004) *Picturing the Social Landscape*, London: Routledge.

Szekeley, M. (2006) 'Rethinking Benjamin: the function of the utopian ideal'. Online. Available HTTP: <http://clogic.eserver.org/2006/szekely.html>.

Tagg, J. (2003) 'Evidence, truth and order: photographic records and the growth of the state', in L. Wells (ed.) *The Photographic Reader*, London: Routledge.

Taylor, G. and Spencer, S. (2004) *Social Identities: Multidisciplinary Approaches*, London: Routledge.

Thomas, B., Pritchard, J., Ballas, D., Vickers, D. and Dorling, D. (2009) *A Tale of Two Cities: The Sheffield Project*, report released 2 November. Online. Available HTTP: <http://www.sasi.group.shef.ac.uk/research/sheffield/index.html>.

Thompson, J. (1994) *The Media and Modernity*, New York: Polity Press.

Threadgold, T. (1997) *Feminist Poetics, Poiesis, Performance, Histories*, London: Longman.

Toren, C. (1996) 'Ethnography: theoretical background', in J.T.E. Richardson (ed.) *Handbook of Qualitative Research Methodology for Psychology and Social Sciences*, Oxford: British Psychological Society of Books, pp. 102–12.

Tumarkin, M. (2005) *Traumascapes*, Melbourne University Publishing.

Tumarkin, M. (2007) 'Traumascapes: places transformed by tragedy', in *Guilt & Pleasure*, pp. 117–21.

Tyler, S. (1986) 'Post-modern ethnography: from document of the occult to occult document', in J. Clifford and G.E. Marcus (eds) *Writing Culture: The Poetics and Politics of Ethnography*, Berkeley: University of California Press.

Urry, J. (1990) *The Tourist Gaze: Leisure and Travel in Contemporary Societies*, London: Sage.

Veblen, T. ([1899] 2008) Martha Banta, *The Theory of the Leisure Class,* Oxford: Oxford University Press, p. 53.

Viola, M. (2002) *Interpreting TV News*, April. Online. Available HTTP: <http://www.aber.ac.uk/media/Students/mlv9802.html>.

Walker, R. (1993) 'Finding a silent voice for the researcher: using photographs in evaluation and research', *Qualitative Voices in Educational Research*.

Warren, C. (1982) 'Field work and film rights: anthropology and ethnographic film', course materials for *Structure Thought and Reality*, Murdoch University, Western Australia.

Waters, M. (1995) *Globalization*, London: Routledge.

Waterscape.com (2009) History of the River Don. Online. Available HTTP: <http://209.85.229.132/search?q=cache:PrMV2nZsZqoJ:www.waterscape.com/canals-and-rivers/riverdon/history+History++Sheffield+apprentices+eating+salmon&cd=2&hl=en&ct=clnk&gl=uk>.

Watkins, C.K. (1975) *Social Control*, London: Longman.

Watson, J. (2006) in A. Brown (ed.) *Historical Perspectives on Social Identity*, Cambridge: Scholars Press, pp. 11–18.

Weedon, C. (1987) *Feminist Practice and Post-structuralist Theory*, Oxford: Blackwell.

Wetherell, M. and Potter, J. (1988) 'Discourse analysis and the identification of interpretive repertoires', in C. Antaki (ed.) *Analysing Everyday Explanation: A Casebook of Methods*, Newbury Park, CA: Sage, pp. 168–83.

Wheeler, H. (ed.) (1935) *Peoples of the World in Pictures*, London: Odhams Press.

Widerberg, K. (2004) 'Institutional ethnography: towards a productive sociology', an interview with Dorothy E. Smith, *Sosiologisk Tidskrift*, 12(2).

Widerberg, K. (2007) 'Among the "others": migration and gender and the ethnographic approach', in *Research Integration,* University of York. Online. Available HTTP: <http://www.york.ac.uk/res/researchintegration/Integrative_Research_Methods/Widerberg%20Ethnography%20April%202007.pdf>.

Wiles, R., Prosser, J., Bagnoli, A. *et al.* (2008) 'Visual ethics: ethical issues in visual research', ESRC National Centre for Research Methods, October.

Wiles, R., Coffey, A., Robinson, J. and Prosser, J. (2010) 'Ethical regulation and visual methods: making visual research impossible or developing good practice', ESRC National Centre for Research Methods, January. Online. Available HTTP: <http://eprints.ncrm.ac.uk/812/2/ethical_regulation_and_visual_methods.pdf>.

Williams, R. (1958) 'Moving from high culture to ordinary culture', in N. McKenzie (ed.) *Convictions*, London: MacGibbon & Lee.

Williamson, J. (1978) *Decoding Advertisements*, London: Marion Boyars.

Williamson, J. (1987) *Consuming Passions: The Dynamics of Popular Culture*, London: Marion Boyers.

Willis, P. and Trondman, M. (2002) 'Manifesto for ethnography', *Cultural Studies/ Critical Methodologies*, 2(3): 394–402.

Wittgenstein, L. (1976) *Philosophical Investigations 1*, Oxford: Blackwell.
Wordley, D. and Blake, W.P. (1959) *The Gap: A Book to Bridge the Dangerous Years,* Adelaide: Applied Journalism.
Yang, C. and Terrill, J.D. (2006) 'Visual analysis of human dynamics: an introduction to the special issue', *Information Visualization*, London: Palgrave Macmillan. Online. Available HTTP: <http://www.cmu.edu/vis/media/pdf/IVJ-Editorial.pdf>.
Yin, R.K. (2003) 'Case study research: design and methods', *Applied Social Research Methods Series*, vol. 5, London: Sage.

Index